E 2

Andrew MacKenzie, who was
and worked in London for more
he served as an infantry officer i
Burma. His interest in psychica
the course of writing a series of
the library of the Society for I
joined the Society in 1962, was
and is at present chairman of the Library Committee. In his
investigations of spontaneous cases he has been greatly helped by
Mr G. W. Lambert, a former President, and other senior figures
in the Society. His five books on psychical research have brought
him hundreds of case histories from readers in many countries,
particularly America. His books are *The Unexplained*, *Frontiers of
the Unknown*, *Apparitions and Ghosts*, *A Gallery of Ghosts* and *Riddle of
the Future*. He has also written *Dracula Country: travels and folk
beliefs in Romania*.

born in New Zealand, has been
than forty years. During the war
in a British regiment in India and
respect, was kindled when, in
article on the subject, he visited
Psychical Research, in 1901. He
elected to the Council in 1934.

ANDREW MACKENZIE

Hauntings and Apparitions

Series Editor: Brian Inglis

Published on behalf of the Society for Psychical Research

A PALADIN BOOK

GRANADA
London Toronto Sydney New York

Published by Granada Publishing Limited in 1983

ISBN 0 586 08430 4

First published in Great Britain by
William Heinemann Ltd 1982
Copyright © Andrew MacKenzie 1982

Granada Publishing Limited
Frogmore, St Albans, Herts AL2 2NF
and
36 Golden Square, London W1R 4AH
515 Madison Avenue, New York, NY 10022, USA
117 York Street, Sydney, NSW 2000, Australia
60 International Blvd, Rexdale, Ontario, R9W 6J2, Canada
61 Beach Road, Auckland, New Zealand

Printed and bound in Great Britain by
Hazell Watson & Viney Ltd, Aylesbury
Set in Baskerville

This book is sold subject to the condition that it
shall not, by way of trade or otherwise, be lent,
re-sold, hired out or otherwise circulated
without the publisher's prior consent in any
form of binding or cover other than that in
which it is published and without a similar
condition including this condition being imposed
on the subsequent purchaser.

Granada ®
Granada Publishing ®

Contents

THE SOCIETY FOR PSYCHICAL RESEARCH

The Society for Psychical Research is the oldest learned society in this field. Its aim is to investigate apparently inexplicable phenomena scientifically. It organizes monthly lectures in London and other activities; it publishes a *Journal*, *Proceedings*, and *Newsletter*. An extensive library and archives are held at the Society's London headquarters where all enquiries, including membership, should be directed to:

The Society for Psychical Research
1 Adam & Eve Mews
Kensington
LONDON W8 6UG

Foreword

Around the year 1873, Frederick Myers was to recall in his *Human Personality*, a small group of Cambridge friends came to the conclusion that neither religion nor materialism had provided satisfactory answers to questions that were puzzling them:

Our attitudes of mind were in some ways different; but to myself, at least, it seemed that no adequate attempt had yet been made even to determine whether anything could be learnt as to the unseen world or no; for that if anything were knowable about such a world in such a fashion that Science could adopt and maintain that knowledge, it must be discovered by no analysis of tradition, and by no manipulation of metaphysics, but simply by experiment and observation – simply by the application to phenomena within us and around us of precisely the same methods of deliberate, dispassionate, exact inquiry which have built up our actual knowledge of the world which we can touch and see.

Along with his friends – chief among them Henry Sidgwick and Edmund Gurney – Myers became one of the founder members of the Society for Psychical Research, when it was formed in 1882 to put these ideas into practice, and this series is being published to mark the Society's centenary.

The phenomena of the 'unseen world' to which Myers referred were originally for convenience put into five main categories, each of which a committee was set up to investigate: telepathy, hypnotism, 'sensitives', apparitions and 'the various physical phenomena commonly called Spiritualistic'. Over the years the emphasis has to some extent shifted – in particular hypnotism, which at that time was dismissed as an occult delusion, was just about to be accepted as a reality, so it ceased to be on the psychic side of the fence. But broadly speaking, the phenomena under investigation are the same, and the ways in which they have been investigated have remained as Myers planned.

The terminology, however, has changed – and changed rather often, which has made for some confusion. Myers himself introduced 'telepathy', as 'thought reading' was ambiguous; it could refer to the way in which Sherlock Holmes picked up what was in Watson's mind by watching his expression. 'Supernormal', however, which Myers thought preferable to supernatural to describe the class of phenomena with which the Society would be dealing, has since itself been replaced by 'paranormal'; and 'parapsychology' has been easing out 'psychical research' – though some researchers prefer to restrict its use to laboratory-type work, leaving 'psychical' for research into spontaneous phenomena. 'Psi' has also come in as an all-purpose term to describe the forces involved, or to identify them – for example, in distinguishing a normal from a paranormal event.

If evidence were lacking for 'parascience' – as it might now more embracingly be described, because the emphasis of research has been shifting recently away from psychology to physics – it could be found in the composition of the Society, from its earliest beginnings. There can be few organizations which have attracted so distinguished a membership. Among physicists have been Sir William Crookes, Sir John Joseph Thomson, Sir Oliver Lodge, Sir William Barrett and two Lord Rayleighs – the third and fourth barons. Among the philosophers: Sidgwick himself, Henri Bergson, Ferdinand Schiller, L. P. Jacks, Hans Driesch, and C. D. Broad; among the psychologists: William James, William McDougall, Sigmund Freud, Walter Franklin Prince, Carl Jung and Gardner Murphy. And along with these have been many eminent figures in various fields: Charles Richet, a Nobel prizewinner in physiology; the Earl of Balfour, Prime Minister from 1902–6, and his brother Gerald, Chief Secretary for Ireland in 1895–6; Andrew Lang, polymath; Gilbert Murray, Regius Professor of Greek at Oxford and drafter of the first Covenant of the League of Nations; his successor at Oxford, E. R. Dodds; Mrs Henry Sidgwick, Principal of Newnham College, Cambridge; Marie Curie; the Hon Mrs Alfred Lyttleton, Delegate to the League of Nations Assembly;

Camille Flammarion, the astronomer, and F. J. M. Stratton, President of the Royal Astronomical Association; and Sir Alister Hardy, Professor of Zoology at Oxford.

Such a list, as Arthur Koestler pointed out in *The Roots of Coincidence*, ought to be sufficient to demonstrate that ESP research 'is not a playground for superstitious cranks'. On the contrary, the standards of research have in general been rigorous – far more rigorous, as psychologists have on occasion had to admit, than those of psychology. The reason that the results have not been accepted is basically that they have not been acceptable: extra-sensory perception and psychokinesis have remained outside science's domain, in spite of the evidence. And although the prejudice against parapsychology has been breaking down, so that it is being admitted as an academic discipline in universities, it is still very far from securing a firm base in the academic world.

Sceptics have sedulously propagated the notion that psychical researchers believe in ESP, PK, apparitions, and so on because they long to believe, or need to believe. Anybody who has studied the Society's *Journals* and *Proceedings*, or attended its meetings, will testify that this is a ludicrous misconception. Many of the most assiduous and skilled researchers have originally been prompted by *dis*belief – by a desire, say, to expose a medium as a fraud. It has to be remembered, too, that many, probably the great majority, of the members have been and still are desirous of showing that paranormal manifestations are *natural*, and can be explained scientifically – though admittedly not in the narrow terms of materialist science, which in any case the nuclear physicists have shown to be fallacious.

No: insofar as a Society containing such a diverse collection of individuals can be said to have a corporate identity, it could almost be described as sceptical; certainly as rational, as this series will show. Not, though, rationa*list*. Unluckily, rationalists, in their determination to purge society of its religious and occultist accretions, often failed to draw a distinction between superstitions and the observed phenomena which gave rise to them – which led them into such traps as refusing to accept the existence of meteorites, because of the association with Jove's thunderbolts; and to this day, they are prone to lapse into support for dogmas as rigid, and as ill-founded, as any of those of the Churches. If the series does nothing else, it will show how rationally – using that term in its proper sense – the writers have examined and presented the evidence.

Apparitions, the subject of the first book of the series, has been one of the Society's preoccupations since it was founded. In some ways it has presented the Society with its most formidable challenge. Whereas the other phenomena which the original committees were set up to explore could be investigated in laboratory conditions, apparitions were spontaneous, and often associated with particular places – notably haunted houses, where ghosts were reported to walk:

> The stately homes of England
>   though rather in the lurch
> Provide a lot of chances
>   for psychical research.

As investigators had already found, even before the SPR was formed, and have continued to find, ghosts are no respecters of research schedules, and rarely turn up when they are expected to.

Ghosts have another disadvantage; they are 'spooky'. Whereas experiences of telepathy or precognition, though they may be momentarily startling, can be accepted with equanimity, seeing a ghost – or worse, feeling its presence – is for most people an alarming experience, 'out of this world'. It is still, in fact, commonly regarded as a supernatural experience, rather than a paranormal one.

Anybody who elects to conduct research into apparitions consequently faces two hazards, if he undertakes fieldwork. 'Ghost-hunting' is immensely time-consuming, and for the most part intensely boring; sitting around, often in the dark, waiting for something to happen with no certainty that anything will happen. And follow-ups of case histories, which also take time, are complicated by the knowledge that good ghost stories, whether real or fictional, tend to be improved in the telling. No evidence can be taken on trust, not even if it is presented by the most truthful of witnesses; it needs to be sifted, and sifted again.

Andrew MacKenzie has devoted countless hours to such work; and in the process, he has become the leading authority on apparitions. Yet he managed to avoid becoming caught up in them, in the sense of growing so attached to any particular account that he cannot see the flaws, or will not accept fresh evidence casting doubt on it.

In one of his earlier books on the subject MacKenzie quoted from Professor H. H. Price, a former President of the Society; and what Price wrote will serve to set the scene.

The tea-party question, 'Do you believe in ghosts?' is one of the most ambiguous which can be asked. But if we take it to mean 'Do you believe that people sometimes experience apparitions?', the answer is that they certainly do. No one who examines the evidence can come to any other conclusion. Instead of disputing the facts, we must try to explain them.

That is what MacKenzie has set out to do — but always bearing in mind that, as Price added, 'whatever explanation we offer, we soon find ourselves in very deep waters indeed'.

Brian Inglis

Preface

This book, written to commemorate the centenary of the Society for Psychical Research (SPR), is composed of material published in the Society's *Journal* and *Proceedings*, with the addition of much hitherto unpublished material from the archives; the results of my own researches which have a bearing on some of the cases discussed; and brief extracts from the works of authors who were, in the main, contributors to the Society's publications. It covers a period of 150 years up to the present day. It should not be thought that everything in a scientific society's publication is necessarily 'as dry as dust' and of interest only to the specialist; Professor William James, the great American psychologist, who was President of SPR in 1894–5, said that the Society's ghost stories 'form the best literature I know of from the point of view of emotional interest' (40b p. 38). W. H. Salter, a barrister, who for more than forty years was a member of the Society and an officer for most of that time, said in his book *Zoar* that 'for a combination of quantity, variety and quality the SPR literature is without a rival, and no writer need apologize if he takes it as the main source of the evidence he cites to support and illustrate his argument' (76b p. 21). Before anything is published it is assessed by referees well versed in the literature of the subject.

Unfortunately, much of this fascinating material is hidden in thick volumes in the Society's library, in a limited number of other libraries, or in the archives, and thus is not readily accessible to the general public. If this book serves no other purpose I hope it will draw attention to the wealth of this material and the opportunity it provides for scientific research.

The object of the Society, set out in every issue of its publications, 'is to examine without prejudice or prepossession and in a scientific spirit those faculties of man, real or supposed, which appear to be inexplicable on any generally recognized hypothesis.' Because of this emphasis on examination, the Society's publications have always served as a forum for debate. The merits of a particular case, such as the experiences of Miss Moberly and Miss Jourdain in the park of the Petit Trianon in Versailles in 1901, or the later and rather better known 'haunting' of Borley Rectory, are in my opinion discussed in a calm and rational manner by members who hold different viewpoints. The opinions expressed are those of the individual, not the Society, which does not have a corporate view.

The material in the book sets out the results of investigations into apparitions and hauntings, subjects which, until the foundation of the Society in 1882, were heavily encrusted with the stuff of folk belief, legend, and superstition. Research into such matters seemed to many then – and still does today, although to a lesser extent than before – to be mere folly, and unworthy of serious minds. However, others take a different view and consider that hauntings and apparitions throw light into unfamiliar aspects of human personality and even of the nature of the universe. Most people, I suspect, do not think at all about apparitions except in the context of tales told at Christmas or films shown on late-night television. This book is written from the viewpoint that what has been revealed in investigations by members of the Society, and others, calls for further study and assessment.

Two questions arise in the minds of most people who have given any thought to the subject of this book. The first, surely, is whether events of the type described here really happen. If the answer is affirmative, the second question relates to their meaning.

It is for the reader to make up his or her own mind on the answer to the first question after studying the case material and my comments on it at the end of each chapter and in the closing chapter. Perhaps I may suggest an approach to a problem in this field in which so much uncritical and sensational material is published.

The first, and most important, point for the reader to consider is 'What is the evidence?', followed by 'Who are the principal witnesses and what value can be placed on their testimony?', and, thirdly, 'Who is the investigator or narrator? Is he widely read in the literature of the subject, does he present his findings in an unbiased manner, and does he present all the relevant evidence and not only that favourable to his viewpoint?'

The value of the literature of the Society for Psychical Research lies in the fact that the criteria set out above, which I give as a personal opinion in my review of Peter Underwood's book *Hauntings* (51f p. 837), are also those which have been taken into consideration by other researchers from the earliest days of the Society.

There is no easy answer to the question of the meaning of the experiences investigated by members of the Society. They have baffled mankind from the earliest times and perhaps, in the light of present knowledge, there are no answers or only very incomplete ones. But this does not mean that we cannot go on asking. We tend to seek simple answers to very complex questions. There are no simple answers.

In order to set the stage for the case histories that follow, I should explain that the most careful enquiry is necessary before a paranormal explanation for an event is accepted. 'Paranormal', as a term, is now preferred to 'supernatural' or 'supernormal'. It refers, according to Robert H. Ashby (2 p. 151), 'to those faculties and phenomena which are beyond "normality" in terms of cause and effect as currently understood.' There are also occasional references to *psi* – the twenty-third letter in the Greek alphabet – in this book. This is a general blanket term, coined by B. P. Wiesner and R. H. Thouless, used as either a noun or an adjective to identify paranormal processes and paranormal causation.

A normal explanation for an experience must first be sought before we accept a paranormal one. All too often what is thought to be a ghost is, in fact, a living person. I could quote case after case to illustrate this point, but will give, briefly, only one example of this common error. In 1968 a woman wrote to me explaining that when she was at the funeral service for her uncle at a crematorium she saw the figure of a woman she did not know in a pew in front of her, but when she came to leave the Chapel with the other mourners this woman had disappeared in an unaccountable manner. On her return home she described this figure to her aunt, who said that it resembled the dead man's mother, who had been dead for many years. I suggested that further enquiries should be made. The result was that the mysterious woman was discovered by my correspondent to be a living person, her uncle's cousin, who had been at the service and had managed to slip away unnoticed. It is easy to make errors of observation at times when people are distraught, such as at a funeral service.

Sometimes there is a physical explanation for what seems to be a ghostly event. Indeed, there are so many possible explanations for such happenings that the Society has issued a booklet as a guide to investigators of spontaneous cases (82k). For instance, mist figures are frequently mistaken for ghosts, with the observer interpreting a white or grey shape as that of a nun or monk. In November 1959, an observer in a top room in Whitcombe Street, London, W.C., saw out of his window at 5.30 a.m. the figure of a young woman in a white flowing nightdress or gown, with an indeterminate hairstyle, 'floating across the floor with her arms out-stretched before her.' It was seen through glass against a large window opposite, and although it may have appeared to be inside the opposite building, the distance could have been misjudged. The figure may have been out in the street at first-floor height from the observer's viewpoint. A mist 'wraith at that point' would not be surprising, as an underground stream crosses beneath Whitcombe Street just there (44h p. 281).

However, this said, there are a great many cases in which the inescapable conclusion is, in my opinion, that the figure seen was that of an apparition, although we are unable to explain satisfactorily, in the light of present knowledge, what is involved in such an experience.

Many people involved in psychical research, and even more outside it, tend to dismiss spontaneous case material on the grounds that it is 'anecdotal' and that little value can be placed on human testimony. Professor D. J. West, a former experimental research officer for the SPR, said in the chapter on spontaneous psychic impressions in his book *Psychical Research Today* that, 'However sure one may be that some of the impressions are genuine examples of ESP [extra-sensory perception], the explanation of many, especially the less well-corroborated cases, must be a normal one. Generalizations based upon all the cases are therefore always hazardous. They make useful starting points for investigation, but firm conclusions have to await experimental confirmation' (93b p. 40). This view may be modified by the fact that just as the percipient is involved in what he sees or hears in an experience which may have paranormal elements in it, in much the same way the experimenter is part of the experiment. In other words, personal elements are involved in work in the field and in the laboratory.

When Sir Alister Hardy, F.R.S., Emeritus Professor of Zoology at Oxford University and a former president of the SPR, produced his recent book *The Spiritual Nature of Man*(30), I asked him if the contents, a collection of accounts of experiences of a spiritual or mystical nature, could be considered a field study. He replied, 'Yes – certainly one can call this a field study: I like to regard our work [that of the Religious Experience Research Unit at Oxford] as similar in nature to that of the great observing naturalists in the last century – Darwin, Wallace, Bates, and many more. The doctrine of evolution was built up by their field observations, brought together to culmination by Darwin in his *Origin of Species* – it came *not* from the biological laboratories.'

Similarly, one may hope that the field studies outlined in this book will contribute something, however small, to an understanding of the true nature of man and the world he inhabits.

Some of the cases in this book contain accounts of happenings so strange that for many people they will strain belief. Yet there is good reason to accept that events happened more or less as set out here; the reason I say this is that the contents reveal a consistent pattern – something the founders of the SPR could not have known, as they did not then have enough reliable material on which to make this assessment. Most of the material will be new to present-day readers, particularly as the *Journal* of the SPR was not available to the public before 1947.

The number in parentheses after the quotation refers to the

source listed opposite that number in the Bibliography. May I stress once more that the Society for Psychical Research does not hold or express corporate views and that any opinions expressed in its publications are, therefore, those of the authors alone. My views should not be considered as those of a spokesman for the Society. This, most emphatically, I am not.

1 Apparitions

The study of apparitions has made little progress since the foundation of the SPR, a century ago, but I think it is fair to say that but for the labours of the pioneers of the Society, and later researchers, the subject would be even more obscure than it is at present. Many members of the general public regard apparitions, or ghosts (the word 'ghost' is mostly applied to figures seen from time to time at haunted places), as the spirits of the dead returned to manifest themselves to the living, whether as an indication of affection or suffering or to draw attention to some wrong done during their lifetime. This is far too simple a view of the phenomena and, moreover, it is not correct. There are apparitions of the living as well as of the dead. F. W. H. Myers, a founder of the Society and one of its most noted figures, said that 'Whatever else, indeed, a "ghost" may be, it is probably one of the most complex phenomena in nature' (60a vol. 2 p. 19).

When the Society for Psychical Research was constituted on 20 February 1882 one of the six committees set up was called on to make 'a careful investigation of any reports, resting on strong testimony, regarding apparitions at the moment of death, or otherwise, or regarding disturbances in houses reputed to be haunted', and another, the Literary Committee, was entrusted with the collection and collation of existing materials bearing on the history of the subjects under investigation by the Society. The first report of the Literary Committee, delivered five months later, showed that much of this material concerned apparitional experiences.

The two honorary secretaries of the Literary Committee were F. W. H. Myers (1843–1901) and Edmund Gurney (1847–88), both outstanding figures in the early life of the Society. Both were classical scholars and Fellows of Trinity College, Cambridge, and the amount of labour – a labour of love – they devoted to the collection of cases and the assessment of them for evidential content was prodigious. Myers was a controversial figure in his lifetime. Dr Alan Gauld, referring to Myers's Cambridge days, says in his book *The Founders of Psychical Research* that 'Few liked him, and some detested him' (23a p. 90). But it is strange that Myers should still be the subject of barbed comments from those opposed to the work of the Society, mainly on the grounds of his alleged sexual peccadilloes. More attention has been given by some writers to such matters than to his outstanding intellectual achievements. I have found myself turning again and again to his most important book *Human Personality and its Survival of Bodily Death* for his perceptive comments on apparitions and hauntings.

Edmund Gurney was much more popular with his contemporaries. He started and abandoned in turn careers in music, medicine, and the law before he found his true role in life in psychical research. He had, in bursts, prodigious energy. As Gauld has pointed out in his book, 'In the course of following up cases he would not infrequently write fifty or sixty letters in one day and in his own hand. He had also not merely to verify the cases, but to sort them, classify them and think about them' (23a pp. 161–2).

Henry Sidgwick, the Society's first president and Professor of Moral Philosophy at Cambridge, had outstanding intellectual gifts. But for his reputation for integrity, the Society would not have attracted the support it did from many influential figures at the time. Indeed, some of the original members joined only on the condition that Sidgwick should accept the presidency. Despite the pressure of his academic work, he took part in many investigations during which he showed himself to be both cautious and sceptical. He had no doubts about the opposition the Society faced. At the second general meeting of the Society on 9 December 1882 he said that he had met people in society who thought 'our evidence for thought-reading looks very strong, and they do not see why there should not be brain-waves or something of the kind; indeed, they have themselves tried some experiments after dinner at country-houses, which seem to confirm our view; and as for apparitions at the point of death, they have always thought there was a case for them.' But as they would tell him, they did not like to see so many superior persons 'spending a serious part of their time on such matters, instead of writing a commentary on Plato, or studying the habits of beetles, or in some other way making a really useful contribution to science or learning ... Some not unfriendly critics have given us to understand that if we had only confined ourselves to thought-reading, and, perhaps, clairvoyance, and similar phenomena of the mesmeric trance, we might have had their countenance; but that by taking in haunted houses, spirit-rapping, and so forth, we make ourselves too absurd' (80a pp. 67–8).

The investigators were not deterred. The Literary Committee composed a circular letter asking for information and sent it to several of the leading London and provincial journals, as well as to private friends. Very many letters were received containing matter 'of more or less value.' No evidence was considered at all unless authenticated by names and dates, not necessarily for publication, and in most cases the members of the committee made the acquaintance of the narrator and heard his story in a manner which pledged his honour to its truth. They also communicated with such other living persons involved in the case, and obtained all independent corroboration possible.

The committee's report stated that 'The very last thing that we expect to produce is a collection of narratives of a startling or blood-chilling character; our pages are far more likely to provoke sleep in the course of perusal than to banish it afterwards. The point in the evidence that impresses us is not its exciting or terrific quality, but its overwhelming quantity – overwhelming, we mean, to any further doubting the reality of the class of phenomena ... Our tales will resemble neither the *Mysteries of Udolpho* nor the dignified reports of a learned society. The romanticist may easily grow indignant over them; still more easily may the journalist grow facetious. The collection may easily be described as a farrago; but it will at any rate be a farrago of facts' (82a pp. 117–18).

The early cases published by the Society were classed as hallucinations experienced by people who were in good physical and mental health. Frank Podmore, one of the founders of the Society and a member of the Literary Committee, calls one of his books *Telepathic Hallucinations: The New View of Ghosts* (66a), and the second chapter is devoted to ghosts as hallucinations. There is an important paper on hallucinations by Gurney in the third volume of *Proceedings* in 1885 and a chapter on the same subject in *Phantasms of the Living* in 1886.

There is a good deal of misunderstanding about hallucinations of the sane. Many such experiences are totally delusive, but some are veridical in the sense that they convey information that can afterwards be verified. We know very little about the mental processes involved in hallucinatory experiences. Even such a distinguished scholar as Professor C. D. Broad, one of the most noted academics of his time, who held the chair of Moral Philosophy at Cambridge once occupied by Henry Sidgwick, confessed himself baffled when it came to explaining how veridical hallucinations occur. He said in his *Lectures on Psychical Research* that, 'up to the present, so far as I am aware, no one has managed to offer an intelligible concept, still less an imaginable schema, of the *modus operandi* of veridical hallucinations, which would enable a psychical researcher to infer what might be expected to happen in assignable circumstances and then to test his inferences by observation' (13c pp. 196–7).

Many doctors and psychologists refuse to regard hallucinations as anything other than the product of disturbed brains. The difficulty we face here, I feel, is to find a word, or term, to describe what happens when we experience an apparition or an apparent example of telepathy (the word coined by Myers to replace thought-transference), clairvoyance, or precognition. 'Hallucination' is, at best, an inadequate label to attach to accounts of such experiences, but it will have to do for the present.

William James's definitions of illusion, delusion, and hallucinations in his *Principles of Psychology* are a help. An illusion he classified as a false perception, giving as an example the illusion of movement experienced by a passenger in a train leaving the station, when all stationary objects visible through the window give him a sensation of gliding in the opposite direction. A delusion is a false opinion about a matter of fact which need not necessarily involve, though it often does involve, false perception of sensible things. Hallucinations, James observed, are often talked of as mental *images* projected outwards by mistake. 'But when an hallucination is complete, it is much more than a mental image. An hallucination is a strictly sensational form of consciousness, as good and true a sensation as if there were a real object there. The object happens not to be there, that is all' (40a vol. 2 p. 115).

James pointed out that 'the hallucination sometimes carries a change of the general consciousness with it, so as to appear more like a sudden lapse into a dream' (40a p. 120). This was a most perceptive comment. Much research has been done in recent years into altered states of consciousness in which someone undergoes an experience which, seemingly, has paranormal content.

The first report of the Literary Committee contained a number of reports of apparitions. One of the best came from Captain G. F. Russell Colt and concerned the death of his brother in the Crimean War. At the time he was home for the holidays and residing with his father and mother at Inveresk House in Midlothian. Russell's brother Oliver, aged 19, serving as a lieutenant in the 7th Royal Fusiliers, had been some months before Sebastopol when Russell, waking suddenly one night, saw him in a kneeling position surrounded by a light sort of phosphorescent mist. Russell tried to persuade himself that he had been deceived by moonlight playing on a towel, or something out of place, but still the apparition persisted, 'looking lovingly, imploringly, and sadly at me.' Russell sprang out of bed, glanced through the window, and saw that there was not only no moon but the night was dark, with heavy rain. When he reached the door he saw that the apparition of his brother had a wound on the right temple with a red stream from it. Russell spent the rest of the night in a friend's room. He told others of his experience, but was ordered by his father 'not to repeat such nonsense'. News of Oliver Colt's death in the storming of the Redan was received more that a fortnight later. The death wound was exactly where Russell had seen it in his vision of his brother.

This is what is known as a crisis case, as the apparition was seen around the time of death. When found, the body was in a kneeling position, propped up by other bodies. Although Russell Colt had been brought up not to believe in ghosts or apparitions, he had asked his brother to let him know if anything had happened to him by appearing to him [Russell] in his room, which he had done (82a pp. 124–6). It may be remarked here that a crisis need not necessarily concern death. It may involve illness, an accident, or an emotional shock.

The themes outlined in the first report of the Literary Committee were continued, and others introduced, in the first major work for the general public produced by the Society, *Phantasms of the Living*, in 1886 (28). The introduction was written by Myers but the principal author was Gurney. The third author, Frank Podmore, was an important figure in the early years of the Society. He had done well at Oxford in both classics and natural sciences, but instead of pursuing a scientific or academic career he joined the Post Office. His attitude towards investigations became increasingly critical, as is shown in his major study, *Modern Spiritualism*, which, although written as long ago as 1902, may still be read with profit today. Some modern researchers take the view that Podmore's influence on the Society was not a good one in that the strictness of his standards led to an attitude of sterile scepticism about all spontaneous phenomena. Others, however, admire him.

Phantasms of the Living, in two thick volumes, is 1,400 pages long and contains 701 cases. These were chosen from over two thousand depositions submitted to the Society, and, as pointed out by Myers in his introduction, 'more than half of them are narratives of appearances or other impressions coincident either with the death of the person seen or with some critical moment in his life's history.'

The approach of the authors to the subject under discussion is typified by the title of the opening chapter, 'Grounds of Caution'.

. . . The endeavour of this book, almost throughout, is to deal with themes that are in a sense familiar, by the aid, partly, of improved evidential methods, but partly also of conceptions which have as yet no place in the recognized psychology. Not, indeed, that the reader is about to be treated to any large amount of speculation; facts will be very much more prominent than theories. Still, the facts to be adduced carry us at least one step beyond the accepted boundaries. What they prove (if we interpret them rightly) is *the ability of one mind to impress or be impressed by another mind otherwise than through the recognized channels of sense*. We call the owner of the impressing mind the *agent*, and the owner of the impressed mind the *percipient*; and we describe the fact of impression shortly by the term *telepathy* ... It is not, however, with the ultimate conditions of the phenomena that the study of them can begin: our first business is with the reality, rather than with the rationale, of their occurrence.

A century has passed since these words were written and the reality of spontaneous cases which involve some ostensible paranormal factor is still a matter of dispute, so much so that other aspects, such as psychological content, have been neglected. It is understandable that the authors, in the prevailing climate of scepticism, made every effort to verify the statements in the narratives sent to them. Supporting evidence was sought where possible and the writers of the reports to be published and their witnesses were often interviewed at length.

In the main section of the book Gurney placed 352 spontaneous (or 'phantasmal') experiences which he regarded as of *high* evidential quality. The remaining cases being of admittedly *inferior* evidential value were relegated to a supplement. The investigation of the cases was an enormous undertaking. Gurney himself travelled far and wide through England, Scotland, Wales and Ireland interviewing percipients and witnesses and once wrote to William James about his 'hundreds of personal interviews' (61 pp. 353–4).

The title of the book requires some explanation. Myers said in his introduction that 'I refer to *apparitions*; excluding, indeed, the alleged apparitions of the dead, but including the apparitions of all persons who are still living, as we know life, though they may be on the very brink and border of physical dissolution.' I feel that what he had in mind here was that, although an apparition may have been seen some hours after physical death, what is experienced are the thoughts and emotions of a dying person as typified by the appearance of a figure, delayed until the percipient was in a suitable state to receive the impression.

There is much of great interest in the book to those interested in theoretical aspects of apparitional experiences: the nature of hallucinatory experiences; dreams which may be reasonably regarded as telepathic; 'borderland' cases which occur in the periods which precede sleep and follow sleep; collective experiences; experimental cases; hypnotic effects at a distance; and, most important, the theory of chance-coincidence with which I will deal later in the chapter. There were, of course, weaknesses in some of the cases, due, in my opinion, to too few investigators trying to do too much too soon: we must bear in mind that the SPR had been founded only four years before the production of this massive book. Commenting on *Phantasms*, Salter said that 'Although every effort was made to verify the cases set out in it, some of them were too old to be unreservedly accepted. The main importance of the book arises from the analysis of different sources of error that had discredited cases of this kind, and the putting forward of the hypothesis that would cover the cases, or most of the cases, that survived critical examination' (76b p. 28). I agree with Gauld in his assessment of the book: 'to pass from even the ablest of previous works to *Phantasms of the Living* is like passing from a mediaeval bestiary or herbal to Linnaeus' *Systema Naturae*' (23a p. 164). The book was, in the true sense of the words, a field study.

The most important work in the first twenty years of the life of the Society was undoubtedly the publication of the Report on the Census of Hallucinations, but as this was confined to *Proceedings* (80c) it did not make the same impact on the general public as did *Phantasms*. The undertaking received the approval of the International Congress on Experimental Psychology, held in Paris in 1889, which formally entrusted it to Professor Sidgwick's direction. He set up a committee, with himself as chairman, and it included such figures as his wife Eleanor Mildred Sidgwick, Miss Alice Johnson, a Cambridge scholar with first-class honours in natural sciences who was to hold several important posts in the Society, Myers, and Podmore. Mrs Sidgwick, a mathematician and sister of A. J. Balfour, the Prime Minister, was one of the ablest women in England and possessed considerable powers of analysis. Her ability to deal with difficult material is shown by her arrangement of it in the Census. Gauld has referred to her 'remarkable gifts for assimilating and analysing large masses of intractable material' (23a p. 168). She became Principal of Newnham College, Cambridge, in 1892, and retained that post until her retirement, at the age of 65, in 1910. An example of her powers of analytical thought is given in Chapter 9 of this book. Mrs Sidgwick's last contribution to *Proceedings* was made in 1932 when she was 87 years old. She died on 10 February 1936 when she was nearly 91. It is significant that she has been spared the personal attacks that have been made on some of the other leaders in the early days of the Society.

The general aim of the Committee that was to undertake the Census was to ascertain what proportion of persons had had sensory hallucinations while awake and not suffering from delirium or insanity or any other morbid condition obviously conducive to hallucination, and, further, to enquire into the nature of these hallucinations and the conditions under which they occur. The question asked was: 'Have you ever, when believing yourself to be completely awake, had a vivid impression of seeing or being touched by a living being or inanimate object, or of hearing a voice; which impression, so far as you could discover, was not due to any external cause?'

Replies were received from 17,000 people. Answers in the affirmative were received from 1,029 women and 655 men, which represented 9.9 per cent of the total. Therefore, approximately one person in ten in the sample had experienced an hallucination.

The Census was an international one. Nearly 16,000 answers came from English-speaking people. The next largest group was Russian and there was also a significant contribution from Brazil. Other replies came from Austria, Germany, France and Italy. An advantage was that recent cases were included: eighty-seven visual apparitions, for instance, had been reported in the previous year, and of these nineteen were within the most recent month. Members of the Committee travelled throughout Britain to interview the percipients and their witnesses in the more important cases.

Far more visual experiences than others were reported. One in twenty had seen a realistic apparition, and one in thirty a realistic apparition of a recognized person. The report revealed the strange fact that in fifteen cases a hand, or hand and arm only, were represented, and in three cases, legs.

A section of the report dealt with the sense of a presence, 'an impression of the near presence of someone, in which no sensation either of sight, hearing, or touch, appears to be involved . . . it is often so strong as to appear to the percipient a very striking phenomenon, and to produce a great effect on his mind.' In some cases the impression of someone being present was not externalized: when an apparition was seen it was the externalization of an impression. In my opinion, both experiences are equally valid in the sense of indicating that someone or something is 'there', but not, apparently, in physical space.

The Committee received twenty-five reports of apparitions of animals: thirteen cats, four dogs, one rabbit, one mouse, one bird, one butterfly, one horse with carriage, besides three recurring cases in which the percipient often saw cats, and two in which both cats and dogs appeared.

Nearly twice as many apparitions of the living were reported as compared with those of the dead. One of the accounts came from Miss Edith Wilson, aged 22. One morning at Christ Church, St Leonard's-on-Sea, Sussex, she looked up from her prayer book, which she was sharing with her brother, and saw the figure of a man she knew standing in what had been an empty seat opposite her. He looked at her with a fixed, agonized gaze and then, to her utter astonishment, vanished. She heard afterwards that at the exact time he was at the deathbed of his mother, a fact established by Mrs Sidgwick, who interviewed the young woman. Mrs Sidgwick said that 'The fact that Mrs— was more clearly passing through a crisis is an argument for supposing that the telepathic impression came from her, but on the other hand there is reason to think that Mr— and the percipient were much more interested in each other than the dying lady and the percipient were, and his thoughts may well have turned to her at the moment of his mother's death.'

We do not know from this account whether Miss Wilson's

brother also saw the figure of the man. The 'mechanism', if that is the word, in such cases is that the thought of a person is directed towards a certain spot, and someone there, and is picked up telepathically. In this case the message was received in visual form, but there are other ways in which a message may be received. One section of the report deals with the effects of noises in producing hallucinations. The case is quoted of a woman, who, at 5 a.m. on 6 April 1881, heard the voice of a man she knew say 'Please silence your dog.' Her dog had, in fact, been barking immediately before this. The man whose voice she recognized was, she knew, lying ill with pneumonia in another part of London. Enquiries made later revealed that he had died at 3.0 a.m. that morning. No one else was awake or heard the noise. A footnote of the report states that 'The importance of the coincidence is of course reduced by the percipient's knowledge that her friend was seriously ill.'

Thirty apparitions were seen in the dark. In seventeen of the thirty cases, the figure alone appeared illuminated, sometimes seeming phosphorescent or emitting a special light of its own; sometimes surrounded by a luminous aura or halo; and sometimes merely appearing as a real person would in the light, but with nothing visible round it. In twelve other cases out of the thirty the room appeared illuminated, though it was really dark; in three of these the figure seemed to emit the light; the remaining case seemed to be between these two types.

Ninety-five out of 1,087 visual cases, and thirty-four out of 493 auditory cases, were reported to be collective, and also two cases involving the sense of touch.

The report stated that reflecting surfaces were apparently favourable as aids to spontaneous hallucinations. 'It seems not improbable that the reason why gazing at a reflecting crystal, or into a refracting body of crystal, is found in practice to be a way of inducing hallucinations is that convenient *points de repère* (guiding marks) without enough meaning of their own distract attention are thus obtained.' Seventeen instances of hallucinations seen in reflecting surfaces were obtained in the Census, 'which seems a large proportion out of the whole number.' Of these seventeen instances, one hallucination was seen in a ship's compass, one in a carafe of water, five in mirrors, and ten in windows of which the two sides were unequally lighted, the figure appearing on the darker side.

Professor and Mrs Sidgwick interviewed a young seaman who, when on board ship in the North Sea, was startled to see reflected in the face of a compass the face of a young lady to whom he was to be married on his return home. When his ship arrived at Berwick the next day he learnt that she had died about the time he saw her.

The Census of Hallucinations throws much valuable light on the circumstances in which apparitions are seen but it is mostly quoted today because of the Report's findings on death-coincidences – an apparition being called 'coincidental' when it occurred within twelve hours either before or after death. The Committee that drafted the Report pointed out that the question of whether there was any connection between the death of a person and the apparition of that person being seen could only be settled by selecting a coincidence between these definite events and seeing how often it would occur by chance and how often it actually does occur. Cases in which an apparition was seen after it was known that a person had died were not taken into account; only those cases in which the death was neither known to the percipient nor expected by him were included.

The Report sets out fully the statistical process that the analysis involved. It can be summarized by saying that corre-spondences between these two events were found to be 440 times as numerous as might have been expected if nothing but chance had to be taken into account.

The Committee considered that 'Undoubtedly the most im-portant part of our work lies in the corroboration . . . on a much wider basis, of the conclusion already drawn by Mr Gurney from his Census in 1885 [Gurney's Census, based on a sample of 5,700 cases, was published in *Phantasms of the Living*]. *Between deaths and apparitions of the dying person a connection exists which is not due to chance alone.* This we hold as a proved fact. The discussion of its full implications cannot be attempted in this paper; nor perhaps, exhausted in this age.'

Discussing the results of the Census, D. J. West said that

although 'the most resolute sceptic could not maintain that chance alone would account for all the cases of apparitions said to coincide with death', a sceptic could still assert that normal factors, which the investigators admitted might account for a high proportion of the cases, might just as well account for all of them.

When large numbers of these cases are studied, one notices that the most striking are usually the ones that are said to have happened long ago. The Census investigators noticed that a disproportionate number of the apparitions which were supposed to coincide with some real event were old cases. Because of this they were prepared to discount half the reported coincidences as probably spurious. With the passing of time, helped perhaps by frequent retelling, coincidences that were not originally remarkable become exaggerated and elaborated out of all recognition. Indeed, it amounts to an almost invariable law in spontaneous cases that the more remarkable the alleged coincidence the worse the supporting evidence, and conversely, the better the evidence the weaker is the coincidence. There can be only one conclusion. Whether one does or does not accept that some cases are instances of genuine ESP, most cases are spurious (93b p. 31).

I cannot agree with West that most cases are spurious, although a great many are capable of a natural explanation, nor can I agree about his 'almost invariable law' as set out above. West bases his argument on the 'invariable law' on a table of non-veridical hallucinations classified according to dates in a long paper on the investigation of spontaneous cases (93a pp. 280–1). The hallucinations he considers were those reported to the researchers who compiled the Census of Hallucinations; but it must be kept in mind that this was a novel and early undertaking and it was inevitable that much old material would be submitted. Enough good material has come to light in recent years to enable me to say with some confidence that certain spontaneous cases do stand up to close inspection. One such case, that of Johnnie Minney, is given in the next chapter. Dr West told me recently (March, 1981) that his view of the 'almost invariable law' is still the same, but 'it does not mean, believing this, that I think that no case is paranormal.'

One of the most important papers produced during the first ten years of the Society's existence was Mrs Sidgwick's 'Notes on the evidence, collected by the Society, for phantasms of the dead' in *Proceedings* in 1885. The Society at that time possessed, as the residue of a much larger number, a collection of about 370 narratives, that seemed to deserve some consideration 'of phenomena, not clearly physical, and which believers in ghosts would be apt to refer to the agency of deceased human beings.' Most of these had to be set aside, for one reason or another, and she confined her attention to twenty-five narratives 'with a view of ascertaining what psychical theories, if any, they seem to point to.'

Mrs Sidgwick considered that the possible non-ghostly explanation of what pass as ghostly phenomena may be conveniently classified with reference to the various sorts of error by which the evidence of such phenomena was liable to be affected. She stated these as (1) hoaxing, (2) exaggeration or inadequate description, (3) illusion, (4) mistaken identity, (5) hallucination, and discussed each in detail (81a p. 71). 'Hallucination' is here used in the popular sense of the term. No rule could be laid down, she thought, as to the light by which ghosts were seen. They were seen in all kinds of light, from broad daylight to the faint light of dawn; from bright gaslight to the light of a dying fire. Sometimes they seem to be self-luminous, and sometimes to bring with them, as it were, an apparition of light. There was even one case where the ghost was described as having been apparently seen in the back of the percipient's head.

As to sounds, again no rule could be laid down. In some cases there were unaccounted-for sounds in houses where ghosts were seen, and in others no sounds beyond what might be noticed anywhere seemed to have been observed. Where there were mysterious sounds they had for the most part no obvious connection with the apparition. The apparition itself rarely appeared to make any noise. To hear footsteps, for instance, seemed to be unusual. Sometimes an apparition seemed to be heralded by a noise – a sound causing the percipients to look in the direction in which they saw the ghost, but it was difficult to say whether these noises were not real, and their connection with the ghost accidental.

The mode of appearance and disappearance of apparitions is also various.

The ghost is usually either seen on looking round, as a human being might be, or seems to come in at the door. Sometimes it forms gradually out of what at first seems a cloud-like appearance. I do not think there are any cases of its appearing suddenly in a spot which the percipient was actually looking at and perceived to be vacant before. It disappears suddenly in this way sometimes, and sometimes if the percipient looks away for a moment it is gone. Sometimes it vanishes in a cloud-like manner, sometimes, retaining its form, it becomes gradually more and more transparent till it is gone. Frequently it disappears through the door, either with or without apparently opening it, or goes into a room where there is no other exit, and where it is not found.

What sort of people see ghosts?

. . . we can again lay down no rules. The power is not limited by age, sex, or profession. It does not, so far as has been ascertained, depend on any obvious conditions of health, temperament, intellect, or emotion. It is not even certain that it is possessed by some persons and not by others, although there are reasons for thinking this probable. If several persons are together when the ghost appears it will sometimes be seen by all and sometimes not, and failure to see it is not always merely the result of not directing the attention towards it. Perhaps the truth may be that we all have potentially the power of seeing such things, but that it requires a special state of mind, or body in us, to coincide with some external cause, and that coincidence rarely, and in the case of most individuals, nevers occurs.

In the quotation given above, Mrs Sidgwick answers the question, so often asked, 'Why can't I see a ghost?' Certain people, with powers of visualization, are more likely to see an apparition than others, but among these may be some, gifted with a certain quality of sensitivity, who are sometimes aware of the presence of a person although this awareness does not take the form of an apparition. There are also people who manage to turn their attention off so completely that they are unable to receive a message, if there is one, in any form. We would be better able to answer the question posed above if we knew more about apparitions – indeed, what is an apparition – than we do. I hope that some of the tentative conclusions set out in the final chapter will make this problem less obscure.

W. H. Salter, who, although qualified in law, served the SPR in a variety of capacities for over forty years and knew all the leading figures in psychical research during this period, pointed out that:

On its foundation in 1882 the Society at once began to follow up two lines of enquiry in which substantial progress had already been made by some of the original members. These were the experimental study of 'thought-reading', as the Founders' Manifesto styled telepathy, and the investigation of apparitions and other spontaneous phenomena. Apparitions are among the oldest of human experiences. As embellished by popular tradition and literary artifice they provided the basis of the familiar ghost story, universally accepted by the western world for centuries, and then almost universally rejected by educated men and women, but in either case without systematic investigation until our Founders undertook the task (82d p. 83).

Reference will be made in later chapters to published studies of apparitions, but I think it is fair to say that the interest of researchers gradually waned as interest in experimental work involving telepathy, clairvoyance and precognition increased, and the Society had to cope with many accounts of precognitive dreams sent in by members of the public, yet people in general have never lost their interest in ghost stories. Lately, the interest of researchers in apparitional experiences has revived.

Anyone who has studied in depth accounts of apparitional experiences will have noticed that very often the act of looking away from an apparition, even for a moment, causes the figure to disappear. The reason for this is that any such act results in a change of consciousness. It is now generally accepted that apparitions are experienced in what are termed altered states of consciousness (ASC), about which there is a large and growing literature. A good introduction to the subject is Dr Adrian Parker's *States of Mind: ESP and Altered States of Consciousness*, with an introduction by Dr John Beloff (65) which has a useful reading list and references. I should point out, however, that there are cases in which a person has diverted his or her attention from an apparition, even to the extent of diving under the bedclothes, and the figure still persists. In such instances it seems that the altered state of consciousness is prolonged, but eventually the figure will disappear.

2 The Debate about Ghosts

A debate about apparitions and ghosts far more vigorous than that being conducted today was carried on in some of the early copies of *Proceedings*, and one such debate is in Volume Six, where Myers engages in a dispute with the more sceptical Podmore, the subject being 'Phantasms of the Dead'. In the course of this Myers attempts some definitions, admittedly incomplete, of apparitions. 'Instead of describing a "ghost" as a dead person permitted to communicate with the living, let us define it as a *manifestation of persistent personal energy* – or as an indication that some kind of force is being exercised after death which is in some way connected with a person previously known on earth,' he said (60c p. 15).

Myers also believed that '"ghosts" must as a rule represent not conscious or central currents of intelligence, but mere automatic projections from consciousnesses which have their centres elsewhere' (60c p. 64).

He also said that 'One true "ghost" story is apt to be very like another; – and all to be fragmentary and apparently meaningless' (60c p. 16).

The automatic behaviour of ghosts has often been the subject of comment. The physicist Dr Raynor C. Johnson, former Master of Queen's College, Melbourne University, shows substantial agreement with Myers's viewpoint when he says in *The Imprisoned Splendour* that:

The apparitional behaviour is usually confined to a semi-automatic type. Anything beyond this is generally of a single idea or purpose – e.g. to stroke hair, to wave the hand, to exhibit a wound, to frequent a neighbourhood or to demonstrate continued existence; having done which the sustaining subsistent thought (or object) has expended the impulse which gave it birth and it fades away (41 p. 212).

Johnson also considered that 'an apparition of a human being is not a centre of consciousness; it is, so to speak, a psychical marionette given temporary life by some quite separate centre of consciousness' (41 p. 213).

Myers introduced the very strange concept of phantasms of the dead being of the nature of dreams of the dead:

To put the matter in a crude way; the behaviour of phantasms of the living suggests dreams dreamt by the living persons whose phantoms appear. And similarly the behaviour of phantasms of the dead suggests dreams dreamt by the deceased persons whose phantasms appear. The actions of these phantasms may therefore be expected to be vague and meaningless, or at any rate to offer little response or adaptation to the actions of the persons who observe them.

He had a message of reassurance to those who think that ghosts may harm them. Discussing hauntings, he said (60c p. 46):

The drift of the evidence . . . makes not for haunted men but for haunted *places*. It tends to show that figures resembling deceased persons are sometimes seen in the former habitat of those persons, under circumstances which make their explanation as after-images or as chance-resemblances improbable. It is plain, however, that these figures can seldom occur under good evidential conditions . . . But there is no part of our enquiry where more care as to evidential conditions is needed, or where less care has actually been used. In our former discussions on apparitions coincident with a death, we found that even the strongest personal interest in the vision was often insufficient to induce the percipient to record it properly, or to collect the most necessary corroborations. And in these cases of so-called 'haunting' the meaning of the apparition is still less the personal concern of any given recipient. Posterity – let us hope – will smile at the tone of many of the accounts which people give of such experiences, – their sense of personal injury at the idea that such a thing could happen to *them*, – their unabashed avowal of having been terribly frightened at a poor phantom which could not hurt a fly.

Answering Myers, Podmore said that it must be admitted that the fact that the figures seen in a haunted house are apt at different times to assume different forms, including those of animals and vague lights, suggests that the phenomena are due not to an alien spiritual presence but to some predisposition to hallucination on the part of the percipients: 'the numerous cases in which it can be shown that the percipients have experienced other hallucinations of various kinds, shared and unshared, give strong confirmation to this view' (66d p. 243). He disagreed with Myers's view that the manifestations in a haunted house seem to reflect 'a dead man's incoherent dream', stating that 'To me it is not obvious why the dreams of the living should possess less potency than the imagined dreams of the unknown dead' (66d pp. 269–70).

Myers's health failed in the autumn of 1900, and he died at Rome on 17 January 1901 in his fifty-eighth year. His great work, *Human Personality and its Survival of Bodily Death*, incorporating the result of many of his investigations for the Society for Psychical Research, was published in January 1903 and reprinted the following month. Various editions, some of them abridged, have appeared since then. 'In this book', Aldous Huxley observed in a foreword to the 1961 American edition, 'Myers brought together an immense store of information about the always strange and often wonderful goings-on in the upper storeys of a man's soul house. And this information he presents within a theoretical frame of reference that takes account not only of the rats and beetles in the cellarage, but also of those treasures, birds and angels so largely ignored by Freud and his followers . . . How strange and how unfortunate it is that this amazingly rich, profound and stimulating book should have been neglected in favour of descriptions of human nature less complete and of explanations less adequate to the given facts.'

Myers's work is attracting increasing attention. In reply to a question from me, Rhea A. White, Consultant to the Library of the American SPR, wrote that 'I think there is more interest in Myers in this country, and probably the world over, now than ever, because of the interest in altered states of consciousness. Certainly Myers was a pioneer in the study of consciousness, just as much as in psychical research.'

Human Personality is, in effect, a summary of the mass of evidence gathered together in the sixteen volumes of *Proceedings* and the nine volumes of the *Journal* of the SPR produced up to that time, as well as case material in *Phantasms of the Living* and in manuscript form. The book is, therefore, an invaluable source of reference for those who do not have access to the early publications of the SPR. At the end of the first volume of *Human Personality* Myers presents some experimental cases, including the deliberate projection of a visual hallucination; and I will give an example of this, because it is a type of case reported in the last century but almost never today. In a survey of cases in *Proceedings* in 1923, Mrs Sidgwick mentioned that no case of this type had been reported to the Society since 1900. I find this puzzling, as other types of apparition are still being reported in considerable numbers, although there are fewer crisis cases than formerly.

The case, which came from the Rev. Clarence Godfrey, first appeared in the second edition of *Phantasms of the Living*, having been sent to Frank Podmore by the experimenter, a friend of his. After retiring to bed at 10.45 p.m. on 15 November 1886 Godfrey had determined to appear, if possible, to a friend, and accordingly set himself to work with all the 'volitional and determinative' energy he possessed to stand at the foot of her bed. Needless to say, he had not given any hint of this intention. His effort was sustained for perhaps eight minutes, after which he felt tired and was soon asleep. He woke at 3.40 a.m., feeling that he had succeeded in his experiment and made a note of that impression at the time. The next day he received from his friend an account of her experience. That morning, about 3.30, she woke up with a start and an idea that someone had come into the room. She rose, lit a candle, and went downstairs to get some soda water. 'On returning to my room I saw Mr Godfrey standing under the large window of the staircase. He was dressed in his usual style, and with an expression on his face that I have noticed when he has been looking very earnestly at anything. He stood there, and I held up the candle and gazed at him for three or four seconds in utter amazement, and then, as I passed up the staircase, he disappeared . . .'

Both witnesses were interviewed by Podmore. Mrs— told him that the figure appeared quite distinct and life-like at first. As she looked it grew more and more shadowy, and finally faded away. Godfrey, at the Society's request, made two other trials, without, of course, letting his friend know of his intention. The first of these attempts was without result, but a trial made on 7 December 1886 succeeded completely. Mrs—, writing on 8

December, stated that she was awakened by hearing a voice cry, 'Wake', and by feeling a hand rest on the left side of her head. She then saw stooping over her a figure which she recognized as Godfrey's.

Commenting on this last experience, Podmore said that the dress of the figure did not seem to have been seen distinctly, but in the apparitional experience on 16 November the dress was that ordinarily worn in the daytime by Godfrey, and that in which the percipient would be accustomed to see him, *not* the dress which he was actually wearing at the time. The conclusion he drew from this was that 'The dress and surroundings of the phantasm represent, not the dress and surroundings of the agent at the moment, but those with which the percipient is familiar' (60a vol. 1 pp. 689–90).

A single modern example of the deliberate projection of a 'body' which was seen by another was published in 1963, and I will outline it briefly here because the absence in modern times of phenomena reported in the early days of the Society must raise doubts either about the reality of such phenomena or the standards of reporting then.

The case concerns Lucian Landau, a member of the Society, and his wife, Mrs Eileen Landau, both now resident in the Isle of Man where I have visited them. Earlier talks were held in London. Both have strong psychic gifts. Over tea, on one occasion, in a lull in a conversation about dogs, I was pondering on the problem of whether animals survive death when Mrs Landau turned to me and said in a positive tone, 'Yes, they do,' thus answering an unspoken question.

At the beginning of September 1955, Landau, who was then living in London, was feeling unwell, but a thorough medical examination failed to show any real trouble. Mrs Landau, as she was later to become, slept in a spare bedroom opposite. One morning she told him that she came into his bedroom during the night (minus her physical body!) to check his pulse and respiration. He asked her to do this again the following night, this time trying to bring some object with her. He gave her his small diary, weighing 38g. That night they left the doors of both bedrooms open because they could hardly expect a physical object to pass through solid wood. Before falling asleep, Mr Landau asked himself to wake should anything unusual occur in his room.

He woke suddenly. It was dawn, and there was just about enough light coming in through the partly drawn curtains to enable one to read. At a point near the door stood the figure of Mrs Landau, looking straight ahead towards the window. The figure was wearing a nightdress; its face was extremely pale, almost white. It moved slowly backwards towards the door with a gliding motion. When the figure reached the middle of the landing Landau left his bed and followed it. He could then clearly see the moving figure, which was quite opaque and looked like that of a living person, but for the extreme pallor of the face, and at the same time the head of Mrs Landau, asleep in her bed, the bedclothes rising and falling as she breathed.

The figure vanished suddenly when it reached a position near the bed. There was no visible effect on Mrs Landau, who did not stir and whose rhythm of breathing remained unchanged. Landau moved quietly back to his room and at the side of his bed found a small rubber toy dog – it weighed 107.5g – which belonged to Mrs Landau and which had stood on a small chest of drawers near her bed in the opposite room when he last saw it.

In the morning, after breakfast, he questioned Mrs Landau about the diary. She replied that she first went to the desk and somehow could not pick it up. As a child she had been told never to handle other people's letters or diaries; possibly for this reason she did not wish to handle this one. Instead, she lifted up the rubber toy dog. She remembered taking it through the door, across the landing, to the other room. Although she did not remember actually walking, she had seen Mr Landau asleep and breathing normally. She felt very tired and wanted to go back to bed. Up to this moment her consciousness appeared to be normal, as did her ability to see her surroundings, which also appeared normal to her. She did not remember anything about going backwards to her room or entering her bed (45 pp. 126–8).

Landau told me that this case was the most unusual one in his experience, 'but its nature makes it difficult to provide the necessary supporting evidence.' I agree with this assessment.

The case is remarkable in that it involves what purports to be the movement of a solid object, a rubber toy dog, by the astral (or etheric) body of Mrs Landau. Some writers would classify this case as an out-of-the-body experience, as Landau did, and others as an apparition of the living, but, if we accept the evidence of both witnesses, the most important point is that it took place in an experimental setting. I should explain that what is described as an out-of-the-body experience refers to an experience, either spontaneous or induced, in which one's centre of consciousness seems to be in a spatial location outside of one's physical body. In this state, percipients have claimed to see their physical body lying inert, to see and hear people while remaining imperceptible themselves, and to perceive and remember people, places, objects, and occurrences which were beyond the reach of their physical senses.

Myers followed up his study of experimental cases in *Human Personality* with an important chapter on phantasms of the dead. He argued that we have no warrant for the assumption that the phantom seen, even though it be somehow *caused* by a deceased person, *is* that deceased person, in any ordinary sense of the word. 'It may bear such a relation to the deceased that it can reflect or represent his presumed wish to communicate, or it may not. If, for instance, its relation to his *post mortem* life be like the relation of my dreams to my earthly life, it may represent little that is truly his, save such vague memories and instincts to give a dim individuality to each man's trivial dreams' (60a vol. 2 pp. 3–4).

It is theoretically possible, Myers maintained, that the force or influence which, after a man's death, creates a phantasmal impression of him, may indicate no continuing action on his part, but may be some residue of the force of energy which he generated while still alive.

Strange as this notion might seem, Myers felt, it was strongly suggested by many of the cases of haunting. 'We shall presently find that there is strong evidence for the recurrence of the same hallucinatory figures in the same locality, but weak evidence to indicate any purpose in most of these figures, or any connection with bygone individuals, or with such tragedies as are popularly supposed to start a ghost on its career. In some of these cases of frequent, meaningless recurrence of a figure in a given spot, we are driven to wonder whether it can be some deceased person's past frequentation of that spot, rather than any fresh action of his after death, which has generated what I have termed the veridical after-image – veridical in the sense that it communicates information previously unknown to the percipient, as to a former inhabitant of the haunted locality' (60a vol. 2 pp. 4–5).

Myers ended his chapter on phantasms of the dead with the strange and convincing case of a woman seen loitering by her husband's tomb by a gardener, who was unaware that she had died seven and a half hours previously. The gardener, Alfred Bard, was on his way home, and on entering the churchyard at Hinxton, Saffron Walden, Essex, on Friday 8 May 1885, he saw Mrs de Fréville, whom he knew well, leaning on the rails of the square stone vault in which her husband was buried, dressed as she normally was in a coal-scuttle bonnet, black jacket with deep crêpe, and black dress, but with a face much whiter than usual. She showed awareness of him. He slightly stumbled on a tussock of grass, and when he looked up she was gone. Supposing that she had gone quickly into the tomb he tried to follow her, but the door was shut. Baffled by what had happened, Bard went home and told his wife that he had seen Mrs de Fréville. His wife later confirmed this fact. News of Mrs de Fréville's death in London was not received in Hinxton until the following day.

This is a good case from an evidential point of view. The local vicar made enquiries immediately after the death of Mrs de Fréville and interviewed the gardener, whom he regarded as a trustworthy person with powers of 'great observation'. Statements were taken and the spot where the apparition was seen was inspected by Myers, who said that the incident suggested that Bard had come across Mrs de Fréville's spirit, so to say, unawares. 'One cannot imagine that she specially wished him to see her, and to see her engaged in what seems so needless and undignified a retracing of current earthly thought. Rather this seems a rudimentary *haunting* – an incipient lapse into those aimless, perhaps unconscious, reappearances in familiar spots which may persist (as it would seem) for many years after death' (60a vol. 2 pp. 66–7).

I am often asked 'How can you prove that anyone has seen an apparition?' The answer is when you see someone you know well in such circumstances that you do not doubt you are seeing a living person. It is worth noting that the gardener considered that Mrs de Fréville's face was much whiter than usual. Mr Landau, it will be remembered, said that the figure he saw looked like that of a living person, but for the 'extreme pallor of the face'. Clues such as this may help us to understand a little more about the phenomena in what are termed visual hallucinations and to trace resemblances between apparitions of the living (Mrs Landau) and of the dead (Mrs de Fréville).

Two hundred reports of phantasms of the living, which had reached the Society since *Phantasms of the Living* was published in 1886, appeared in *Proceedings* in 1923. Analysing them, Mrs Sidgwick said she had accepted only cases in which the interval between experience and record did not exceed five years. Her classification differed in some respects from that of Edmund Gurney in *Phantasms of the Living*, where he treated separately dreams, 'borderland' cases (that is, experiences occurring when the percipient was in bed but believed himself to be awake), and hallucinations when the percipient was up and about. She treated these three classes together (81f p. 27).

Impressions, as I have pointed out, are sometimes externalized in the form of an apparition. Sometimes, however, information is conveyed in a manner in which it is not possible to ascertain the source. One such case concerned a little boy, aged just over three, who, while lying quietly in bed, suddenly sat up and said, 'Daddy's dead', his father at that time (1918) being a serving officer. News of the death of the person concerned, Captain Edward Stanley Russell, reached his family several days later. Mrs Sidgwick commented that in this case evidence of any exact coincidence was wanting, but there was no doubt that the little boy's experience occurred some time before the news of his father's death was received, 'and it is almost if not quite certain that it did not occur before the death itself' (81f pp. 133–5).

A case that impressed Mrs Sidgwick concerned the death of Lieut. David E. McConnel, who was killed in a flying accident on 7 December 1918. The percipient was one of his fellow officers,

Lieut. J. J. Larkin, RAF. She considered it perhaps the best-evidenced death coincidence in the collection of 200 reports, having been spoken of by the percipient to another person, who corroborated it, before it was realized that the figure was not that of the living man; and it was recorded in writing within fifteen days of the event.

On the morning of 7 December 1918 Lieut. McConnel, aged 18, a trainee pilot, was unexpectedly asked by his Commanding Officer at Scampton, Lincolnshire, to fly a Camel aircraft to Tadcaster, sixty miles away. At 11.30 a.m. McConnel took leave of his roommate Lieut. Larkin, saying that he expected to be back for tea. At Tadcaster aerodrome, in dense fog, McConnel apparently lost control of his plane, 'nose-dived', and crashed with the engine full on. A girl who saw the plane crash ran to the plane and found McConnel dead. The violence of contact seemed to have stopped his watch, which registered 3.25 p.m.

Lieut. Larkin was reading and smoking in his room when he heard someone walking up the passage. The door opened with the usual noise and clatter which McConnel always made and Larkin heard his greeting, 'Hello, boy!' He half turned round in his chair and saw McConnel standing in the doorway, half in and half out of the room, holding the doorknob in his hand. He was dressed in his full flying clothes but wearing his naval cap – an unusual item of apparel. The two young men exchanged a few words. McConnel said, 'Well, cheero!', closed the door noisily, and went out. Larkin did not have a watch, but was certain the time was between quarter and half past three, because shortly afterwards a Lieut. Garner-Smith came into the room and it was then a quarter to four. Garner-Smith came to enquire whether McConnel was back because they planned to go to Lincoln that evening. Larkin replied, 'He *is* back, he was in the room a few minutes ago!' Garner-Smith then went off to search for McConnel. Larkin discovered that McConnel was dead when he overheard a group of officers discussing the crash in the Albion Hotel, Lincoln, that evening.

The only normal explanation which could be made to cover the facts in this case would be one of mistaken identity; but, Mrs Sidgwick commented, this hypothesis 'seems very difficult to maintain in face of the recognition, not only of appearance, but of voice and of manner of entering the room.'

She added:

It will be observed that we know the apparition to have been seen within a few minutes of the death, but not whether it occurred before or after or at the actual moment. If it preceded the death, Lieutenant McConnel dreaming in a fainting condition may have imagined his expedition successfully accomplished and himself returned to his quarters. In this case the details of the apparition may have been due to the agent. They are, however, also what might naturally be supplied by the percipient, given the time and place (81f pp. 152–60).

Mrs Sidgwick raises in the last sentence a most important point which I will discuss in the closing chapter.

Dr West, a most sceptical investigator, was impressed by this case and considered that it was unusually well corroborated; 'indeed, there are few others in the SPR collection which reach the same standard.' He said that the McConnel apparition was unusual in being so very lifelike, and in being talked with as well as seen. 'In most cases the apparition is seen as a mute figure, often misty and unreal. Sometimes an apparition is not "seen" at all, but felt as a "presence". Apparitions are not physical phantoms that can be photographed. They are subjective and, in the strict sense, hallucinations.'

West considered that one of the least implausible explanations was that Larkin's hallucination was induced by an expectant state of mind. There was no doubt, he said, that expectancy sometimes produces hallucinations. In the McConnel case, Larkin was expecting his friend to return around teatime. If news of the fog had reached Scampton, he may have been a little anxious. A condition of anxious expectancy was just that state of mind most likely to induce an hallucination in persons inclined to have these experiences. The weak point in this explanation, West observed, was that Larkin stated that the experience *was* for him quite exceptional. 'There is no doubt that had he been questioned on the point he would have vigorously denied that he was subject to hallucinations, expectant or otherwise' (93b pp. 25–9).

When Lieut. Larkin heard footsteps in the passage, followed

by the appearance of the figure of David McConnel, he had been reading. Time and again I have been struck by the fact that people have been reading – 'lost in a book' is a very telling phrase – when they looked up to see an apparition. This suggests that conditions in which the busy world is shut out and attention diverted elsewhere are conducive to experiences of the type described in this book. It is significant that Celia Green's analysis of spontaneous cases in the last major census conducted by the Society, in 1959, revealed that thirteen people were reading in a library or a classroom when they had their 'fully awake' experience, which did not necessarily involve an apparition.

When I referred this point about reading to Dr Robert H. Thouless, the Cambridge psychologist, he replied that my observation of the frequency with which apparitions are seen while reading was an interesting one:

It seems to suggest that detachment of attention from the immediate problems of adapting to the external world may be a favourable condition for a *psi*-experience. It suggests the possibility of experimental verification. If one interrupts a person reading and asked him to guess a card, would this be a favourable condition for being right? I think that noting such a fact is, in the present condition of psychical research, more important than thinking of an explanation. Every new oddity is a contribution to the pattern of *psi* phenomena. When we know the total pattern, the explanation of all its parts will become clear.

The next important survey of experiences involving apparitions and haunting ghosts was made by G. N. M. Tyrrell in preparation for his seventh Myers Memorial Lecture, delivered to the SPR on 31 October 1942. This involved the study of sixty-one principal cases. Tyrrell's conclusions from this study formed the basis of his book *Apparitions*. It has proved to be one of the most influential in modern psychical research and its significance, in my opinion, lies in the attention Tyrrell gives to theoretical aspects of the subject. Tyrrell, who devoted forty years of his life to psychical research, was President of the SPR in 1945–6. He took a degree in physics and mathematics at London University and was one of the early students of wireless under Marconi. In his view, the primary task of psychical research was nothing more or less than 'the exploration of human personality', and particularly, as Professor Price pointed out in his preface, the exploration of its subliminal or unconscious strata (91d p. 10).

In her Presidential address to the SPR in October 1980, read in her absence, Dr Louisa E. Rhine, the noted American parapsychologist who has collected thousands of spontaneous cases, said that Tyrrell concentrated on the processes that seemed to be involved in spontaneous cases, especially in apparitional experiences, in a way that nobody before him had attempted to do.

In a logical analysis of what must go on in a psychic experience, Tyrrell simplified the concept of that process by thinking of it as involving two stages. In Stage I, the information secured by the living person, the percipient in a *psi* experience, would have to be acquired by him without sensory mediation. This stage, of course, was an unconscious one and entirely inexplicable. It was the essentially parapsychological one.

But then, in Stage II, the information from Stage I was processed into consciousness. This was obviously a more explicable stage for it was accomplished by familiar psychological means, which Tyrrell called vehicles; dreams and certain waking experiences, which, as he recognized, were the same as those used in ordinary cognition.

Tyrrell introduced a rather involved concept, that of the Producer and Stage Carpenter, as an explanation for what he called an apparitional drama. The Producer and Stage Carpenter may be thought of as psychological constituents of the percipient's personality which operate in a quasi-autonomous manner below the level of consciousness, and are Tyrrell's rather whimsical names for the unconscious mental factors which are responsible for the apparitional drama.

According to Price, Tyrrell's theory offered a solution to the problem of why apparitions were clothed and were sometimes accompanied by horses and carriages, dogs, and other apparently physical appurtenances. The clothes, horses, etc., were as hallucinatory as the 'ghost' itself was. They were there because they were required by the 'theme' or 'motif' of the apparitional drama, just as they would be there in a dream if the theme of the dream-drama required it. They were dramatically appropriate. The same explanation applied to the behaviour of the apparition itself. The door was locked; yet the apparition opened it and walked into the room. Physically, the door did not move. Its movement was as hallucinatory as the apparition itself was. But the opening of the door was dramatically appropriate, if the theme of the drama was the idea of *going* into the room where Mr X was. Similarly if the apparition cast a shadow, or was reflected in the mirror, or made the noise of footsteps as it moved, this was because the Stage Carpenter was efficient at his job. His instructions were to provide as lifelike a representation as possible of what would be seen and heard if the agent were physically present and physically moving about in the room, Price maintained.

Tyrrell drew up a list of nineteen characteristics of what he termed the 'perfect apparition'. The figure was imaginary only in one sense, he said. Each of its features rested on solid evidence; but they were not all to be found in any actual single case, although there were cases which contained a good many of them. For instance, if an apparition stood beside a normal human being, both figures would stand out in space and would appear equally real and solid. The apparition would be just as clear and vivid in matters of detail, such as the colour and texture of skin and clothing, as the material person. He pointed out (characteristic No. 17) that if we were to take a photograph of the two figures, only the real man would come out. And if we had sound-recording apparatus, only the sounds made by the real man would be recorded. 'It is true that these are inferences and do not rest on direct evidence. But the non-physical character of apparitions is so clear that the inference seems to be inescapable.'

Tyrrell ended his list with the statement that this was 'a picture of what an apparition would be like at its best, according to our collected evidence; and this is what, throughout the ages, has been called a "spirit". But clearly it is in reality a psychological phenomenon, the explanation of which must be caught in the processes of sense-perception.' Apparitions, he considered, divided themselves into four main classes:

1. Experimental cases, in which the agent had deliberately tried to make his apparition visible to a particular percipient.

2. Cases in which a recognized apparition was seen, heard, or felt at a time when the person represented by the apparition was undergoing some crisis (these cases were briefly referred to as 'Crisis-cases' or 'Crisis-apparitions').

3. Cases in which a recognized apparition was seen or heard so long after the death of the person represented by the apparition that no coincidence with any crisis, such as the death of the person, could be supposed (these are referred to as 'post-mortem' cases).

4. Ghosts, or apparitions, which habitually haunt certain places.

The classes, Tyrrell pointed out, were not sharply differentiated. There were some cases which did not clearly belong to any class; as, for example, unrecognized figures seen on only one occasion, or recognized figures of living people which did not coincide with any crisis in their lives.

I feel that Tyrrell's classification does not make sufficient allowance for the large number of reported cases of apparitions of the living. It should be amended to read:

1. Experimental cases.
2. Apparitions of the living.
3. Apparitions of the dying and those undergoing a crisis.
4. Haunting and apparitions of the dead.

The case of Canon Bourne is a good example of an apparition of the living. Canon Bourne and his two daughters were hunting in Worcestershire in 1887 when the daughters decided to retire home early with the coachman. A short while later all three distinctly saw the Canon waving his hat to them and signing them to follow him. He was on the side of a small hill and there was a dip between them. As the Canon waved his hat his daughters clearly saw the Lincoln and Bennett mark inside, though from the distance they were apart it should have been 'utterly impossible' for them to have seen it. The Canon's horse looked so dirty and shaken that the coachman thought there had been a nasty accident. The three hurried to the spot but the

Canon was not to be seen. After they had returned home the Canon arrived to tell them that he had not been in the field where they thought they saw him, he had never waved to them, and had not met with an accident (60a vol. 1 pp. 651–2).

It was curious that the Misses Bourne should have been able to read the makers' name inside the hat at a distance. Another example of this strange faculty is an experience involving an apparition given by Una, Lady Troubridge, who recounted how she and Miss Radclyffe Hall, author of the controversial novel *The Well of Loneliness*, had agreed to meet a friend at a garage to inspect a car. When approaching the garage she appeared to see her friend pointing to a car and gesticulating, and recognized familiar details of her dress, the distance being about thirty feet. But her friend was not to be found in the garage and arrived ten minutes later, dressed as Lady Troubridge had seen her. 'I not only saw her with normal distinctness,' said the narrator, 'but in a way too detailed in my opinion to be possible for normal vision at some 30 feet away. [Lady Troubridge remarked that she was very short-sighted] . . . When I described what I had seen to Miss Radclyffe Hall . . . I realized that I had noticed details in a manner which I thought, and still think, exceeded my normal visual powers at a distance' (29 p. 7).

Tyrrell discussed at some length the theory of apparitions, and his theory was, in turn, discussed in 'Six theories about apparitions', a co-operative report by Professor Hornell Hart, an American sociologist, and associated collaborators in the International Project for Research on ESP Projection. This report is, in my opinion, the most important document on theoretical aspects of apparitional appearances published to date. It is in the form of a debate conducted by correspondence in *Proceedings* in 1956 by some of the leading theoreticians in this field (31b).

Five alternative hypotheses were considered. They were:

1. The Gurney hypothesis, which interpreted apparitions as mental hallucinations, created by individual percipients in response to telepathic impulses directly or indirectly received from the appearer.

2. The Tyrrell hypothesis, which regarded apparitions as

idea-patterns produced currently or very recently by the subconscious levels of the percipient, with or without the co-operative assistance of the unconscious of the appearer.

3. The Myers-Price Theory, further developed by Raynor C. Johnson, which suggested that apparitions were etheric images, created currently, or in the past, by some mental act.

4. The occultist theory, which held that apparitions consisted of the astral or etheric bodies of the appearers, with clothing and accessories created *ad hoc*.

5. The spiritualist theory, which assumed that apparitions of the dead were the spirits of the departed.

The contributors to the debate considered that the fact that each of the above five theories failed in various ways to account for the observed data did not mean that all of them – nor indeed any of them – needed to be discarded *in toto*. Each of them might be modified in various ways so as to take account of the characteristics which the cruder statements of the hypotheses seemed to miss. 'But such modifications would bring all of the theories into convergence towards a common, operationally accurate and adequate theory, making use of the valid aspects of the previous ones, but supplementing them so as to account adequately for all the clearly established types of observations.'

This proposed convergent and operational theory involved two basic propositions:

1. Apparitions and their accessories are semi-*substantial* in the sense that they tend to have the following characteristics:

(a) They are described as 'solid', 'real', or the like, and their visible details are often said to be vivid.

(b) They are often perceived tactually and audibly as well as visibly, and these three kinds of perception are consistent with one another.

(c) As thus perceived, they appear to be recognizably similar to – and often identical with – material human bodies and physical objects.

(d) Their observed details may be otherwise unknown to any living person, and yet may prove to be verifiably correct.

(e) They make adjustments to their physical surroundings and to physically embodied people, in much the same ways in which physically present people would do.

(f) They are seen in normal perspective, both when stationary and when moving; they may be reflected in mirrors, may obscure other objects and be obscured by other objects, and in other ways they fit into the physical environment as physical objects do.

(g) They are often seen collectively by two or more persons at the same time.

2. Apparitions and their accessories are only *semi*-substantial, in the sense that they tend to have the following characteristics:

(a) Their visibility is erratic, in that they are likely to appear or disappear suddenly and inexplicably, to be invisible to people who would see them if they were physically embodied, to fade in or out, and to be self-luminous.

(b) They may pass through solid walls or locked doors.

(c) They may rise into the air without physical support, and may glide instead of walk.

(d) They may communicate ideas without words, gestures or other symbols – i.e. telepathically.

This semi-substantiality went beyond the mere etheric images which the Myers-Price theory regarded as being specially created in the case of every apparition, and would seem to have called for a new theory which the authors of the report called the revised 'etheric-object' hypothesis. Let us suppose, they said, that every physical object (including human bodies, and other living animals) has an etheric counterpart, similar to it in every detail. Let us also suppose that etheric objects may be created by imagination, by imitating, modifying, or combining the etheric objects found in nature. If so, they exist in psychic space rather than in physical outer-world space, but these two kinds of space may have converging intersections. Etheric objects must be regarded as having four dimensions, including a time dimension, but these dimensions were not usually co-ordinated with those of the physical world.

The differences between etheric objects and physical objects were matters of degree and might vary through the whole range between those of sheer subjective imagination and those of completely materialized forms. Collective percipience of apparitions, materializations and dematerializations, and physical phenomena in general (so far as genuine) involved relatively high degrees of approximation to physical traits on the part of etheric objects. On the other hand, 'purely mental' imaginings and dreams on the part of individuals represented points towards the other end of the same scale.

Professor C. D. Broad, one of the contributors to the debate, referred to it in his Presidential address to the Society in 1958. Discussing the significance of collective hallucinations, he said he felt that an explanation in terms of nothing but 'telepathy' and 'clairvoyance' would tend to become extremely complex and artificial, and would moreover have to stretch the meaning and application of these terms far beyond anything for which we have independent evidence.

If really well attested cases of these kinds were to accumulate, I think we might be compelled to take some form of the hypothesis of an 'astral double' to the normal human body as much the simplest working hypothesis. I do not think that the evidence at present available is such as to force anyone to that decision, but I do consider that it might even now be a working hypothesis worth serious consideration by sane and critical psychical researchers [13b pp. 77–8].

One of the most original contributions to the debate in *Proceedings* came from Professor Price (not to be confused with the late Henry Price, the 'ghost hunter'), Emeritus Professor of Logic at Oxford University, and a very distinguished academic philosopher, twice president of the SPR. Price considered the possibility that some apparitions might be 'real objects' – spatial though not physical – and that one function our ESP powers might have is to make us aware of such 'real objects'. Such apparitions were neither mental nor physical, but betwixt and between.

If once it is granted that an apparition is at least sometimes a 'real object' – real in the sense of not just being a hallucinatory construct – the further step you want to take, that this object is, or may be, a genuine 'vehicle of consciousness' follows fairly easily . . . But of course the survival which such apparitional evidence would point to (if we could get it) would not be the survival of a *disembodied* mind, but of a mind which was still embodied though in . . . a non-physical sort of body with certain 'ideoplastic' properties . . . [31b p. 238].

Price had earlier discussed his suggestion that apparitions were sometimes 'real objects' in his Preface to Whately Carington's *Matter Mind and Meaning* in which he said that we were inclined to say that an hallucinatory entity was something 'purely mental', as opposed to a 'real object' which was physical. But according to Carington's philosophy, Price observed, the difference between the hallucinatory and the physically real was only a difference of degree.

A hallucinatory entity, the celebrated pink rat for instance, is composed of sense-data or appearances ('cognita') just as a 'real' object is. What is wrong with it, what inclines us to call it 'unreal', is the fact that there are not *enough* of them. For example, the hallucinatory rat can be seen from the front but not from the back; it is visible but not tangible; it can be perceived by one percipient but not by more; and it endures for only a minute or so. But some hallucinations do better than this. Apparitions, for example, are sometimes public to several percipients, can be seen from different points of view, and endure for considerable periods of time – though not as long as they would if they were 'real' human beings. Now suppose there was an apparition which had unrestricted publicity, i.e. was public to an indefinite number of points of view and an indefinite number of observers: suppose that there are tangible as well as visible particulars among the appearances (or 'cognita') which are its constituents; suppose it endures for half an hour and then disappears. We should not know whether to call it an unusually prolonged and complex hallucination, or a very queer 'real' object (queer, because we should not know how it got into the room, or why it abruptly vanished into thin air). In point of fact, it would be something intermediate between the two: a complex system of 'cognita', but not quite complex enough to count as a complete material object [15 pp. xix–xx].

These points raised by Price are of the greatest theoretical interest when we try to consider what an apparition might be. In the chapters on haunting I will give two examples (the Cheltenham case and the Ramsbury, Wiltshire case) in which an apparition *was* on view for half an hour. I will discuss the significance of such cases in the final chapter.

One of the most significant passages in *Six Theories about*

Apparitions contains the view of Hart and his associates, that the hypothesis that apparitions usually constitute some sort of objective image seems to be fairly well substantiated by an impartial summary of available evidence. On physical psychic phenomena they said:

The present study is concerned primarily with visually perceived apparitions. But in collecting cases of this type, the number of more or less parallel cases involving physical phenomena has been impressive. The overturning of furniture, the shattering of glass and crockery, the ringing of bells, the stopping of clocks, and the like appear to be so frequent that it is a distortion of the picture to ignore them. Such cases correspond logically to the psychokinetic phenomena of the Parapsychology Laboratory [psychokinesis, or PK, is the mental, but non-muscular, influence exerted by the subject on an external physical process, condition, or object]. They appear to be so well authenticated that they need to be recognized as part of the total factual picture. They add further weight to the conception of apparitions as objective phenomena [31b p. 215].

The results of the last important census of spontaneous cases are contained in the Report (1959) on Enquiry into Spontaneous Cases, published in *Proceedings* in 1960. Possibly because of changing social conditions and lack of leisure or inclination for letter-writing, the response was far below that of the great Census of Hallucinations in the last century, when 17,000 replies were received. A questionnaire sent to interested members of the public elicited only about 300 cases, of which few approached the high standard of corroboration that had been hoped for, but to these were added over 1,300 cases sent to the Society by Chapman Pincher, then scientific correspondent of the *Daily Express*. Nearly half the cases were reports of hallucinations of some kind, and 27 per cent concerned apparitions.

Several thousand reports of apparitions are in the archives of the SPR, but, because of high printing costs, which limit the size of the *Journal* and *Proceedings*, only a handful of the better modern cases have been printed. One of the most convincing of these is about the death of Johnnie Minney. This case was investigated by G. W. Lambert, a former President of the Society, who has devoted a lifetime to psychical research. Lambert, who was born in 1889, was until his retirement Assistant Under Secretary of State for War, and is a distinguished example of the many non-academics – George Tyrrell was one and Rosalind Heywood another – who have given notable service to the Society. I followed up Lambert's paper on the case in the *Journal* (44i) with a visit to Vicarage Farm in the village of Waresley in Huntingdonshire, where Johnnie died, and was able to add some of my own findings to Lambert's.

The case concerns an Australian, Mrs Stella Herbert, who, after having been only three days in England, went to stay with her fellow Australian, Mrs Shirley Ross, at the farm on Wednesday, 7 July 1965. Mrs Herbert was introduced briefly on arrival to Miss Margaret Minney, who had lived on the farm all her life and who occupied separate quarters there. The two women exchanged only a few words, none of a personal nature.

On her first night at Vicarage Farm Mrs Herbert fell quickly asleep and thought she had been asleep for some time when she was awakened by a little boy kneeling at the side of her bed and looking at her with a pleading look. 'I can still see his face, so thin and drawn, and he gave me the impression that had he stood up he would have been tall and bony. His hair was fair and straight and falling to one side,' Mrs Herbert said in her statement. She sat up in bed, and although the boy did not speak she could feel that he was asking her to call his mother. She could also feel his hands clawing at her arm, almost hurting it. Eventually Mrs Herbert called 'Mummy' rather loudly and at that moment the boy disappeared.

The following evening Mrs Ross called on Miss Minney and asked if a little boy had ever died in the house.

'Yes, my brother Johnnie,' Miss Minney replied.

'Come to my room and listen to Mrs Herbert,' Mrs Ross said. Mrs Herbert repeated the account of the apparition and stressed the appearance of the boy. 'His arms were so thin, like bones with only the skin stretched over them, and I can still feel his hands on my shoulders,' she said, and was so moved by the memory that tears came to her eyes.

Miss Minney seemed speechless until the end and said, 'But I know that was Johnnie, my brother, who died when he was five.'

She then told the two women that Johnnie had been sleeping in the room where Mrs Herbert had her experience when he was taken ill in February of 1921. He had meningitis and became terribly ill. He had periods of lucidity when he seemed quite normal, she recalled, and then times when he would shout and cry with pain and call constantly for 'Mummy'. His parents were away at an exhibition in London at the time. Those in the house were awakened in the night by his calls, and he became worse from then on until he died. When Johnnie's mother returned he was moved to the other room [the one occupied by Mrs Ross]. She could not remember his going back to the room where he became ill.

Johnnie Minney's death certificate confirmed that he died on 21 August 1921, aged four years – not five, as Miss Minney had thought – of cerebro-spinal meningitis. This disease, if prolonged over some months (February–August in this case), usually leads to severe emaciation. Mrs Ross compiled a written account of what had taken place two days after the event.

Lambert visited Vicarage Farm and interviewed Mrs Ross and Miss Minney, Mrs Herbert having returned to Australia. He was given a statement from Mrs Kitty Hampton, then aged ninety-five, the only surviving member of a family of eleven which included Miss Minney's mother. 'I am the Aunt' she told him, 'who was keeping house at the time of his [Johnnie's] illness. I took him into my bed during the night, before his parents returned. He was a very lovable child – everyone loved him. At his death he was wasted to skin and bone.'

We must, of course, try to seek a natural explanation for what took place at Vicarage Farm, but I find it difficult to think of one. Mrs Herbert had recently arrived from Australia and had not been in the village long enough to pick up gossip about the death of a little boy in the house where she was staying. Miss Minney had never mentioned the subject to Mrs Ross. The only photograph of Johnnie, a snapshot taken when he was three, was kept in a drawer and was never seen by Mrs Ross. Critics of cases of the type described in this book will argue that it was 'merely a coincidence' that a boy had died in the house where Mrs Herbert had her experience, but surely it is stretching the argument of coincidence too far when the appearance of the boy was so distinctive?

Although we know very little about such matters, it seems to me that Mrs Herbert's experience should be classed as an example of retrocognition, which has been defined as 'paranormal knowledge of past events beyond the range of inference or memory on the part of the subject' (Chapters 8, 9, and 10 have particular reference to retrocognition). Myers considered the problems it poses in *Human Personality* where, discussing Phantasms of the Dead, he said 'I think that the curious question as to the influence of certain *houses* in generating apparitions may be included under the broader heading of retrocognition. That is to say, we are not here dealing with a special condition of certain houses, but with a branch of the wide problem as to the relation of supernormal phenomena to *time*. Manifestations which occur in haunted houses depend, let us say, on something which has taken place a long time ago . . .' (60a vol. 2 p. 76).

Not only houses could be haunted, Myers thought; he advanced the concept of what he called 'a phantasmogenetic centre', which he described as 'a point in space so modified by the presence of a spirit that it becomes perceptible to persons materially present near it. The concept of *psychical excursion* or *invasion* implies that some movement bearing some relation to space as we know it is accomplished; that the invading spirit modifies a certain portion of space, not materially nor optically, but in such a manner that specially susceptible persons may perceive it' (60a vol. 1 p. xix).

A Committee on Haunted Houses was set up on the foundation of the Society, and in its first report in *Proceedings* in 1882 said that its labours in obtaining, from trustworthy sources, evidence bearing upon the subject had been 'fruitful beyond our expectations'. Since then cases have continued to accumulate until today there are nearly 700 accounts of hauntings in the archives of the SPR, not all of which have been investigated; indeed, many are of poor quality from an evidential point of view.

Theories about haunting, with a number of examples of haunted houses quoted in support of her argument, are given by

Mrs Sidgwick in a long and important paper. Her conclusion was that 'I can only say that having made every effort – as my paper will, I hope, have shown – to exercise a reasonable scepticism, I yet do not feel equal to the degree of unbelief in human testimony necessary to avoid accepting at least provisionally the conclusion that there are, in a certain sense, haunted houses, i.e., that there are houses in which similar quasi-human apparitions have occurred at different times to different inhabitants, under circumstances which exclude the hypothesis of suggestion or expectation' (81a p. 142).

Professor Broad also accepted the reality of haunting, although not without reservations. He said in his *Lectures on Psychical Research*, 'When one studies the details of the best cases of "haunting" they do not, I think, on the whole suggest the presence of any persistent desire or intention. They suggest, rather, an aimless mechanical repetition of the dreams or waking fantasies of a person brooding over certain incidents and scenes in his past life' (13c pp. 136–7).

Some very experienced investigators are dubious about most reports of haunted houses. Salter, who handled a great many such reports during his long term of office in the SPR, said in *Zoar*, 'Haunted houses are much more numerous in fiction than in fact, and more thrilling too. I do not number among them houses where the husband had a stomach-ache in the night, or the wife, having mislaid the saucepan or finding a chimney smoke, promptly calls in the aid of the nearest journalist, to be followed, according to their inclinations, either by one of the local clergy or a medium from a neighbouring town. This is an imaginary psychic incident, but each item of it could be paralleled from my own, and doubtless many other investigators' experience' (76b p. 48). I can understand Salter's scepticism about many cases. Once, investigating a building reported to be haunted, I was asked if ghosts did not like smoking. When I asked why, I was assured solemnly that ash trays containing cigarette ends had been moved when the smoker was not looking. I can think of several ways in which this might have happened without involving the agency of ghosts. However, the cases presented in this book are not based on evidence as trivial and flimsy as that referred to by Salter, and he conceded that some cases, such as the Cheltenham one, deserved serious consideration.

What explanation can we offer for hauntings? Mrs Sidgwick offered one which she considered 'corresponds best to a certain part of the evidence':

> It is that there is something in the actual building itself – some subtle physical influence – which produces in the brain that effect which, in its turn, becomes the cause of a hallucination . . . If there be any truth in the theory, I should expect in time to obtain a good deal more evidence of this kind, combined with evidence that the same persons do not as a rule encounter ghosts elsewhere. I should also expect evidence to be forthcoming supporting the popular idea that repairs and alterations to the building sometimes cause the haunting to cease [81a p. 148].

The belief that 'there is something in the actual building itself' which causes people to experience apparitions there is an old one and it has been advanced, in different forms, by writers who may not have read Mrs Sidgwick's study of hauntings. One who did was Professor Price, who developed Mrs Sidgwick's concept in his Presidential address on 'Haunting and the "psychic ether" hypothesis'. This is the only Presidential address I know in the present century which has been devoted to haunting and should be read by all interested in this subject (67b).

Price's theory of haunting concerns *mental images* and he puts forward the idea that once it has come into being, the image has a tendency to *persist* in being, and that it is not dependent upon the mind for its continuance, as it was for its origination. Price went on to propose that images were not only persistent entities, but were endowed with *causal properties*: 'If you prefer to put it so, we will say that they are "dynamic" rather than "static" entities, endowed with a kind of "force" of their own.'

Psychic ether, he suggested, consisted of traces which were not material in the ordinary sense, but somehow interpenetrated the walls or the furniture: 'something which was like matter in being extended, and yet like mind in that it retained in itself the *residua* of past experiences.'

It will be seen that there is some connection between Myers's conception of a ghost as 'a manifestation of persistent personal

energy' and Price's view that a person who comes into contact
with images which are 'persistent and dynamic entities' may see
an apparition. Both concepts involve energy.

Price admitted that the theory of haunting he advanced was
'much too narrow' in that he had spoken as if images were the
only sort of psychical contents, which was far from true. Again,
the theory had in any case been restricted to one special type of
haunting, the type in which there were no physical effects; it
could only be extended to cover other types by introducing
additional assumptions, which might have to be 'very out-
rageous'.

Hauntings in which there are physical effects are akin to
poltergeist cases in certain respects. 'Poltergeist' is an old
German word meaning 'noisy spirit', and poltergeist activity is
the occurrence of (a) production of noises such as tappings,
sawings, bumpings; and (b) movement of objects by no known
physical force. In this book I propose to deal with only a single
case involving the movement of objects, but in some there is
certainly the suggestion of poltergeist-type activity. For instance,
in Chapter 5, 'Two Haunted Parsonages', we read how a curate
who, disturbed by knocks, answered them with taunts which
resulted in more furious knocking. This suggested mode of
communication reminded me of the famous Derrygonnelly Case
in 1877, investigated by Sir William Barrett, one of the founders
of the SPR and Professor of Physics at the Royal College of
Science, Dublin, who received what seemed to be answers to his
questions in the form of knocks (6a pp. 390–5). Another case in
this book, that of the haunted mill house at Willington (Chapter
4), contains an account of an ostensible physical happening, the
raising of a bed with two women in it.

One of the best-attested poltergeist cases in the early literature
of the Society concerns strange happenings in the house of a
small horse-dealer named Joe White in Worksop, Nottinghamshire, in March 1883 (66e). It was investigated by Frank
Podmore, who went to Worksop in April at the request of the
Haunted Houses Committee. By that time the phenomena had
ceased, but he was able to take statements from the principal
witnesses of the events. Podmore could not have enjoyed his visit

to the house, which was hung with bacon. He described it as 'filthy dirty'.

On Thursday night, 1 March, at about 11 p.m. Tom White, Joe White's brother, went up to bed – the children having gone up some hours before. Mrs White and Eliza Rose, the child of an imbecile mother, were left alone in the kitchen. Half an hour later various things such as a corkscrew, clothes pegs, and a salt cellar which had been in the kitchen only a few minutes before, came tumbling step by step down the kitchen steps. Tom White positively and solemnly denied having thrown the articles, and the mystery was increased when, at least twenty minutes after he had gone upstairs, no one else having left the room in the interval, some *hot* coals were thrown down.

On the following night, 2 March, Joe White, Mrs White and Eliza Rose were in the kitchen when knives, forks and other objects were thrown down the stairs. The girl picked them up, but others followed still faster. Joe White left the room to go up to his brother Tom. During his absence one of the ornaments flew off the mantelpiece into the corner of the room near the door. Nothing was seen by the two women, but they heard it fall and found it there. Their screams summoned White down; as he entered the room his candle went out, and something struck him on the forehead. The girl picked up the candle, which appeared to have left the candlestick, and two new ones which had not been in the house previously, from the ground; and as soon as a candle was lit, a little china figure of a woman left the mantelpiece and fell into the corner, where it was seen by Joe White. As soon as it was replaced it flew across the room again, and was broken. Other things followed. The women were very frightened, and Joe White, thinking that the disturbances presaged the death of his child, who was very ill from an abscess in the back, sent Tom, who was afraid to go alone, with Ford, a neighbour, to fetch the doctor. Mrs White meanwhile took one of the children next door. Eliza Rose approached the inner room to fetch one of the other children when things immediately began to fly about and smash themselves in that room.

After this, all appear to have been absent from the house for a short time. White then returned with Higgs, a policeman and, while they were alone in the kitchen, standing near the door, a glass jar flew out of the cupboard into the yard; a tumbler also fell from a chest of drawers in the kitchen, when only Higgs was near it. Both then went into the inner room, and found the chest of drawers there turned up on end and smashed. On their return they found Eliza Rose, Solomon Wass (the next-door neighbour), and Tom White in the kitchen, and all saw a cream jug, which Eliza Rose had just placed on the bin, fly four feet up in the air and smash on the floor. Dr Lloyd and Mrs White then entered, and in the presence of all these witnesses a basin was seen to rise slowly from the bin, no person being near it except Dr Lloyd and the police constable. The basin went up two or three times in the air, rising slowly a few inches or perhaps a foot, and then falling plump. Then it got higher, and went slowly, wobbling as it went, up to the ceiling, after which it fell down and broke. Dr Lloyd looked in the bin, said the devil must be in the house, and left.

The disturbances continued the following day. At about 2.0 p.m. a Salvation Army woman came and talked to White. Eliza Rose was alone with them in the kitchen. A candlestick flew from the bin and fell behind the Salvation Army woman as she stood near the pantry door, causing her to leave the room in terror. At intervals, a full medicine bottle fell without breaking, an empty medicine bottle and a lamp glass fell and broke. By 4.0 p.m. Joe White could stand it no longer. He told Eliza Rose she must go; she did in fact leave before 5.0 p.m. After her departure nothing whatever of an abnormal character took place and the house remained undisturbed.

It will have been noticed that the phenomena seemed to centre around Eliza Rose and that they ceased after she left the house, where she had been staying. Such people seem to serve as what has been termed a poltergeist 'focus' or 'agent'. Although, as Myers said, there is ordinarily no need to be frightened of ghosts, some poltergeist outbreaks can be terrifying; and a number of cases are on record in which people suffered injury, rarely serious, sometimes from flying objects.

Some critical investigators still adhere to the 'naughty little girl' theory, which implies that *all* so-called poltergeist-type cases are the results of trickery; but the evidence makes this view hard to sustain. However, this is not a book about poltergeists, so I can do no more than hint at the problems involved in this fascinating subject, and list some of the more authoritative recent books dealing with it in the Bibliography.

3 The Cheltenham Hauntings

In the opinion of Dr Robert H. Thouless, 'the best study of an apparitional haunting is still the report of the "Morton" ghost observed during the first seven years after the founding of this Society' (88a p. 8). There has been little disagreement among serious writers on psychical research, even from those who take a highly critical view of reports of haunting, such as D. J. West and W. H. Salter, who treat the case with respect. The account of the hauntings, which lasted seven years, by a 'Miss R. C. Morton', appeared under the title of 'Record of a Haunted House' in SPR Proceedings, in 1892 (volume eight), but there are references to the case by Mrs Sidgwick in Proceedings in 1885, published while the haunting was still in progress – most unusual, as nearly all such accounts appear after a haunting has ended.

'Miss Morton' was encouraged in her investigation by F. W. H. Myers. The identity of the family concerned, and the location of the house, were revealed in 1948 by B. Abdy Collins (16). The house, then known as Donore and now as St Anne's, still stands on the corner of Pittville Circus Road and All Saints Road, Cheltenham, and the 'Morton' family's name was Despard. The Despard family consisted of Captain F. W. Despard; his wife, 'a great invalid'; the narrator, Rosina C. Despard, aged 19, then studying to be a doctor (she afterwards qualified); Edith Despard, then aged 18; Lilian and Mabel Despard, then 15 and 13; Henry Despard, then 16, who was absent most of the time at school; and Wilfred Despard, then aged 6. (I have obtained these names from Lilian Despard's daughter, Mrs Joyce Rynd, and will give real names throughout the narrative that follows.) Another sister, Mrs Freda Kinloch, who was older than Rosina, was a visitor from time to time.

The apparition, that of a tall woman in black, was seen, I estimate, by seventeen people, and heard by more than twenty. It was thought to be that of Imogen Swinhoe, the second wife of Henry Swinhoe, the first occupant of

An artist's impression of the Cheltenham Ghost (by courtesy of Psychic Press).

the house. There has been a good deal of controversy, however, about the identity of the apparition, mainly because the lower part of the face was hidden by a handkerchief held there, and the features could not be seen clearly.

Rosina Despard's account was compiled from a series of letters she wrote to a friend, Miss Catherine M. Campbell, who was asked to present them to the Society, but she declined because they contained 'so many allusions to private matters'. This is regrettable, although understandable; the letters did not later come into the possession of the Society, and it is not known if they still exist. If they could be found they would provide invaluable evidence of the haunting.

Frederick Myers said in his preparatory note to Miss Despard's account that the first intimation he received of the phenomena described by her was in a letter of December 1884, from J. W. Graham, then Principal of Dalton Hall, Manchester. Graham had heard an account from Captain Despard, written this account out from memory, and had it revised by Captain and Mrs Despard. This account, and Miss Despard's letters to Miss Campbell, which began with the first appearance of the figure, were the earliest written records. Myers was later able to interview members of the household and the staff. 'In this case', he wrote, 'it is observable that the phenomena as seen or heard by all the witnesses were very uniform in character – even in the numerous instances where there had been no previous communication between the percipients. I have found no discrepancy in the independent testimonies, when collected, with the unimportant exception of General A's [Annesley's] inability or unwillingness to recall one incident, which was already included in Mr Graham's first account, soon after its occurrence, and six years before General A, an old man, was asked to repeat it.'

Myers added that Captain Despard and the members of the family in general, 'while feeling little scientific interest in the apparition, were unusually free from superstitious fears'.

According to Rosina Despard the house was a typical modern residence, square and commonplace in appearance. It was separated from the road in front only by railings with high gates and a short carriage-sweep. On one side, but completely detached, was another residence; on the other ran a cross road, shut out from the house by the small orchard referred to in the account, and by the fair-sized garden, which also extended some way at the back.

At the end of the garden were stabling and a small cottage, neither of which was in use. The whole was in thoroughly good repair; neither rats nor mice had ever been seen in the house, and there were no owls in the neighbourhood to account for any of the sounds heard.

When Captain Despard took the house in March 1882, no one had heard then of there being anything unusual about it. The family moved in towards the end of April, and it was not until the following June that Rosina Despard first saw the apparition:

I had gone up to my room, but was not yet in bed, when I heard someone at the door, and went to it, thinking it might be my mother. On opening the door, I saw no one; but on going a few steps along the passage, I saw the figure of a tall lady, dressed in black, standing at the head of the stairs. After a few moments she descended the stairs, and I followed for a short distance, feeling curious what it could be. I had only a small piece of candle, and it suddenly burnt itself out; and being unable to see more, I went back to my room.

The figure was that of a tall lady, dressed in black soft woollen material, judging from the slight sound in moving. This is all I noticed then; but on further occasions, when I was able to observe her more closely, I saw the upper part of the left side of her forehead, and a little more of the hair above. Her left hand was nearly hidden by her sleeve and a fold of her dress. As she held it down a portion of a widow's cuff was visible on both wrists, so that the whole impression was that of a lady in widow's weeds. There was no cap on the head but a general effect of blackness suggests a bonnet, with long veil or a hood.

During the next two years – from 1882 to 1884 – Rosina Despard saw the figure about half a dozen times; at first at long intervals, and afterwards at shorter, but she only mentioned these appearances to one friend, who did not speak of them to anyone. During this period, so far as was known, there were only three appearances to anyone else.

The first, in the summer of 1882, was to Rosina Despard's sister, Mrs Kinloch, when the figure was thought to be that of a Sister of Mercy who had called at the house, and no further curiosity was aroused. Mrs Kinloch was coming down the stairs rather late for dinner at 6.30, it then being quite light, when she saw the figure cross the hall in front of her and pass into the drawing-room. She then asked the rest of the family, already seated at dinner, 'Who was that Sister of Mercy whom I have just seen going into the drawing-room?' She was told there was no such person, and a servant was sent to look; but the drawing-room was empty. Mrs Kinloch persisted that she had seen a tall figure in black, with some white about it; but nothing further was thought of the matter.

In the autumn of 1883 the figure was seen by the housemaid about 10.0 p.m. She declared that someone must have got into the house, her description agreeing fairly with what Rosina Despard had seen. After a search when no one was found, her story received no credit.

On or about 18 December 1883 the figure was seen in the drawing-room by Rosina's brother and another little boy. They were playing outside on the terrace when they saw the figure in the drawing-room close to the window, and ran in to see who it could be that was crying so bitterly. They found no one in the drawing-room, and the parlourmaid told them that no one had come into the house.

After the first sighting, Rosina Despard followed the figure several times downstairs into the drawing-room, where she remained a variable time, generally standing to the right-hand side of the bow window. From the drawing-room she went along the passage towards the garden door, where she always disappeared. The first time Rosina Despard spoke to the figure was on 29 January 1884:

I opened the drawing-room door softly and went in, standing just by it. She came in past me and walked to the sofa and stood still there, so I went up to her and asked her if I could help her. She moved, and I thought she was going to speak, but she only gave a slight gasp and moved towards the door. Just by the door I spoke to her again, but she seemed as if she were quite unable to speak. She walked into the hall, then by the side door she seemed to disappear as before.

During these two years the only *noises* Rosina Despard heard were those of slight pushes against her bedroom door, accompanied by footsteps. 'Her footstep is very light, you can hardly hear it, except on the linoleum, and then only like a person walking softly with thin boots on.'

During July and August 1884 the appearances became much more frequent; indeed they were then at their maximum. Of these two months Rosina Despard had a short record in a set of journal letters written at the time to a friend. On 21 July she has the following account:

I went into the drawing-room, where my father and sisters were sitting, about 9 in the evening, and sat down on a couch close to the bow window. A few minutes after, as I sat reading, I saw the figure come in at the open door, cross the room and take up a position close behind the couch where I was. I was astonished that no one else in the room saw her, as she was so very distinct to me. My youngest brother, who had before seen her, was not in the room. She stood behind the couch for about half an hour, and then as usual walked to the door. I went after her, on the excuse of getting a book, and saw her pass along the hall, until she came to the garden door, where she disappeared. I spoke to her as she passed the foot of the stairs, but she did not answer, although as before she stopped and seemed as though *about* to speak.

On the night of 2 August the footsteps were heard by Rosina Despard's three sisters and by the cook, all of whom slept on the top landing, and also by her married sister, Mrs Kinloch, who was sleeping on the floor below. They all said the next morning that they had heard them very plainly pass and repass their doors. The cook was a middle-aged, sensible woman; on being asked the following morning if any of the servants had been out of their rooms the night before, after coming up to bed, she said that she had heard these footsteps before, and that she had seen the figure on the stairs one night when going down to the kitchen to fetch hot water after the servants had come up to bed. She described it as a lady in widow's dress, tall and slight, with her face hidden in a handkerchief held in her right hand. 'Unfortunately we have since lost sight of this servant; she left us about a year afterwards on her mother's death, and we cannot now trace her. She also saw the figure outside the kitchen windows on the terrace-walk, she herself being in the kitchen; it was then about 11 in the morning, but having made no note of the occurrence, I cannot now remember whether this appearance was subsequent to the one above mentioned.'

These footsteps were very characteristic, and were not at all like those of any of the people in the house; they were soft and rather slow, though decided and even. Rosina Despard's sister would not go out on the landing after hearing them pass, nor would the servants, 'but each time when I have gone out after hearing them, I have seen the figure there.'

On 5 August Rosina Despard told her father about what she and others had seen and heard. 'He was much astonished, not having seen or heard anything himself at that time – neither then had my mother, but she is slightly deaf and an invalid.' Captain Despard made enquiries of the landlord, who lived close by, as to whether he knew of anything unusual about the house, as he had himself lived in it for a short time; he replied that he had only been there for three months, and had never seen anything unusual.

On 6 August a neighbour, General Annesley, who lived opposite, sent his son to enquire after Rosina Despard's married sister, Mrs Kinloch, 'as he had seen a lady crying in our orchard, which is visible from the road. He had described her to his son, and afterwards to us, as a tall lady in black, and a bonnet with a long veil, crying, with a handkerchief held up to her face. He did not know my sister by sight, as she had only been with us a few days, and had been out very little, but he knew that she was in mourning for her baby son. My sister was not in the orchard that day at all, is rather short, and wore no veil.'

This was the second time the figure had been mistaken for that of a real person, the outlines being very distinct, and the whole appearance solid. The same evening General Annesley, who was a friend of the landlord's and was later to say that he had no recollection of the incident, came to the Despard home. 'We all took up various stations to watch for the figure, which was not seen by anyone.'

On 12 August, while coming up the garden, Rosina Despard was walking towards the orchard during the evening when she saw the figure cross the orchard, go along the carriage drive in front of the house, in at the open side door, across the hall and into the drawing-room. She followed and saw the figure take up her usual position behind the couch in the bow window. Captain Despard came in soon after, and Rosina told him she was there. He could not see the figure, but went up to where his daughter told him she was. 'She then went swiftly round behind him, across the room, out of the door, and along the hall, disappearing as usual near the garden door, we both following her. We looked out into the garden, having first to unlock the garden door, which my father had locked as he came through, but saw nothing of her.'

That same evening, about 8.0 p.m. and while it was still quite light, Edith Despard was singing in the back drawing-room.

[Rosina] heard her stop abruptly, come out into the hall, and call me. She said she had seen the figure in the drawing-room, close behind her as she sat at the piano. I went back into the room with her, and saw the figure in the bow window in her usual place. I spoke to her several times, but had no answer. She stood there for about 10 minutes or a quarter of an hour; then went across the room to the door, and along the passage, disappearing in the same place by the garden door.

My sister Mabel then came in from the garden, saying she had seen her coming up the kitchen steps outside. We all three then went out into the garden, when Mrs Kinloch called out from a window on the first storey that she had just seen her pass across the lawn in front, and along the carriage drive towards the orchard. This evening, then, altogether 4 people saw her. My father was then away, and my youngest brother out.

On the morning of 14 August the parlourmaid saw the figure in the dining-room, about 8.30 a.m., having gone into the room to open the shutters; it was quite light. The shutters did not fit well, letting sunlight through the cracks; so the room was very sunny even with all the shutters closed. She had opened one shutter when, on turning around, she saw the figure cross the room. 'We were all on the look-out for her that evening, but saw nothing; in fact, whenever we had made arrangements to watch, and were especially expecting her, we never saw anything. This servant, who afterwards married, was interviewed by Mr Myers at her own house.'

On 16 August, about 8.30 p.m., Rosina Despard saw the figure on the drawing-room balcony. She did not afterwards come into the room, as on the former occasion. On looking out at the side door, nothing could be seen. The gardener said that he had seen the figure on the balcony that morning early, about 6 o'clock.

Three days later all the Despards went to the seaside for a month, leaving three servants in the house. When the family came back the servants said they had frequently heard footsteps and noises, 'but as the stair carpets were up part of the time and the house was empty, many of these noises were doubtless due to natural causes, though by them attributed to the figure.' The cook also spoke of seeing the figure in the garden, standing by a stone vase on the lawn behind the house.

During the rest of that year and the following year, 1885, the apparition was frequently seen, especially during July, August, and September; the appearances being of exactly the same type, seen in the same places and by the same people, at varying intervals. The footsteps continued, and were heard by several visitors and new servants, who had taken the places of those who had left, as well as by Rosina, four sisters and brother; in all by about twenty people, many of whom had not previously heard of the apparition or sounds.

Other sounds were also heard in addition which seemed gradually to increase in intensity. They consisted of walking up and down on the second-floor landing, of bumps against the doors of the bedrooms, and of the handles of the doors turning. The bumps against the bedroom doors were so marked as to terrify a new servant, who had heard nothing of the haunting, into the belief that burglars were breaking into her room, while another servant, who had a slight attack of facial hemiplegia, attributed it to terror caused by attempts at her door worse than usual one night; the doctor, however, thought the attack was caused by cold rather than fright.

A second set of footsteps was also heard, heavy and irregular, constantly recurring, lasting a great part of the night, often three or four times a week. On the first floor the same noises were heard, especially in the front right-hand room formerly used by Mr and Mrs Swinhoe. And in the summer of 1885, heavy thuds and bumpings were heard, especially on the upper landing.

These facts were kept quiet for the sake of the landlord, who feared they might depreciate the value of the house. New servants were not told of them, 'though to anyone who *had* already heard of them we carefully explained the harmless nature of the apparition. Some left us on account of the noises, and we never could induce any of them to go out of their rooms after they had gone up for the night.'

During the year, at Myers's suggestion, Rosina Despard kept a camera constantly ready to try to photograph the figure, but on the few occasions she was able to do so she got no result. 'At night, usually only by candlelight, a long exposure would be necessary for so dark a figure, and this I could not obtain. I also tried to communicate with the figure, constantly speaking to it and asking it to make signs, if not able to speak, but with no result. I also tried especially to *touch* her, but did not succeed.' When cornered, she disappeared.

On one night in July, 1886 (my father and I being away from home), my mother and her maid heard a loud noise in an unoccupied room over their heads. They went up, but seeing nothing and the noise ceasing, they went back to my mother's room on the first storey. Then they heard loud noises from the morning-room on the ground floor. They then went half way downstairs, when they saw a bright light in the hall beneath. Being alarmed, they went up to my sister Edith, who then came down, and they all three examined the doors, windows, etc., and found them all fastened as usual. My mother and her maid then went to bed. My sister Edith went up to her room on the second storey, but as she passed the room where my two sisters Lilian and Mabel were sleeping they opened their door to say that they had heard noises, and also seen what they described as the *flame* of a candle, without candle or hand visible, cross the room diagonally from corner to door. Two of the maids opened the doors of their two bedrooms, and said that they had also heard noises; they all 5 stood at their doors with their lighted candles for some little time. They all heard steps walking up and down the landing between them; as they passed they felt a sensation which they described as 'a cold wind', though their candles were not blown about. They *saw* nothing. The steps then descended the stairs, reascended, again descended, and did not return.

The family heard from a carpenter who had done jobs in the house in Mrs Swinhoe's time that she had wished to possess herself of the first Mrs Swinhoe's jewels. Her husband had called him in to make a receptacle under the boards in the morning-room on the ground floor, he had placed the jewels in it, and then had it nailed down and the carpet replaced. The carpenter showed them the place. Captain Despard made him take up the boards; the receptacle was there, but empty. And when Captain Despard, thinking there might be something hidden near the garden door, where the figure usually disappeared, had the boards taken up, nothing was found but the original shavings and dust.

During 1887 there were few records of appearances and in 1888 and 1889 the figure was very seldom seen, though footsteps were heard; the louder noises, too, gradually ceased. From 1889 until this account was written, in 1892, the figure had not been seen at all. The lighter footsteps had lasted a little longer, but even they had ceased.

The figure became much less substantial on its later appearances. Up to about 1886 it was so solid and life-like that it was often mistaken for a real person. It gradually became less distinct. At all times it intercepted the light; we have not been able to ascertain if it cast a shadow. I should mention that it has been seen through window-glass, and that I myself wear glasses habitually, though none of the other percipients do. The upper part of the figure always left a more distinct impression than the lower, but this may partly be due to the fact that one naturally looks at people's faces before their feet.

Rosina Despard gave a list of 'proofs of immateriality'.

1. I have several times fastened fine strings across the stairs at various heights before going to bed, but after all others have gone up to their rooms. These were fastened in the following way: I made small pellets of marine glue, into which I inserted the ends of the cord, then stuck one pellet lightly against the wall and the other to the banister, the string being thus stretched across the stairs. They were knocked down by a very light touch, and yet would not be felt by anyone passing up or down the stairs, and by candle-light could not be seen from below. They were put at various heights from the ground, from 6 inches to the height of the banisters, about 3 feet.

I have twice at least seen the figure pass through the cords, leaving them intact.

2. The sudden and complete disappearance of the figure, while still in full view.

3. The impossibility of touching the figure. I have repeatedly followed it into a corner, when it disappeared, and have tried to suddenly pounce upon it, but have never succeeded in touching it or getting my hand up to it, the figure eluding my touch.

4. It has appeared in a room with the doors shut.

On the other hand, the figure was not called up by a desire to see it, for on every occasion when we made special arrangements to watch for it, we never saw it. On several occasions we have sat up at night hoping to see it, but in vain, – my father, with my brother-in-law, myself with a friend 3 or 4 times, an aunt and myself twice, and my sisters with friends more than once; but on none of the occasions was anything seen. Nor have the appearances been seen after we have been talking much of the figure.

A section of Rosina Despard's report is devoted to the conduct of animals in the house. A retriever who slept in the kitchen was several times found by the cook in a state of terror when she went into the kitchen in the morning. He was also seen more than once coming from the orchard thoroughly cowed and terrified. A small Skye terrier who usually slept on Rosina Despard's bed undoubtedly heard the footsteps outside the door. On 27 October 1887 the dog was suffering from an attack of rheumatism, and very disinclined to move, but on hearing the footsteps it sprang up and sniffed at the door. She twice remembered seeing this dog suddenly run up to the mat at the foot of the stairs in the hall, wagging its tail, and moving its back in the way dogs do when expecting to be caressed. It jumped up, fawning as it would do if a person had been standing there, but suddenly slunk away with its tail between its legs, and retreated, trembling, under a sofa. The family had no horses; and nothing peculiar was noticed about the behaviour of the cat which, as a rule, lived only in the kitchen.

In conclusion, Rosina Despard remarked,

In conclusion, as to the *feelings* aroused by the presence of the figure, it is very difficult to describe them; on the first few occasions I think the feeling of awe at something unknown, mixed with a strong desire to know nore about it, predominated. Later, when I was able to analyse my feelings more closely, and the first novelty had gone off, I felt conscious of a feeling of *loss*, as if I had lost power to the figure. Most of the other percipients speak of feeling a cold wind, but I myself have not experienced this.

Statements in support of Rosina Despard's account were taken from Catherine M. Campbell, Edith Despard, Freda Kinloch, Wilfred Despard, Mrs Brown, a former parlourmaid, and Mrs Twining, a charwoman, 'a sensible, trustworthy person, who had worked for the Despards for eight or nine years', according to Myers, who interviewed her. She described the Despard family as 'very good, kind people'.

Evidence from an independent source of the hauntings at Cheltenham was to come more than fifty years after the publication of Rosina Despard's account in *Proceedings*. George Gooding, a successful solicitor, wrote to the SPR in November 1944 to say:

I will gladly give you any information I can, but I fear it is very meagre, though perhaps slight confirmation of what must be already on record . . . My main difficulty is to separate clearly in my mind my own actual experience from knowledge acquired at the time or subsequently from older friends or other sources. It must be remembered my experiences are of events of over fifty years ago when I was only a small boy who did not reg ard such things very seriously, and at this distance of time it is not easy to separate actual first-hand knowledge from the contemporary hearsay. However, for what it is worth, here it is.

I saw the ghost on a number of occasions, of which two are very clear in my mind. It was a harmless ghost – at any rate it did not appear to upset or affect people and those immediately concerned took little notice of it. I remember, however, the dogs disliked and apparently feared it.

It was a tall female figure dressed in black and with a handkerchief held to her face as if crying. To the best of my knowledge 'she' was substantial and I have no impression of translucency.

I believe 'she' was known in her lifetime to my godmother with whose family I lived for a time when I was a boy, but she would *never* speak of her. If this is so (I have no reason to doubt it) the ghost's original could not when I saw her have been long dead.

She was not particular where or when she appeared. The two occasions I clearly remember were (1) in the garden in bright sunlight walking about and (2) in the drawing-room when we made a ring round her by joining hands, from which she appeared merely to walk out between two people and then disappeared.

I feel sure there were other occasions, but as I have said I was very small – the youngest of those with whom I was associated – and I dare say I was not encouraged much to join in and had doubtless more important interests elsewhere. And I expect it is all on record. I cannot remember the name of the ghost lady, if I ever knew it; the people who afterwards had the house for a time were named Despard . . .

The suggestion conveyed in Gooding's letter is that his experiences with the apparition were before the arrival of the Despard family. He was born on 17 October 1878, so would have been between three and four years old before the Despards moved into the house in April 1882. It is most unlikely that he and other boys could have gained access to the drawing-room of a house which the landlord was trying to let, so it is possible that the experience of the drawing-room took place after the Despards had taken up residence. The dogs who disliked the ghost were probably those belonging to the Despards.

George Gooding did not wish his name to be revealed, but as he is dead I feel that this restriction may be lifted. His statement is valuable because, as a solicitor, he would understand the importance of not relying on hearsay evidence in a matter such as this.

Rosina Despard gave some details of the history of the house and I will supplement her account with the results of my own research from 1966 onwards. It was built about 1860, on a site occupied by a market garden. While it was still unfinished it was bought from the builders by the first occupant, Henry Swinhoe, a solicitor who had been in Calcutta. He had five children from his wife, Elizabeth Frances Swinhoe, 'to whom he was passionately attached', and when she died, aged 35, on 11 August 1866, 'to drown his grief [he] took to drinking.'

Henry Swinhoe's next marriage, on 16 February 1870, was to Imogen Hutchins, of Clifton, Bristol. Rosina Despard said that his second wife 'was in hopes of curing him of his intemperate habits, but instead she also took to drinking, and their married life was embittered by constant quarrels, frequently resulting in violent scenes. The chief subjects of dispute were the management of the children . . . of the first Mrs Swinhoe, and the possession of her jewellery . . . Finally, a few months before Mr Swinhoe's death on 14 July 1876, his wife separated from him and went to live in Clifton. She was not present at the time of his death, nor, as far as it is known, was she ever at the house afterwards.'

Quite a different story about the cause of Henry Swinhoe's drinking habits was given to me by his granddaughter, Mrs Violet Rhodes James, of Crowthorne, Berkshire, the daughter of Rodway Swinhoe. According to the children, their father discovered on his honeymoon that Imogen was a heavy drinker, and it was she who introduced him to intemperate drinking, not the other way round; the children had 'years of tyranny and misery under Imogen'. She died, aged 41, on 23 September 1878 at 1 Clifton Hill, Bristol, the cause of death being given as dipsomania, followed by subacute gastritis. Imogen Swinhoe was buried in the churchyard of Holy Trinity Church, Portland Street, Cheltenham, about five hundred yards from her former home, and there is a commemorative tablet to her in the church.

After Henry Swinhoe's death his affairs were found to be much involved, and the house was sold as soon as a purchaser could be found. According to Rosina Despard, 'it was bought by Mr L., an elderly gentleman, who, after thoroughly doing up the house, which was in a very dirty state, went there to live, with his wife, a lady of about his own age; two sons were there from time to time, but never for long together. Old Mr L. died rather suddenly . . . and, rather a curious coincidence, in the same small sitting-room . . . in which Mr Swinhoe had also died, and where the jewels had been hidden, but in which the figure has never been seen.'

This 'Mr L.' was Mr Benjamin Littlewood, of The Greenway, Shurdingham, near Cheltenham. He lived only one month in his new home, dying there on 5 August 1879. His widow moved to a smaller house at Pittville Circus, only a few hundred yards away.

The house remained empty until the Despards took possession of it in 1882. Rosina Despard said:

During this time there is no direct evidence of haunting, but when enquiry was made later on much hearsay evidence was brought forward: for example, an old job gardener, who often worked at the house opposite, is said to have frequently seen the figure of a tall lady in black in the garden of — . This old man was on enquiry found to be dead and his widow could not be traced. A lady (Mrs P.) who had at one time resided in the same town, and after an absence of some years returned there to live, was met by me at a friend's house, and expressed great interest in the apparition, which she said seemed to be identical with one seen in the same house shortly after the death of Mrs Swinhoe. After the lapse of time it was, however, found impossible to trace this story to its source. I was also told by a friend that during the summer of 1879 or 1880, the house was offered to a lady at a rental of £60, which is less than half of what is now asked and given.

Rosina said that the figure had been connected with the second Mrs Swinhoe, on the following grounds:

1. The complete history of the house is known, and if we are to connect the figure with any of the previous occupants, she is the only person who in any way resembled the figure.
2. The widow's garb excludes the first Mrs Swinhoe.
3. Although none of us had ever seen the second Mrs Swinhoe, several people who *had* known her identified her from our description. On being shown a photo-album containing a number of portraits, I picked out one of her sister as being most like that of the figure, and was afterwards told that the sisters were much alike.
4. Her step-daughter and others told us that she especially used the front drawing-room in which she continually appeared, and that her habitual seat was on a couch placed in a similar position to ours.

5. The figure is undoubtedly connected with the house, none of the percipients having seen it anywhere else, nor had any other hallucination.

Captain Despard went to Bristol to examine the register of Mrs Swinhoe's death. He called on the doctor who had attended her, and asked him if there had been any disfigurement of the face which would account for its persistent concealment. The doctor remembered the case and said there had not been, though the face had become more full and round.

This ends Rosina Despard's account in *Proceedings*. Three years after it was published she passed, with Third Class Honours in Medicine, Obstetrics, and Forensic Medicine, her final examination. In December, 1897, she passed the examination for the M.D. Commenting on this in the SPR *Journal* (34), Mrs Pamela M. Huby said that 'even for a man' it would have been a creditable performance. 'For a woman, at the end of the nineteenth century, it is a distinguished achievement. The London School of Medicine for Women, where she studied, had only opened its doors in 1874, and women had only been admitted to London degrees in 1878. Even at the beginning of 1895, the year in which she qualified, there were only 200 women on the medical register.'

Dr Despard's interest in psychical research continued after the cessation of the haunting. She became a member of the Society, an account of her experiments in thought transference which she carried out with her friend Miss Campbell at intervals from November 1891 to October 1892 was published in the SPR *Journal* in 1893 (82e pp. 4–9), and further experiments between the two young women were published in the *Journal* in 1896 (82f pp. 234–8).

She died at Yarmouth, Isle of Wight, in 1930, aged 67.

The Despard family left the house in 1893. It remained empty until 1898 when, under the name of Inholmes, L. M. Wallich opened a preparatory school for boys there, and a strange story about it is included in Abdy Collins's book. A correspondent told him that the building was persistently haunted by the apparition of a woman. 'The old lady was encountered on the stairs – in the corridors – even in the boys' dormitories – always leaving the house in broad daylight from the garden door and wandering down the short drive. The maids left in terror and eventually the place was again closed. One small boy was very ill from fright and nearly died' (16 p. 257). Whether this was so I have been unable to confirm. I have searched copies of local papers of the time in Cheltenham library, and appealed for information about the school in the press, but without result.

The school lasted for nine years, and the building then stayed empty until 1910, when it was taken over by nuns of the Order of Ursulines. They moved out in 1912, and in the following year St Anne's Nursery College, probably used for the training of nannies, was opened there. In 1935 St Anne's was bought by the Diocese of Gloucester for use as a diocesan house. It was closed on 31 December 1970 and in 1973 was bought by a housing association for conversion into flats.

I feel it is significant that in fifty-three years the building had five names ('Garden Reach' under the Swinhoes, 'Pittville Hall' when owned by Mr Littlewood, 'Donore' during the occupancy of the Despard family, 'Inholmes' as a school, and finally 'St Anne's', the name by which it is known today. This suggests difficulties in letting the building because of its reputation. It is also significant that between 1860 and 1913 the building was empty for nine years at varying periods. I have confirmed by enquiries at the Cheltenham library that no other building in Pittville Circus Road was empty for so long.

Mrs Joyce Rynd, daughter of Lilian Despard and the only surviving grandchild of Captain and Mrs Despard, told me that her grandfather had the building exorcized by Canon Gardner, the vicar of All Saints Church. With the possible exception of the time when the building was used as a boys' school, there have been no reports of haunting at St Anne's. However, there have been persistent reports of the apparition of a tall woman in black having been seen in the neighbourhood. The Spring 1958 number of *Light*, the magazine of the College of Psychic Studies, contains a statement from Percy Wilson that Mrs Maisey, who was then still alive and living in Cheltenham, had seen the ghost on many occasions thirty-five years earlier. Mrs Wilson's father also saw the ghost many times, as also, according to Mr Wilson, did his wife's Uncle George, now living in America, who told them during their visit to Connecticut in 1958 that he had often seen the ghost when he was a boy in Cheltenham. 'We used to go and see the ghost dancing across the lawn on many occasions when I was a boy. It used to be quite a common experience with the boys of the town.'

Mr Wilson cross-examined him as to what the figure looked like and was told 'it was just a lady, who walked and sort of danced, if not floated, across the lawn.'

This, of course, is secondhand evidence; but some reliable first-hand reports have been obtained. The question is whether the figure seen by the percipients whose accounts follow was the one reported by Rosina Despard.

The figure of a woman was seen in 1958 and 1961 in Cotswold Lodge, a building now demolished, which stood on the opposite side of the road from St Anne's and within sight of it. The case was brought to my notice by William Thorne, an executive officer of Customs and Excise at London Airport, and I give details of it in *Apparitions and Ghosts*. In late November 1961 Mr Thorne, who lives at Maidenhead, drove with his wife and son John, then aged fifteen, and daughter Sally, aged four, to Cotswold Lodge, where his brother, also named John, had a flat. They were persuaded to spend the night there, instead of returning to Maidenhead as they intended. William Thorne and his son shared a couch in the drawing-room. They went to bed just before midnight. Ten minutes later, when William Thorne was almost asleep, he heard footsteps in the carpeted corridor. Thinking that they were made by his brother's wife, Mrs Paulette Thorne, he called out, 'Is that you, Paulette?' There was no reply. The footsteps were heavy but muffled. He looked at the open door, expecting to see his sister-in-law, but instead there was the figure of a woman in a long black dress which extended to the ground. The features were not clearly defined because the 'woman's' right hand, with a handkerchief in it, was held to the face. The figure was seemingly solid but the upper part was more clearly defined than the lower. The 'woman' was looking into the room but not directly at him. Although he shut and opened his eyes several times the figure did not disappear.

Young John Thorne was not asleep when he heard his father ask, 'Is that you, Paulette?' He raised himself on his right elbow and looked over his shoulder to see the figure of a woman in a long black dress standing in the doorway, completely outlined in phosphorescence. The dress was so long that it hid the feet. Unlike his father, he did not hear footsteps. He could not see the features or the hands and did not notice the hand with a handkerchief raised to the face as his father had. The figure, which was seen against a dark background, appeared to be solid. He estimated the 'woman' to be five feet four to six inches tall.

John Thorne did not feel alarmed. He said to his father, 'Did you see that?'

'Yes, go and close the door,' his father replied.

He looked away while he was getting off the couch and when he went to the door the figure was not there. Before he closed the door he looked up and down the corridor, which was twenty to twenty-five feet long, but it was empty.

William Thorne and his family did not mention this experience to their hosts, as they did not wish to cause alarm, and it was only later that they discovered that the older John Thorne, the sales manager of a large brewery company, had also seen the figure, in October 1958. In a letter to me from Scotland, he wrote:

I awoke one night, time approx. 2.30 a.m. (I am normally a heavy sleeper) and standing between me and the window was a woman. Natural reaction, with beating heart, was to dive under the bedclothes! Summoning sufficient courage, I peeped again; she remained standing there . . .

Shape suggested a woman in a long dress, as one imagined the Victorians dressed, but I could not or at least cannot remember whether features were at all discernible. I went under the clothes a second time and cowardly tugged at my wife's nightdress. She put on the light and hearing what I had to describe told me 'I had been dreaming'. I was not convinced by any means, although as time passed I did not treat the matter with much consequence.

Before going to Cheltenham William Thorne had never heard about the Cheltenham Ghost, nor had his brother before his experience. I interviewed William Thorne and his son and took statements from them. Both impressed me as being reliable witnesses, and although I was unable to interview John Thorne, as he was in Scotland, he supplied answers to sixteen questions I addressed to him, and was anxious to confirm the reality of his experience.

Cotswold Lodge was later converted into an hotel. I went there with G. W. Lambert to see if any later experiences had been reported, but the manager said that none had been brought to his attention. A block of flats now occupies the site.

Early in 1974 I received a letter from Mrs Jane Harding (pseudonym), a doctor's wife, who spent her childhood in Cheltenham. In 1933, when she was twelve years old, she spent a few nights at Weston House in Pittville Lawn, the home of her uncle, Colonel Walter Fitzgerald Bourne, and his wife Hilda, her mother's sister. Weston House, which was built around 1830, is about half a mile from St Anne's. Mrs Harding's account is as follows:

I slept in the spare room on the first floor front next to my aunt and uncle's room. One night I was awake and my aunt – as I thought – came into my room and stood by my bed. I pretended to be asleep while watching her through one half-closed eye, and teased her at breakfast next morning that I had tricked her into thinking I was asleep when really I was awake at the time – it was not until some years later (either '40 or '41) during a university vacation that my mother told me that my aunt had not been to my room on that night and had told my mother that she firmly believed I had seen an 'apparition'. She could never be induced to say if she had seen 'her' herself, but it was always my mother's belief that she had.

It was only then that I learned that noises 'of furniture being dragged across bare boards' on the top floor of Weston House (called by my aunt 'The Commotion) was [*sic*] a frequent cause of disturbance to both my uncle and aunt, but she seldom mentioned the occurrences for fear of losing 'cook' and 'Brewer', the aged parlourmaid, who both slept on the top floor. My aunt had often gone up in the night to investigate, but found both sleeping heavily.

I sent Mrs Harding a long questionnaire, which she answered, and have had several interviews with her. She impressed me as being an excellent witness and not fanciful, and one with a good memory. The figure, she said, appeared to be tall and was wearing what she imagined was a dressing-gown. The experience did not last longer than two minutes. Asked if the figure was seemingly solid, Mrs Harding replied, 'Yes, it appeared to be my aunt'.

Mrs Harding assumed the figure was that of her aunt because she could not think it belonged to any other person. She was certain the servants had not visited the room: 'Brewer (the parlourmaid) was very small and I never saw the cook out of the basement. I never even remember seeing Brewer upstairs. She and cook used the back stairs which were shut off from the hall by a baize door, and went up behind a stained glass window on the half-landing. They would not have been allowed on the first floor at night!'

Her aunt, she said, was about five feet six inches in height. She did not see the features of the figure, which was in view for about two minutes. She added:

I was consciously feigning sleep during the episode, which seems a rather unlikely 'dream'. My aunt, as she told my mother, had no doubt that I had seen something other than her – she never entertained the idea that I had been dreaming, as this would have been her first rejoinder when I told her at breakfast. Instead, she must have instantly recognized that I had experienced what she had herself, in all probability (as my mother believed) seen previously. It could even have occurred to her before I went to stay that I might experience something, so that when I spoke she was immediately on her guard not to alarm me, and allowed me to continue to think that it had been her.

Mrs Harding said that during World War II a school from Birmingham was evacuated to Cheltenham and shared Pate's Grammar School building. Two girls aged about eleven were billeted on her uncle and aunt. Her uncle would not allow them to occupy the spare room on the first floor, where she had slept, but instead decided that they should sleep together in the cook's old room in the attic next to Brewer. Her aunt was very much against this arrangement because she was convinced the children would be frightened by 'the commotion'; it did occur while they were there, but they apparently slept through it.

After Colonel Bourne's death in April 1948, the house was divided into flats. Since 1967 Weston House has been used by doctors as a surgery. Through the kindness of Dr Michael Martyn I was able to interview other doctors in his partnership and women members of the staff. When they moved into the building nothing was known about the previous history of haunting, which had not then been published, but it was soon apparent that there was something strange about it. Noises were heard on the upper floor when no one was there, the sound of rustling paper came from rooms that were unoccupied, and one doctor who has since left the practice confessed to me that he 'felt very uncomfortable in the building at night'; indeed, he refused to stay there. Another doctor said to me:

I never liked coming in at night. It was an awareness more than anything else. The atmosphere was electric. It felt like watching a horror film on TV when you sit on the edge of the seat. I have not noticed it so much in the last eighteen months or two years. I did not like to go upstairs at all. When I drove in late at night to get records I would look up at the windows to see if anyone was there. Then I have turned and looked back again.

This doctor described himself as being 'more factual than imaginative', but said that he had felt 'on edge' in certain buildings.

The last reported experience at Weston House was in the summer of 1979. A woman member of the staff was alone in the office on the ground floor about 7.15 p.m. when she heard the sound of footsteps. She felt, understandably, 'a bit nervous', and decided to return to her home.

This is the first time anything has been published about the haunting of Weston House, which has lasted about fifty years. The phenomena are not as pronounced now as they were in Colonel Bourne's time and seem to be dying out. The Colonel, I gather from Mrs Harding, was most reticent about what had happened in his house and did not like the case discussed – hence his wife's unwillingness to admit that she had seen the apparition later experienced by Mrs Harding as a child.

Cheltenham seems to be unusually rich in haunted houses. The report of a haunting which had some unusual features appeared in the magazine *Merry England* for December 1883, written by 'a lady who lived in it'. This house was in a row 'in one of the best-known and most central parts of the place.' The woman, who took up residence there in 1874, heard 'extraordinary noises;

noises as of someone running up and down stairs: crashing sounds as if heavy substances were falling: and, night after night, distinct talking in the bedroom next to my own. At first I reproved my two children who occupied this room for talking so late; but they always said they must have been fast asleep.' The maid and the children later reported hearing raps and loud whispers. The apparition of a girl was seen, and the figure of a woman whom the girls mistook for their mother.

The younger daughter, when an adult, added some details to her mother's narrative. She said, 'My sister always teased me for being afraid of ghosts; but, one night, she herself got really frightened. She was standing by my bed, and mother and the maid were talking outside in the passage, when I heard something under my bed, and asked my sister to look. She laughed, and said it was nothing; but while she looked, about a dozen black creatures, like toads, only with horns and a tail, came out from under the bed, and ran over my sister's foot and across the room, disappearing down the wainscot, to return no more.'

The Society made enquiries about this case. The house was No. 30 Montpellier Terrace, but as the street has been renumbered it is not possible to say with certainty which of the houses there was the haunted one. The tenant or owner was Mrs Charlotte E. Field, who said that her narrative was in every respect 'an accurate record of facts'. She added that 'as my daughters are much more country than town girls they are not likely to mistake toads, or what looked like toads, "with a tail and horns", for rats, as the reviewer is pleased to doubt in *The Tablet*.'

Miss Ellen Christine Luard, then living at Brighton, gave her own account of this incident. Writing on 10 December 1884 she said:

My sister was in bed or standing, I forget which, and I was sitting by her, and our mother was outside with a servant. Suddenly my sister said to me, 'There is something under the bed, do look.' I did so and these creatures ran out and one of them ran over my foot with a distinct underlined touch. I have always thought it was something got up to frighten us by the next door neighbours, who might have had their own reasons for wishing to keep the house empty or only inhabited by whom they choose. There was a great deal in that house that seems as if it must have been supernatural but these creatures were likely some magnetized india rubber contrivance got up on purpose to terrify women and children – at any rate that is the most pleasant supposition. Black things, with horns and a tail, could not have come from a good place, if they were supernatural.

Miss Luard attempts a natural explanation for the experience, but it is hardly likely that india rubber animals would disappear under a wainscot. The experience was probably a very complex collective hallucination, including the hallucination of the sense of touch by one of the girls. This will not be the only account of phantom animals in this book.

Is there a natural explanation for the strange happenings at the house now known as St Anne's? Lambert thinks that there is. He points out in an article in the SPR *Journal* (44G) that a noise at the door preceded the first appearance of the figure, and that sounds described as 'footsteps', 'knocks', 'twisting of door handles' and so on, were frequently heard afterwards, suggesting very strongly that the primary phenomena were of the 'haunted house' variety, and that the apparition was a secondary result of the mystification caused by the noises.

He maintains that a study of a six-inch Ordnance Survey map made as a result of a survey in 1885, when the phenomena were most pronounced, indicates that a stream could have passed very close to or under the Despards' home. This stream was fed by the river Chelt when in flood, and 'it is a reasonable inference, then, that the Chelt was the cause of the noises at Garden Reach [the name by which the house was known in Henry Swinhoe's time], creating disturbance by excessive flooding that passed under the east end of the house.'

Lambert also maintains that this theory provides a very convincing answer why the noises practically stopped in 1886. Until that year floods swept down the Chelt unchecked except for mill dams, which must have aggravated the mischief locally, but at that time the Dowdeswell reservoirs, which impounded the headwaters of the Chelt, were opened. Up to that time a very intermittent stream might have caused the 'rather slight' noises complained of by the Despard family, at times when it was active. Lambert admits that the foregoing circumstantial evidence was inconclusive, but leaves open the possibility that the noises at Garden Reach were due to a natural cause. It was hardly possible, he said, to explain all the appearances of the Cheltenham Ghost in terms of a physical phenomenon, but something of the kind may well have been the trigger which set off a chain of psychological reactions.

Lambert's theory should certainly be taken into consideration in assessing the phenomena in and around the house, but the noises were at times very far from 'slight'. Heavy thuds and bumpings, especially on the upper landing, were heard in the summer of 1885, and some servants left because of them. One witness, Mrs Kinloch, said she was 'much terrified' by the sounds. I have examined maps of present-day Cheltenham at the municipal offices and discussed them with the officials there. Pittville, at least today, is not a 'wet' district, so, by and large, Lambert's physical theory does not, it seems to me, offer an adequate explanation for what took place in the Despards' home. It is, of course, possible that an underground stream was responsible for some of the noises that frightened the family and servants.

Could the tall woman in black have been a living person? This theory is advanced by Peter Underwood, a member of the SPR, in his book *Hauntings* (London: Dent, 1977). He suggests that the figure was that of 'a real person living in the house with the willing connivance of Captain Despard (and possibly Mrs Despard), but unknown to the rest of the house; an illicit lodger, in fact?'

Underwood said that no one seems to have considered this possibility, but that very astute observer Mrs Sidgwick had, and she dismissed it.

Without revealing the address of the haunted house or the identity of the people concerned, Mrs Sidgwick discussed the case in *Proceedings* in 1885 while the haunting was still in progress, and pointed out that the figure 'has once been seen by two together, and on another occasion by one only, although others were present. This, and its apparently disappearing through a closed door, preclude the idea of its being any real person.' Again, when discussing the apparent progress of the figure through the house and garden, Mrs Sidgwick used the phrase, 'If it had been a real woman whom the Miss D's were observing' in assessing the possibility that the 'woman' was seen by different people in different places at the same time (81a). There is no reason, Mrs Sidgwick considered, why a ghost should not appear in two or more places at once.

In my review of Underwood's book in the *Journal* I state that 'As the haunting was to continue for four years after the publication of Mrs Sidgwick's paper there was ample opportunity to remove any doubts that still remained on whether the figure was an apparition or a living woman, but, judging by the character of the narrative published in 1892, there were none' (51f p. 840). We must also bear in mind that a living person could not have passed through the threads on the staircase without disturbing them, as the figure seen by Rosina Despard was reported to do.

Dr D. J. West, discussing the Cheltenham haunting in his book *Psychical Research Today*, said that 'the appearances and noises that were reported after Miss Morton's [Despard's] experiences became known to the other persons in the house might have been caused by suggestion', and W. H. Salter, in his discussion of the case in *Zoar*, said that 'After Miss R. C. Morton's first experience had become known to other members of the Morton family, ordinary suggestion might induce hallucinations in them.'

It might indeed, and some purported appearances of the figure could have been due to the effects of light and shade in a particular spot being interpreted as an apparition. For instance, Wilfred Despard said in his evidence that 'Another time I was in the morning-room, and had a momentary glimpse of the figure, but not long enough to be absolutely certain of having seen it. This was in the evening, the gas having been lit both in the room and in the passage outside.' On the other hand, Rosina Despard once saw the figure for half an hour, and maids who, for obvious reasons, had not been told about the ghost, reported seeing the figure.

We must also bear in mind the evidence of the solicitor, George Gooding. His recollection of what he saw as a small boy is quite clear, and as presumably it was before the arrival of the Despards, the effects of suggestion would not come into it.

Thouless, discussing this case in *Psychical Research Past and Present*, stated:

The psychical researcher is handicapped by the fact that the average person living in a haunted house generally looks at the haunting in much the same way as he would an invasion of his larder by black beetles: not as an interesting and rare occurrence to be carefully studied but as an unbearable nuisance to be got rid of as quickly as possible. He is more likely to send for an exorcist than for a psychical researcher.

We have also the difficulty that many of the cases of alleged hauntings reported to the Society are of a trivial nature, and may possibly be explained as due to misunderstanding of entirely normal events. But if a good haunting were presented to us, our resources for investigation are quite inadequate. In order to have a really illuminating investigation which could give us some understanding of the laws of hauntings, more is required than a visit by a senior member of the Society or even by the Research Officer. A prolonged occupation of the house by a team of research workers with full equipment of recording devices would be necessary, and few householders would welcome that. It is not often that a psychical researcher has the advantage that Miss Morton [Despard] had of living in a haunted house, and it was this fact that gave Miss Morton's account its pre-eminent position. If a real attack on this problem were to be made, it would be necessary that the Society should be able to buy haunted houses and to put a properly equipped research team into them. Until we are in a position to do that it is unlikely that the study of such problems will advance far beyond where it was in the early days of the Society [88a pp. 8–9].

Alas, the Society does not have funds for the purchase of haunted houses in these days of high property prices: all it can hope for is the willing co-operation of the occupants of such houses. In Chapter 14 I give details of the equipment installed by a group of researchers in a house in a mining village reported to be haunted. It is instructive to compare this equipment with that available in the Despard household a century ago. However, Miss Despard's investigation was sufficient to establish the non- physical nature of the figure.

The evidence in this case may be considered to be good. It was extremely fortunate for the Society that Myers, who lived in Cheltenham, came into contact with a family as sympathetic and helpful as the Despards and that there was on the spot a researcher as conscientious and intelligent as Rosina Despard. What I find particularly interesting about this case is that after the cessation of the haunting at the building now known as St Anne's – the present residents may sleep there in peace – the phenomena apparently continued from time to time elsewhere in the neighbourhood. This is an indication that when conditions become unsuitable for a haunting at one spot the haunting apparition will manifest itself at some other spot. I count myself to be extremely fortunate in receiving, from reliable informants, two separate reports of appearances of a female figure which bears a resemblance to the apparition seen by the Despards. This being so, I cannot help wondering how many other people have also seen the apparition but, for fear of ridicule, have kept silent. Let me assure them that I will be delighted to receive accounts of any such experiences. Details may be sent in confidence.

If the Despards could return to their former home and the neighbourhood today they would find a great many changes. The house has been repainted and looks very smart, but the garden and orchard at the rear have gone and in their place are seven bungalows. Many Victorian houses in the vicinity have been demolished and others have been converted into hotels. Blocks of flats give a modern air to parts of Pittville Circus Road. It is perhaps significant that the appearances of the apparition described by Mrs Harding and the Thorne family were in houses which were in existence when the Despards lived in Cheltenham. This suggests that the increasing modernization of the district may affect the occurrence of phenomena of the type described here.

4   The Haunted Mill House at Willington

The 'haunted house at Willington', near Wallsend, was a familiar story on Tyneside in the last century, and was referred to in print while the haunting was still in progress: an unusual feature of such accounts, which are so often produced long after the haunting has stopped. The most authentic and full account of the haunting appeared in the SPR Journal, for 1891–2, based on the diary of Mr Joseph Procter, a mill owner who lived in the house until 1847, when the commotion there caused him to move with his wife Elizabeth and family to North Shields. Mr Procter's diary covered the period of the haunting from 1834 to 1841, when the phenomena were most pronounced.

Edmund Procter, Joseph Procter's son, found the diary among his father's papers after his death in 1875. Publication was delayed for two reasons: his mother's objection to the publicity during her lifetime; and Edmund Procter's hope that he would find the continuation of the diary and conclusion, which had been lost. Edmund Procter, who was born in the haunted house, left there when he was seven, but he was able to remember his pursuit, with other members of the family, of what was apparently a phantom monkey. The Procters were a Quaker family, known locally for their integrity; this lends value to Joseph Procter's account of the phenomena which plagued the family for so long.

This case has often been referred to as 'the haunting of Willington Mill', but the haunting was mostly confined to the Mill House, which was built in 1800. The house stood in a hollow near a large steam corn mill in full view of the Willington viaduct on the Newcastle and Shields Railway. The fact that the building was detached is important when we consider the possible origin of the strange – indeed alarming – sounds heard in the house. A particularly important feature of the account that follows is the description by a Sunderland doctor of his experience with an apparition during the one night he spent in the house. The Editor of the Journal said in a brief introduction to Joseph Procter's account, 'It is a very complete and typical *case of what is commonly called "haunting", consisting of unexplained noises, generally heard by all within earshot, and continued at intervals through a period of years, in the course of which various visual phantasms were seen by different people.' Professor Sidgwick was able to interview a visitor to the house fifty years after the haunting started, and she had vivid recollections of it. I regard this as one of the best accounts of a haunting on record, mainly because Joseph Procter described what happened without exaggeration and frills.*

The disturbances at the Mill House, Willington Mill, began in the autumn of 1834. The first person to be affected by them was the nursemaid, who, in December of that year, told Mrs Procter of 'the state of dread and alarm she was kept in, in consequence of noises she had heard for about two months, occurring more particularly nearly every evening', when left alone to watch the child, a boy then about two years old, in the nursery on the second floor. She declared that she distinctly heard a dull heavy tread on the boarded floor of the unoccupied room above, pacing backwards and forwards and, on coming over the window, giving the floor such a shake as to cause the window of the nursery to rattle violently in its frame. The disturbance generally lasted ten minutes at a time, and though she did not heed it at first she became convinced that it was supernatural and 'it quite upset her.' This was evident to Mrs Procter in the girl's agitated manner.

The kitchen girl said that the nursemaid had called her upstairs when frightened in this manner, and that she had found her 'trembling much and very pale.'

'On examining her further in reference to this improbable tale', Joseph Procter wrote, 'she did not vary her statements, but on searching the rooms above and finding nothing to cause such results, but little credit was attached to this story. Before many days had elapsed, however, every member of the family had witnessed precisely what the girl described, and from that time to the present, nearly every day, sometimes several times in the day, the same had been heard by one or more of the inmates, varying unimportantly in the nature of the sound.'

On 23 January 1835 Mrs Procter, when in the nursery after

dinner, heard a noise in the room above like a person stirring about, which she took for granted was the maid cleaning out the chamber; but, to her surprise, she afterwards found that neither of the girls had been upstairs at all. In the meantime the nursemaid who first heard the noise had left and another had been engaged, 'from whom the affair was carefully concealed.' However, this girl also heard the noises and 'somewhat alarmed, enquired who or what was in the room above.'

Mrs Procter, kept at home by indisposition, was in the nursery at 11.0 a.m. when she heard in the room above a step as of a man with a strong shoe or boot going towards the window and returning. The same day, when the family was at dinner, the maid, being with the child in the nursery, 'heard the same heavy tread for about five minutes; she came into the sitting room to satisfy herself that her master was there, thinking it must have been he who was upstairs. The following day the dull sound was resumed . . . It may be noted that frequently the room has been examined immediately after the occurrence of the noise; it has been sat in, in one instance slept in all night, and in every case nothing has been elicited. Several of our friends who have waited up to hear the invisible disturber have all, with one exception, been disappointed.'

The noise was thought to come from a room on the third floor. Procter considered there could not be what he called 'any trick' in the case. There was a garret above and the roof was inaccessible from outside the house, which stood alone. The chimney was closed by a fireboard which was so covered over with soot 'as to prove that not a pebble or a mouse had passed.' No rat had been seen in the house for years. The noise had been heard at every hour of the day, though most often in the evening. It had no connection with the weather nor with the operations of the mill, which was divided from the house by a road. In short, 'it is difficult to imagine a natural cause having a shadow of pretension to belief.'

The phenomena consisted of sounds such as those which could have been made by a mallet in the Procters' bedroom; footsteps; a peculiar whistle; the sound of a clock being wound; sounds as if a person were stamping in a passion; and the sound of voices uttering meaningless phrases. Some of the thumping sounds caused beds to vibrate. Procter made enquiries about the possible origin of the haunting. He and his wife were told by their cousin Unthanks – the firm was known as Unthanks and Procter – that the house, and the room where the noises occurred, were said to be haunted before they entered it in 1806, but nothing had occurred during their occupancy of twenty-five years.

The diary contains a number of accounts of disturbances in the bedrooms. Mrs Procter, when sharing a bed with a nurse named Pollard, felt the bed raised up and let down three times. She did not speak to the nurse, nor the nurse to her, each thinking the other was asleep, but it was established at breakfast time that both had felt the movement of the bed. Mrs Procter, discussing this incident with her son Edmund, said that 'the bed was lifted up as if a man were underneath pushing it up with his back.'

Little Joseph Procter, who had been in bed about half an hour, called for someone to come to him and begged for a light; he said that something under the crib raised him up very quickly many times, and he wished to know what it could be.

Another night Jane Carr (Mrs Procter's sister) felt the bed raised up under one side as if to turn her over, giving two lifts. Nurse Pollard, in another room on the same floor, heard a noise which roused her as she was going to sleep; something then pressed against the high part of the curtain and came down on her arm, which was weighed down with the same force; in great terror she called out, 'Lord, have mercy upon me!' Nothing further occurred to her that night, nor was the maid who slept with her aroused.

Two of the children, Joseph and Henry, were several times disturbed in their cribs during the course of one evening; once they heard a loud shriek which seemed to come from near the foot of the bed, and Joseph was found 'trembling and perspiring from the fright.' On another evening their father heard a very peculiar moan or cry in the same room.

Another time little Joseph said that his bed moved backwards and forwards; also, a voice by the foot of the bed said, 'Chuck' twice, and then made a noise like a child sucking. He described other voices and was very inquisitive as to the origin of these sounds.

One of the most alarming experiences took place early one February in a room which Jane Carr shared with her companion, Mary Young (who was also the cook), because she did not dare to sleep alone in such a house. The cook was described by Edmund Procter as a most respectable and intelligent woman.

Between eleven and twelve at night Miss Carr heard a thump on the landing near the bedroom door, upon which she awoke the other woman.

Mary Young heard the slot in the door apparently slide back, the handle to turn and the door to open. A rushlight was burning on the dressing-table, but the bed was an old four-poster, and the curtain being drawn, nothing could be seen. A step then went to the rushlight, and appeared by the sound to snuff it and then lay down the snuffers. In the act of snuffing the light was transiently obscured, as when that act is customarily performed. Jane C. then felt it raise up the clothes over her twice; then they both heard something rustle the curtains as it went round the bed; on getting to Mary Young's side she distinctly saw a dark shadow on the curtain. On getting to the bed-board where Jane C. lay a loud thump as with a fist was heard on it; something was then felt to press on the counterpane on M. Young's side of the bed, the bed curtains being pushed in but nothing more seen. Whatever the visitor might be was then heard to go out, seeming to leave the door open. In the morning they found the door still bolted as it was left when they went to bed. In this occurrence Jane C. heard and felt everything described, but having her head under the bedclothes could not see the shadow as her companion did.

One night, while her husband was asleep, Mrs Procter felt a heavy pressure 'which unnerved her very much; it seemed to take her breath away and she felt quite sick after it,' but she did not tell her husband about it until the morning. On a previous night Mr Procter was awakened by feeling a pressure of icy coldness on the face over the eye; 'it was suddenly laid on with a good deal of force and as suddenly withdrawn.'

The phenomena were not confined to the house. More than once Procter, coming through the garden at night, heard a sound like someone stepping down the gravel walk, but he had been unable to discover anyone. The step on the gravel had been heard by one or two others, but nothing was seen. Thomas Mann, the foreman of the mill, 'a man of strict integrity and veracity', one night heard the sound of a cistern on iron wheels, used for bringing water to the horses, moving along the yard towards the gates, creaking excessively as it went. Fearing that the cistern was being stolen, he ran towards the spot, only to find, to his astonishment, that it had not moved.

Apparitions, too, were reported. A 'respectable neighbour' saw a transparent white female figure in a window in the second storey of the house. Some days later Mrs Mann, on leaving the house to get coal, saw a figure in the same window; 'it was very luminous and likewise transparent and had the appearance of a priest in a white surplice.' She drew her husband's attention to the phenomenon, and he in turn called his daughter and a relative of the Procter family, Mrs Christiana Wright, of Mansfield, Nottinghamshire, who was staying at the Manns' house. When they came the head was nearly gone, and the brightness somewhat abated, but it was 'fully ten minutes' before it quite disappeared by gradually fading downwards. Mrs Wright was still alive in 1892 and confirmed this account taken from the diary.

Jane Procter, about four and a half years old, told her parents that when sleeping with her aunt she one night saw, by the washstand at the foot of the bed where the curtains were drawn, a queer looking head, she thought that of an old woman; she saw her hands with two fingers of each hand extended and touching each other; she also had something down the sides of her face and passed across the lower part of it. She saw it plainly though it was darkish in the room. She was afraid and put her head under the clothes and eventually fell asleep. Later that month about dusk, she described having seen a head on the landing as she was coming downstairs, 'and appeared to be very much terrified.'

On 26 October 1841, about 9.0 a.m., Joseph and Henry Procter were playing at the foot of the stairs when they both saw a white face looking down upon them over the stair rails leading to the garret. Joseph called for his aunt, Christiana Carr, to come and see it, 'but just as she was coming he saw it hop away. Henry heard it give a great jump, but Joseph, being very hard of hearing, did not. They both agreed in the description of what they saw.'

On 24 November 1841 Joseph, aged eight, who had gone to bed about 8.0 p.m., called to his father in some alarm. He said a man had just gone to the window, thrown up the sash, put it down again and then walked out; he had light or grey hair and no hat on. He was astonished his father had not met him. Within a few minutes he called out again; he had heard a step from the door to the closet at the far side of the room where he heard something like a cloak fall. He did not dare to look up to see who it was.

In August of that year Joseph, on two or three occasions, said he had heard voices from underneath the bed and from other parts of the room, and described how once he had seen a boy in a drab hat much like his own, the boy very much like himself too, walking backwards and forwards between the window and the wardrobe. He was afraid but did not speak. 'If any readers exclaim that these are but the dreams and nightmares of children', Edmund Procter commented, 'I will only remind them that I am simply transcribing from my father's diary, written on the dates given by his own hand, and that they must form their own conclusions.'

A Sunderland doctor, Edward Drury, had a dramatic encounter with an apparition in the house. Fortunately, he gave an account of it in correspondence with Mr Joseph Procter which is quoted in an appendix to the *Journal* (the letters were originally published in the *Local Historian's Table Book*) (71).

On 17 June 1840 Dr Drury wrote to Procter to say that, having heard of unaccountable noises in the house at night, his curiosity was 'excited to a high pitch', and he wanted to satisfy this by remaining alone in the house all night with his watchdog as a companion. He had read Wesley's account of such things, he explained, but with no great belief.

Procter invited the doctor to spend a night in the house on or after 24 June, when the family would be away. He warned him, however, that the disturbances were only occasional and quite uncertain, 'and therefore the satisfaction of E.D.'s curiosity must be considered as problematical.'

Procter left home with his family on 23 June, leaving an old servant in charge of the house in their absence. He returned alone on 3 July on account of business and that evening Drury arrived unexpectedly with a friend to carry out his investigation. The house was locked up and every corner of it was minutely examined. An account of what happened is contained in a letter from Dr Drury to Mr Procter, dated 13 July.

Having received your sanction to visit your mysterious dwelling I went, on the 3rd of July, accompanied by a friend of mine, named T. Hudson. This was not according to promise, nor in accordance with my first intent, as I wrote to you I would come alone; but I felt gratified at your kindness in not alluding to the liberty I had taken, as it ultimately proved for the best. I must here mention that, not expecting you at home, I had in my pocket a brace of pistols, determining in my mind to let one of these drop, as if by accident, before the miller, for fear he should presume to play tricks upon me; but after my interview with you I felt there was no occasion for weapons, and did not load them, after you had allowed us to inspect as minutely as we pleased every portion of the house. I sat down on the third-floor landing, fully expecting to account for any noises I might hear in a philosophical manner. This was about eleven o'clock p.m. About ten to twelve we both heard a noise, as if a number of people were pattering with their bare feet upon the floor; and yet so singular was the noise that I could not minutely determine from whence it proceeded. A few minutes afterwards, we heard a noise, as if someone was knocking with his knuckles among our feet; this was immediately followed by a hollow cough from the very room from which the apparition proceeded. The only noise after this was as if a person was rustling against the wall in coming upstairs. At a quarter to one, I told my friend that, feeling a little cold, I would like to go to bed, as we might hear the noises equally well there. He replied that he would not go to bed till daylight. I took up a note, which I had accidentally dropped, and began to read it, after which I took out my watch to ascertain the time, and found that it wanted ten minutes to one. In taking my eyes from the watch they became rivetted upon a closet door, which I distinctly saw open, and saw also the figure of a female attired in greyish garments, with the head inclining downwards, and one hand pressed upon the chest, as if in pain, and the other, viz., the right-hand, extended towards the floor, with the index finger pointing downwards. It advanced with an apparently cautious step across the floor towards me; immediately as it approached my friend, who was slumbering, its right hand was extended towards him; I then rushed at it, giving at the time . . . a most awful yell; but instead of grasping it, I fell upon my friend, and I recollected nothing distinctly for nearly three hours afterwards. I have since learnt that I was carried downstairs in an agony of fear and terror.

I hereby certify that the above account is strictly true and correct in every respect.

The following day Mr Procter wrote to his wife with an account of his own part in these dramatic happenings.

Dear Elizabeth . . . Last night Dr Drury came with T. Hudson, a shopman of Joseph Ogilvie, chemist, and no dog. After a long chat they sat on the high landing; I went to my own bed; Bell [presumably the servant who had been left in charge of the house] in the Camp room. About one o'clock I heard a most horrid shriek from E.D., slipped on my trousers and went up. He had then swooned, but came to himself again in a state of *extreme nervous excitement*, and accompanied with much coldness and faintness. He had seen the G.; had been struck speechless as it advanced from the closet in the room over the drawing-room to the landing, and then leapt up with an awful shriek and fainted. The other young man had his head against the easy-chair and was dozing, and as the G. made no noise in coming up he did not awake until the yell of his friend called him to his help.

I called up Bell to make up the fires, get coffee, etc., but he continued in a shocking state of tremour for some hours, though not irrational. He had a ghastly look and started at the smallest sound – could not bear to see anything white; he had not been in the least sleepy, and was not at all frightened till the moment when the G. met his gaze. They had both previously heard several noises, but all had been quiet for about a quarter of an hour, and E.D. was thinking of getting his companion to go to bed, not expecting anything more that night . . . E.D. has got a shock he will not soon cast off.

The closet from which the apparition appeared, Edmund Procter was to observe, was too shallow to contain a person.

Professor Sidgwick interviewed Mrs Hargrave, one of Mrs Procter's sisters, on 3 January 1884, who told him that on one occasion she saw an apparition similar to that seen by Dr Drury. She described it as the figure of a woman in a grey mantle which came through the wall of her room from the next. There was a light in the room; her sister who was with her was asleep. The feet of the figure appeared to be about three feet from the floor. It came close up to the bed. She also saw in the daytime 'a large white cat' in the garden; it was larger than a real cat and with a long snout. It appeared to go through the closed garden door or through the wall into the engine-house and disappear as if it had gone into the fire. It was also seen in one of the bedrooms, going through a closed door.

Procter's diary had a note that on 13 November 1841, about 4.30 p.m., Joseph was in the nursery with his brothers and sisters. He had seated himself on the top of a chest of drawers and was making a pretended speech to them when he suddenly jumped down, and, the nursery door being ajar, Procter, who was in his own bedroom adjoining, heard him exclaim that there was a monkey and that it had pulled his leg by his shoestrap. Procter himself did not see the monkey, but coming out of his room saw the children peering under the curtains of the bed in the blue-room where, they alleged, the animal had disappeared. Joseph afterwards stated that the monkey had given a sharp pull at his shoestrap, and had tickled his foot; he did not suppose it was other than a real monkey. 'Edmund, who is under two years old, was frightened a short time before by what he called "a funny cat", and showed a good deal of timidity the rest of the evening, looking under chairs, etc., lest it should be lurking there, and it is to be noted that he has no fear of a cat.'

As it happened, Edmund Procter remembered this incident perfectly, young as he was. He said that his parents had told him that no monkey was known to be owned in the neighbourhood, and that after diligent enquiry no organ-man or hurdy-gurdy boy, either with or without a monkey, had been seen anywhere about the place or neighbourhood.

The diary ended abruptly in 1841. Edmund Procter said he knew that disturbances of a varied character continued for years. Finding life in the house no longer tolerable, and fearing also an unhappy effect, if not a permanent injury, in the minds of their children should they remain longer 'in such a plague-ridden dwelling', the Procter family left in 1847 and went to reside in Camp Villa, North Shields. Edmund Procter said that his parents repeatedly told him of the happenings during the last night they slept in the old house, the rest of the family having preceded them to the new one. There were continuous noises during the night of boxes apparently being dragged with heavy thuds down the now carpetless stairs, non-human footsteps stamped on floors, doors were, or seemed to be, clashed, 'and impossible furniture corded at random or dragged hither and thither by inscrutable agency; in short, a pantomimic or spiritualistic repetition of all the noises incident to the household flitting.'

Edmund Procter outlined the subsequent history of the house. The foreman and chief clerk in the flour mill, 'less sensitive perhaps to the disturbances, and with families of maturer years,' raised no objection to occupying the Mill House after a time, and it was divided into two separate dwellings, and inhabited by them for nearly twenty years. They were occasionally disturbed by unaccountable noises, and Thomas Mann, the foreman, on one or two occasions saw what appeared to be apparitions, but both families were 'designedly reticent on the subject, and I believe suffered but little throughout their occupancy.'

About 1867 the mill and the house were let for a few months to a firm from an adjoining town whose mill had been burnt down. Edmund Procter was told that those occupying the house were 'much troubled,' one family declining to stay on any terms. Not long afterwards Joseph Procter sold the entire premises to a firm of guano merchants, and information reached the Procter family that two machinists, one of them a German, who were fixing machinery in the mill, spent some 'restless evenings and unhappy nights in the house in fruitlessly trying to discover the origin of fitful and exasperating disturbances.'

The mill was used only as a warehouse, and later the house was divided into small tenements. When in 1890 Edmund Procter interviewed three or four of the tenants, he was told that no disturbances had been experienced.

Information about the haunting was obtained by a clairvoyante called 'Jane', the wife of a pitman in the county of Durham, and an account was given by Mrs Sidgwick (81c pp. 53–4, 82–4, 86–7, 91). According to Myers, whom Mrs Sidgwick quoted, 'Jane' had never received any fee, or made any exhibition of her powers. She was mesmerized at intervals for many years from 1845 onwards for the sake of her health, and when in the mesmeric state she almost always began to talk in a childish language, and to ask to 'travel', that is, to be guided by suggestion to places which she should clairvoyantly visit.

'Jane', when in trance, accurately described the flour mill at Willington in action and the location of the Mill House. She asked why the gentleman who had occupied it went away and, answering her own question, said, 'It was a vision that frightened him away. The lady was only a vision.' At a later session, in which she was asked to return to the haunted house, 'Jane' said that she did not like what she saw. The lady had a very white face, 'but she moves about so quick; she has eyes, but no sight in them; she is just like a shadow.' Asked if the vision had a name, 'Jane' replied, 'No, she has no name and no brains; she is just like a shadow and flits about so quickly from place to place.'

'Jane' purported to describe the figure of a man who also troubled the occupants of the Mill House. It was a vision: 'he has no brains in his head; he looks very fierce, his eyes flash like a tom cat's – like a tiger; he has a white dress on like a surplice. Oh, how angry he is!' The clairvoyante said there were two or three kinds of animal in the house: one was like a monkey, and another like a dog . . . 'What is that other one? Do we know what we call it? It is not a pussy, it runs very fast, and gets among feet. It is a rabbit but a very quick one.'

This is an interesting account, well documented, of a haunting which lasted at least thirteen years, and is based mainly on a diary kept by a man of known integrity for seven years. Although the sounds heard so frequently in the house caused vibrations, it does not appear from Joseph Procter's account that objects were physically moved.

It is tempting to speculate that some of the strange noises in the house could have been caused by nearby water. I have not visited the spot, but William Howitt, a contributor to M. A. Richardson's *Local Historian's Table Book*, described it as standing on 'a sort of little promontory, round which runs the channel of a watercourse, which appears to fill and empty with the tides'.

Possibly some of the sounds complained of were caused by water, but we must bear in mind that the Unthank family, who occupied the house for twenty-five years, did not complain about strange noises, so this seems to rule out a natural explanation for them. We should also note that the strange sounds were heard *before* the Newcastle and Shields Railway, which runs near the house, crossing a viaduct, was opened on 19 June 1840.

Not only were the strange happenings experienced by members of the Procter household but also by visitors, such as the Carrs of Carlisle. However, what I find most interesting about the whole affair was Dr Drury's encounter with the ghost. He went to the house hoping to solve the mystery of the strange sounds and actually encountered an apparition, something he never expected. This is the only reliable account I know of someone whose one-night vigil in a haunted house was rewarded in this fashion. Dr Drury's reaction to the experience was one of great terror; this is unusual.

In assessing the evidence given by the clairvoyante, 'Jane', in trance we must bear in mind that she lived in Durham, which is reasonably close to Willington, and that she could have read about the haunting. The author of *The Night Side of Nature* (17), Mrs Catherine Crowe, quotes William Howitt's statement on 22 July 1847 that the 'strange visitations' at the Mill House 'were of such a nature that they soon became rumoured over the whole neighbourhood. Numbers of people hurried to the place to enquire into the truth of them . . .' Knowledge of the happenings at Willington, even if not consciously remembered, could have been reflected in 'Jane's' utterances in the trance state. Even so, her account of the 'visions' is remarkable, particularly when she said of the apparition of the woman, 'she has eyes, but no sight in them; she is like a shadow . . . she has no name and no brains'. This is what one would expect of a certain type of haunting ghost.

The clairvoyante also described spectral animals of the type reported by the children. If it is argued that the monkey seen by them could have been a living one we must ask why it was not found when it was searched for after it had disappeared under a bed. It is difficult to know what to make of the large white cat, with a long snout, described by Mrs Hargrave. 'Jane' decided that it was a rabbit, but surely Mrs Hargrave would know what a rabbit looked like. There is no doubt that this 'cat' or 'rabbit' was a phantom because it was seen to go through a closed door.

There were some strange features in this haunting. For instance, little Joseph saw what could have been his own apparition. When the children were playing in the rooms upstairs, Mrs Hargrave and her sister, playing with them, used to see a door banged in their faces, the windows being shut and there being no draughts to cause it.

The haunting of the Mill House started more than thirty years after it was built, and why this should be so remains a mystery, but we must bear in mind that two different families were involved. The house itself is no longer in existence, but the Mill is still there, being part of the Hood Haggie Ropery (now Bridon Fibres). The haunting was apparently motiveless and nothing is known of the identity of the apparitions reported to have been seen there. In a case such as this, it is difficult to attribute the haunting to a former occupant of the house.

5 Two Haunted Parsonages

'Twelve Months in a Haunted House' was the title of a manuscript sent to the SPR in May, 1883. It must have been prepared for publication at some time in the past, probably 1868, because the writer, Canon Robinson, of York, was dead. Anonymity was requested then by the Canon's widow, so the account, which appeared in Proceedings *in 1884, was attributed to 'a well-known Church dignitary.' The events described took place about 1850 in a vicarage in Shropshire, which I will not name for the sake of the present incumbent and his family. Canon Robinson's daughter, Miss Edith Robinson, said that her mother was fully able to corroborate every fact mentioned in the story. The manuscript was copied for the archives before being returned to Miss Robinson. The narrative that follows was described in* Proceedings *(82g pp. 144–51) as 'a remarkably clear account of a haunted house where noises were heard, but nothing was ever seen . . . The case is remarkable as showing a periodicity in the noises, which is, as we have previously stated, by no means a common feature.' It is, in fact, very rare, as later investigations indicate. Canon Robinson's report is given mainly in full.*

About eighteen years ago, having completed the probationary period of two years from my ordination as deacon, I was in search of a curacy. Amongst others that came under my notice was one in the south-west of the county of S. The parish was extensive and the situation very retired. It was a sole charge, and a commodious house was at the disposal of the curate. The curacy was accepted, and in due time my wife and I proceeded to take possession of our new home. We reached it on the afternoon of a dull February day.

The vicarage we were to occupy was a square spacious building, surrounded by lawn and shrubberies, garden and orchard. The house was detached, situated a short distance from the village, and separated by a road from two or three cottages which were the nearest dwellings. Our rooms were large and sufficiently lofty, everything was in good repair, and we congratulated ourselves on having secured a comfortable home.

It was, I remember, a Friday afternoon on which we arrived, and we

worked with a will, and had two or three rooms fit for occupancy by
Saturday evening.

Night fell, shutters were fastened, bolts shot and keys turned, and my wife
and I retired to bed on that Saturday, not reluctantly, for we had worked for
a couple of days as hard as porters in a warehouse.

We had not as yet engaged a servant, and had, therefore, availed
ourselves of the help of an honest country woman, who lived hard by. When
I made all fast on the Saturday night, the honest country woman, my wife,
and myself were – to the best of my knowledge and belief – the only three
living beings within the four walls of the vicarage. Long before twelve we
were all in the land of dreams, and probably some way beyond it, in that
realm of sleep to which no 'extravagant and erring' dream ever finds its way.
Suddenly, however, there broke on our drowsy ears a sound which
murdered sleep. In a moment, almost before consciousness had come, I was
out of bed and on my feet, and even then it seemed as if that strange noise
was only just passing into the accustomed silence of deep night. My wife was
as abruptly and completely roused as myself, and together we listened for
some repetition of what had disturbed us, or for some further token to guide
us to the discovery of the cause. But nothing came. It was obviously my
business to make an investigation without delay, for the natural solution of
the mystery was that some one or more persons had made their way into the
house.

Accordingly I hurried on a few articles of dress and set out on an
exploring expedition. Before doing so, however, I looked at my watch, and
found that it was just 2.5 a.m. I wish to call particular attention to this fact.
I made a thorough search over the whole house. I examined the fastenings
of the doors, the shutters of the windows. All was safe, all was quiet,
everything was in its place. There was nothing left for me to do but to return
to my room, go to bed, and think no more of the disturbance. This last was
not so easy. Neither my wife nor I could persuade ourselves that it was a
mistake. The sound was so palpable, broke on our sleep with so peremptory
a summons, pealed on our half-awakened senses with so prolonged a crash,
that neither could its reality be doubted nor its impression thrown off.

It struck me, then and afterwards, as being like the crash of iron bars
falling suddenly to the ground. Certainly there was a sharp metallic ring
about it. Moreover, it was prolonged, and instead of coming from some fixed
point, it seemed to traverse the house like a succession of rattling echoes,
treading hard on one another's heels.

I speak of it not specially as it impressed me on the particular occasion to
which I am referring, but from my general estimate of its character; for I
may as well say at once that my acquaintance with it was not limited to the
experiences of that one early Sunday morning. Of course – on my return to
my room – when we talked the matter over, it occurred to us to ascertain
whether the good woman from the village had also been roused by the din.
However, as she had not herself given any signs of alarm, we resolved to
wait to see whether she had any tale to tell in the morning.

Well! the remaining hours of darkness passed away quickly enough, and when morning came we found that the third member of our household had been a sharer with ourselves in the mysterious visitation. She, like us, had been rudely awakened, and had long lain awake in a state of considerable disquietude and alarm.

To her, however, the thing was not quite so strange and unlooked for as to us. 'Oh dear,' she said, 'I've heard tell of it afore, but never till last night did I hear it, and don't want to again.'

She had heard tell of it before. But there was not much more to be got out of her, and she seemed unwilling to discuss the subject. 'It was a conceit,' she said, and that was all she chose to say about it. On one point, however, she was clear enough, and that was the necessity of going home that evening to look after her house and children. She would give us her services during the day, but she could not well be spared from home at nights. To this effect, therefore, an accommodation was made with her, and my wife and I stood committed for the coming night to be the sole garrison of the vicarage, whether it was to be assailed by tangible force or impalpable sounds.

The Sunday duties were duly discharged. I met my parishioners in the church for the first time; looked round with satisfaction on a large and attentive, though not perhaps especially intelligent congregation, and could not help wondering whether any of those stolid young farmers and peasants, whose faces were turned so impassively towards the pulpit, had been indulging in a grim practical joke at my expense.

In due time, my wife and I found ourselves alone in the vicarage: the darkness of a winter night without, a snug wainscoted parlour, a bright fire, and sundry creature comforts within. Thus we sat, till about eight o'clock. It then occurred to us to make an examination of the house, though we had taken care – as soon as it became dark and our handmaid had left us – to make everything, as far as possible, secure. We rose, then, and set off together, and passing out of our sitting-room, found ourselves in the square entrance hall, the door of which opened into the garden.

Scarcely were we there before we heard a noise which made us pause and listen. The sound came from the long passage upstairs into which all the bedrooms opened, and was simply the sound of human footsteps walking slowly but firmly along the passage. There was no mistake about it. Bold, distinct, and strong, each footfall reached our ears. At once, candle in hand, I dashed upstairs, three steps at a time, and in a moment was on the landing and in full view of the passage. But there was nothing to be seen. My wife, of course, followed me, for she was becoming nervous.

Together, therefore, we entered and searched the bedrooms. But our search was fruitless. If anybody had been there he had contrived in some way inexplicable to us to make his escape. A more complete and anxious examination of the house was the necessary consequence of the adventure, and we pretty well satisfied ourselves that, whatever might have caused the sounds we had heard, we were not the involuntary entertainers of any unbidden guest of flesh and blood. To make assurance doubly sure, I unbarred the yard door and took a survey of the outside premises.

From this work, however, I was rather hastily recalled by my wife, who announced that the inexplicable footsteps were again in motion, and though on my return they had ceased, yet once more that night they did us the favour of letting us hear them before we went to bed. Now at this point I am bound in honesty to say that when we returned to our parlour fire, which had a very encouraging and comforting look about it, my wife and I, in discussing the matter, did hint at the possibility of our having fallen in with 'a haunted house'. And it is only fair to add that we neither of us was so settled in all unbelief of the supernatural, as without further consideration to scout the notion as absurd. But assuredly we did not jump at once to any such conclusion, and were content with simply passing a resolution to the effect that the disturbances were somewhat extraordinary and rather disagreeable than otherwise.

That night we experienced no further annoyance, and indeed for a week or two there is nothing of any particular significance to record.

In the meantime we found ourselves fairly settled. One strong and willing female servant did all that we needed to have done indoors, and a lad of about fourteen years of age was engaged to look after a couple of ponies and to do the sundry odd jobs. This boy, it must be observed, did not sleep in the house, so that unless we had a visitor, which did not often happen, the number of the inmates was only three. Our female servant was a stranger from a village at some distance, and had not, as far as we knew, any acquaintances in the place.

For some little time, as I have intimated, we were not much disturbed. The unexplained sound of footsteps we occasionally heard, but we troubled ourselves as little as possible about it, believing that whatever it might be it was at all events very inoffensive and not likely to interfere much with our comforts or prerogatives.

However, in due time we were favoured with a new development and that, too, of a kind which was sufficiently distinct and obtrusive. There was, it must be understood, a range of attics at the top of the house reaching over the full extent of it. We found them empty and in good repair, and we converted them into store-rooms for our boxes, packing cases, etc. They were reached by a small staircase opening off the main passage upstairs; and having deposited in them everything that we wished to put out of the way we secured the staircase door.

We had gone to bed one night as usual, and were about quietly to drop asleep, when all at once there commenced a tumult overhead, which very soon made us wide-awake as we had ever been in our lives. The noise was, confessedly, of the most vulgar, commonplace, and substantial kind. It was – or rather I should say it seemed to be – the result of the tossing about over the attic floor of all the boxes, cases, and bundles stored there. It was loud, boisterous, and persistent. There was a bump, and a rattle, and a roll, and a crash. Of course an investigation was an obvious necessity, but an investigation discovered nothing. All was quiet. Everything was apparently undisturbed and as much in order as it had ever been, or, in such a place, could be expected to be. We were confessedly perplexed, and moreover – as far as that, as well as the other occurrences went, we were condemned to the humiliation of remaining in a state of unrelieved perplexity.

But, besides, some supplementary entertainments were provided for our benefit. From time to time a succession of distinctly audible knocks would greet our ears. These knocks varied in their type. At one time they were hurried, eager, impatient; at another, slow and hesitating. But, however, in one style or another we were treated to them, I should say on the average, four nights a week during our sojourn at — . These were, of all the phenomena, the commonest. I am bound, in justice to the unknown cause of them, to say that we were seldom disappointed in our expectation of hearing them. They were not very alarming, certainly, and after a little familiarity had bred the requisite measure of contempt, they were not particularly disturbing.

One feature about them, however, deserves to be noticed. Sometimes, while lying awake, an involuntary listener to their tattoo, I was provoked to the use of a little sarcasm or what schoolboys would call 'chaff'. I would, for instance, address the hypothetical agent and bid it 'be quiet, and not disturb honest people in their beds', or I would challenge it, if it had any request to make or any complaint to lay, 'to come out and do it in a manly, straightforward way'. Somehow or other these remonstrances were not well received. They always led to louder, more hurried, and if we may use such a term, more passionate knocking. The reader may smile at the notion of any connection between any wild words and the intensified rappings, and I do not wish to assert that there must necessarily have been any connection. I simply state the fact that coincidentally with my challenge, the rappings intensified. I do not theorize, I tell a round, unvarnished tale. Possibly it was a coincidence and nothing more.

Did we – it may be asked – say anything to our neighbours about what we were so frequently experiencing? For a considerable time we did not. We had determined to hold our tongues for several reasons. In the first place if we talked about what had so much of the mysterious about it, we might give rise to exaggerations, and excite alarms which would make it a difficult matter to keep a servant or get one. Moreover, we knew little of the characters of the people amongst whom we had come, and we thought that if it was the result of a trick we should, by saying nothing about it, be more likely to discover it, or to tire out the performers by assumed indifference. Hence, though our servant, who was a stout-hearted country wench, sometimes dropped hints of nocturnal disturbances, we always put aside the subject and discouraged her attempt to talk about it. So far I have strictly confined myself to what came under my own observation – to what I heard with my own ears. And I think that the experience of my wife and myself does not reach beyond the rappings, the confused noises in the attic, and well-defined pacing of footsteps about the house, and that grand satanic crash. On these the changes were from time to time rung.

They began soon after our arrival, they were kept up with tolerable activity during our stay, and for anything I know we left them behind us when we departed. The great noise which greeted us on the first Sunday morning, as it was the most startling of all the phenomena, so it was the least frequent. Weeks sometimes passed without our hearing it at all. But whenever we did hear it – if we took the trouble to ascertain – we always found that it occurred at *two o'clock on a Sunday morning*. In the course of time, we had incontrovertible evidence that it might manifest itself to some persons in the house, without my wife or myself being conscious of it. Knowing how overwhelming the sound always appeared to me when I did hear it, I cannot but consider this fact one of the most wonderful things in the whole business. I will show, however, that it was so.

As the winter passed away, and our country became more attractive, we had a few visitors; amongst the earlier comers was a young lady, a very near relative of my wife. We agreed to say nothing to her about our own experiences, partly because we did not want her to be frightened by anticipation, and partly because we wished for a little independent, unprejudiced and spontaneous testimony.

We very soon got it; our friend had not been many nights with us, before she began to put questions as to why we had made such a stir in the house after everybody, as she supposed, had retired to rest. Our answers to these enquiries were, as might be expected, a little vague and unsatisfactory. Once or twice she asked whether there was to be a funeral, for she had heard under her window what she had concluded to be the sexton digging a grave, and she expressed a little surprise that he should choose to ply his melancholy trade during the hours of darkness. She was, of course, assured, as was indeed the case, that no funeral was about to take place, and, moreover, that whatever she heard under her window, it was at all events not the process of grave-digging, for the churchyard lay on the other side of the house. This was conclusive enough, no doubt, against her theory, but she did not the less persist in asserting that on several occasions she had heard a noise beneath her window, and that the noise was, in her judgement, the result of some form or other of spade-husbandry. I have no doubt of the reality of the impression made on her mind, but I never myself heard the sound which she described.

I was not, however, particularly surprised, when, on another occasion, she told us that someone had walked along the passage, and knocked at her door, but that in answer to her call of 'Who's there?' no reply had been vouchsafed, and no attempt at entrance into her room had been made.

At length Sunday morning arrived, and we met at the breakfast table.

'Whatever was the matter last night?' was our kinswoman's earliest greeting. 'What a clatter somebody made! I was so thoroughly awakened, that I got up and should have come out of my room to see what had happened had it not been that I was afraid of encountering your dogs! However I was so much disturbed that I could not easily compose myself again to rest, and as I stood at my window, peering into the darkness, *I heard the church clock strike two.*' Hereupon my wife and I exchanged very significant looks. Our friend had heard that night – though we had not – what we had begun to call 'The Great Sabbath Alarum'. We then told her something of our own experience, and her impression of the sound harmonized with our own. I shall only mention one more incident collateral to what we ourselves observed, for it is on our own *personal* experience that I rest the value and the interest of my story.

The curate and his wife were absent 'for a week or two' during the autumn, and on their return were told by the servant of strange happenings during their absence. Once, when she had gone to the village, the servant boy left in sole charge of the house was disturbed by the sound of footsteps tramping round the passages. He investigated, but no one was to be seen. The third time he was disturbed by the footsteps, 'it was too much for boyish flesh and blood.' He rushed out of the house 'and never stopped till he told his breathless tale to the gaping inmates of his father's cottage.'

The curate eventually spoke about the disturbances to 'a very excellent Christian woman' whose cottage was just opposite the vicarage. The window of the little room in which she lay commanded a full view of it, and she had at times seen flickering and intermittent light at the attic windows. She said that there had often been talk of these disturbances and that some, at least, of his predecessors in the curacy had been a good deal annoyed by them. She also told him of 'certain transactions' which had taken place in the past century, and of which she had heard from her elders.

What was the explanation for the disturbances?

The first explanation, said the curate, was the possibility of a practical joke. He dismissed this on the grounds that had any persons gained admission to the house, 'they must have been the most patient and dreary jokers that ever gave their unrequited and unappreciated services to the genius of mischief.' The curate also considered, and dismissed, the possibility that some of the noises could have been caused by rats. 'If . . . they really achieved all that came under my own observation, then I must say that their abilities are wonderful. How, for instance, did they accomplish – and how did they so exactly time – the Great

Sunday Crash? There is a circumstance that deserves to be considered by anyone who may care to suggest an explanation of what I have related.'

The curate pointed out that at the time he had two Skye terriers of pure breed, excellent house dogs, and uncompromising foes to vermin. The winter was a rough one, times were not good, and there were several robberies of houses in the neighbourhood. An attempt was made on the vicarage. 'My trusty dogs, however, gave prompt alarm, I was roused by their fierce barking, reached the window in time to see more than one dark figure on the lawn below, and was able to address such a remonstrance to them as led to a retreat, expedited in some measure by the discharge of a few shots from a pistol.'

He mentioned this incident, he said, to contrast the behaviour of the dogs on that occasion with their conduct in the presence of the mysterious noises, 'for when at such times, in making search about the house, I came where they were, I always found them cowering in a state of pitiable terror. Of this I am quite sure, that they were more perturbed than any other members of the establishment. If not shut up below they would make their way to our bedroom and lie there, crouching and whining, as long as we would allow them.'

The curate ended his account by stating:

Our experience of the phenomena, which I have described, extended over a period of twelve months. At the end of that time I was appointed to a benefice in another part of England, and consequently resigned my curacy. We turned our backs on the vicarage, not sorry, it must be confessed, to be done with our nocturnal alarms, but disappointed at not having been able to discover the cause of them.

I have never visited the place since, and never had the opportunity of learning whether the attentions paid by those secret and invisible agents to us have ever been renewed in favour of our successors.

For some months the papers relating to this case could not be found in the archives; and as the location of the haunted vicarage had never been given, I wondered whether the rectory at Polstead, in Suffolk, could be the building concerned, as it has been much in the news in recent years. For instance, the *Sunday Express* of 30 July 1978 carried an account of how a new rector and his wife were driven out, after residing only three days in the rectory, by the sound of noises in the night and by unexplained feelings of terror. Church officials, the paper said, knew that previous occupants had experienced similar sensations, and a year earlier a service of exorcism was carried out in a bid to drive the 'evil spirits' from the house. The widow of a former rector, Mrs Mary Neads, who lived in the building from 1960 until 1976, was quoted as saying that with her husband she had heard heavy footsteps on the stairs and on other occasions on the gravel drive outside, but there was never anyone there.

Mr Thomas Bannister (pseudonym) wrote to the Society in 1980 about the varying mystifying incidents which occurred over an eight- or nine-year period on his visits to Polstead Rectory about twenty-five years previously. 'I should explain that at that time I was the complete sceptic and anything of the supernatural never entered my head,' he said. 'In fact, I thought it all a lot of nonsense.' Once he woke up in the night and heard what sounded like rats running about on the attic floor above his bedroom. A ratcatcher was called in but he said there were no signs of rats anywhere in the house. On another visit he woke up again in the middle of the night to hear what sounded like heavy furniture being trundled across the floor of the attic above, which was strange because he knew the attic was empty and not being used.

Another time he was awakened in the night to hear the handles on a chest of drawers beside his bed being lifted up and violently banged down. In the bright moonlight he could see that there was nobody in the room. The banging down of the handles stopped when he looked in the direction from which the noise came. 'Rectories are often cold places, but this was the first time I noticed how cold the bedclothes felt in spite of having been in bed for several hours without feeling cold,' he stated.

On yet another visit, Bannister recalled, he was woken up in the middle of the night by what sounded like half a dozen stones rattling down the chimney and hitting the iron grate in the fireplace with a loud metallic clang. Because of the cold he decided to stay in bed and investigate the cause of the sound when he got up in the morning. An inspection then indicated that there was nothing in the grate.

The phenomena he listed fit into the general pattern of haunting. One experience in the open air, however, was quite distinctive.

My only frightening experience occurred in the garden in broad daylight. It happened at about 10 o'clock on a bright sunny morning in October. I was digging . . . in the vegetable patch. If a weed did not get buried when I turned the earth over with the spade, I would stoop down and pick it up and throw it into a wheelbarrow. When I stooped down to pick up a rather large weed that had not got buried (I cannot remember the species) it moved about a yard away from me along the ground. So I stepped on the ground I had already dug to retrieve it and it moved another yard out of my reach. I stood up to think out how this could occur as there was no wind at all that could have moved it. Then I felt a very heavy weight on my shoulders forcing me to the ground. I was so taken by surprise that my first reaction was to remain on my two feet, to do which needed all my strength. I cannot say how long the struggle lasted, perhaps less than a minute. At the stage when I began to feel exhausted and frightened because I could not see what was happening to me I prayed. It was a quick mental prayer: 'Please God help me'. Whatever it was on my shoulders forcing me to the ground left off instantly and I experienced a marvellous sense of peace and calm with all sense of fear completely gone.

But had the weed *physically* moved? When I was reading Bannister's account of his experiences I came across a typescript of a lecture which Dr James McHarg, a consultant psychiatrist, of Dundee, gave on the subject of 'The recognition of personal distress' to a study day meeting arranged by the SPR in October 1980. In this Dr McHarg pointed out that objective disturbance of brain function, as distinct from objective mental disturbance, quite commonly gives rise to pseudo-*psi*-phenomena. What are called 'sub-delirious states', due to a variety of toxic conditions, may well come to the notice of the psychical researcher, he said. 'The visual hallucinations in delirium and sub-delirious states are not infrequently of small objects which tend to occur not at the point of visual fixation but in the peripheral visual field as they are caused by local disturbance of the visual cortex of the brain. They appear to move away when the subject moves his eyes in the vain attempt to get a good look. In fact they remain at the same peripheral point within the visual field. That is why they are commonly interpreted as small actively moving animals such as rats or mice. They are not usually given a paranormal explanation, but I recall one lady, suffering in this way from a sub-delirious state, who felt that small objects in her house were being moved about in the manner she had heard reported in poltergeist cases.'

I referred Thomas Bannister's experience to Dr McHarg, and he replied that what had happened at Polstead 'certainly is suggestive of something similar to what I said often occurs, in delirious and sub-delirious states . . . Perhaps I should add that other forms of localized brain disturbance, as well as delirium, could cause localized cortical excitation in a part of the visual cortex representing a point in the visual field which is peripheral to the point of fixation, and giving the illusion of an object moving away when one tries to "pin it down".'

It is possible that the fright caused by the apparent movement of the weed helped to induce the feeling of being forced to the ground reported by Bannister. However, it should not be assumed that because there was apparently a natural explanation for the incident of the 'moving weed' there was a natural explanation for other events he related.

At the time of writing Polstead Rectory is being converted into a private dwelling. Although it transpired that Polstead was not the place referred to in *Proceedings* in 1884, I feel that it has been well worth while publishing these two separate accounts because both have a certain amount in common which indicates a pattern in such hauntings, separated, as they are, by more than a century.

Miss Robinson said in her letter to the SPR that 'the story the old woman told to my father was that years ago a man had kept his mother chained in the attic until she died of starvation: his reason for doing so was that she had won large sums of money in lotteries, which he wished to appropriate.' As no evidence of the truth of this story was offered, and the young curate does not seem to have made any enquiries, it must be treated with reserve. Old copies of *Proceedings* show how often a murder or suicide, without accompanying details, is advanced by witnesses as the cause of a haunting. Before this is accepted, full enquiries should be made into the truth of such a story.

Hauntings confined to noises of unknown origin are uncommon: all too often people mystified by bangs, crashes and noises for which no physical cause can be found start 'seeing things'. In such cases apparitions are the secondary result of a disturbance. The reaction of Canon Robinson's dogs to the noises is revealing: they were terrified. A comparison may be made here with the behaviour of the dogs in the Cheltenham case. It is possible to suggest a physical origin for the 'flickering and intermittent light' seen by the old woman in the attic windows; they could have been caused by lamps held by the curate's predecessors while they sought to establish the origin of the sounds that disturbed them. However, we must bear in mind that strange lights are sometimes reported in haunted houses.

It was remiss of officials of the Society not to have made enquiries about whether the vicarage in Shropshire was still haunted when Miss Robinson's letter was received in 1883, but possibly this was because they were overwhelmed with case material at the time. Wherever possible, new occupants of a building reputed to be haunted should be encouraged to report further developments, in confidence if necessary, to the Society. Canon Robinson's report is yet another indication of the value of an account prepared by an occupant as compared with one by an outside investigator. The latter more likely than not, will not be able to share, during occasional visits, the phenomena reported by the occupants, who are in a much better position than others to observe what is happening.

6 Beavor Lodge: an old ghost story retold

The account of the apparent haunting of Beavor Lodge, Hammersmith, West London, that follows contains a number of interesting features, and I have chosen it because it provides an excellent opportunity for discussion of physical factors which should be taken into consideration in assessing whether a house is haunted or not. Mr W. B. Richmond, a rising young artist – later to become Sir William Richmond, R.A. – took up residence in the Lodge in 1870, when Hammersmith still contained many farms, and died there on 11 February 1921, by which time the house had become surrounded by houses and factories. He was the last occupant of the house. The Richmonds were a gifted family – two of the sons were knighted – and the occupation of a house for over fifty years gave them excellent opportunities for observing and reporting on the phenomena. The narrative that follows is based on an extract from a paper by Mrs Sidgwick in Proceedings *in 1885 (81a pp. 115–17) an extract from* Phantasms of the Living *(28 vol. 2 p. 194), and, in particular, from G. W. Lambert's paper 'Beavor Lodge: an old ghost story retold' in the Society's* Journal *in 1964 (44h pp. 273–82). For the family history of the Richmonds I have referred to* The Richmond Papers, *a large volume based on the correspondence of George Richmond, R.A., and his son Sir William Richmond, R.A., K.C.B., edited by Mrs A. M. W. Stirling (86a). William Richmond, who is best remembered for his mosaics in St Paul's Cathedral, London, made notes at the time of various happenings at Beavor Lodge. When he was old and ill he wrote his 'Recollections' but, as Mrs Stirling makes clear in the foreword to the* The Richmond Papers, *unfortunately it was impossible to publish the manuscript in its original form, and she had 'to eradicate the superfluous, to elucidate the obscure, and to knit the whole into a certain sequence.' Mrs Stirling devotes a chapter of her book* Ghosts Vivisected *(86b) to the haunting of Beavor Lodge, and*

includes extracts from Sir William Richmond's papers with some of her own
observations and interviews of witnesses.

Beavor Lodge was a simple rectangular building of two storeys, with brick walls and slate roof. Certain of the rooms had some interesting eighteenth-century decoration, but its main feature was its spacious garden near the Thames. This was entered by a doorway in the wall which separated it from Beavor Lane (formerly known as Green Lane) and which towards the end of the last century still retained something of its country aspect. When the Richmonds went there it still had the aspect of a country house, and many of the streets with which it was afterwards surrounded did not yet exist.

The first account of the haunting, sent to the Society by Mrs W. B. Richmond, later Lady Richmond, was written in the summer of 1883 (the name of the writer, and the address of the house concerned, were not given in *Proceedings*).

When we went to live in our house at Hammersmith, we had never heard a word of its being haunted, nor had we any sort of feeling that it was a ghostly house or anything of the sort, nor had we ever in any other house experienced any phenomena of the kind. Almost immediately after taking possession, all members of the household complained of hearing noises in the lower part of the house – windows would be violently shaken every night between 2 and 4 o'clock, and steps were heard apparently going about the house. I myself frequently had doors opened for me before entering a room, as if a hand had hastily turned the handle and thrown it open. Then occasionally we used to hear sounds as of someone sobbing and sighing (deep long sighs at all times of the day).

I used to hear these sounds in my bedroom, and on the little staircase leading to it, and my husband would hear it in the dining-room underneath. Sometimes I would hear a sound of stitching in the room out of my bedroom, as if some hard and very coarse work were being done, and then a sound as of something being dragged across the floor. I got to have a feeling which was most uncomfortable, at times, as of being *watched*.

These sort of things went on for about five years, when, in October 1875, about 3 o'clock one afternoon I was sitting with three of my children in the dining-room, reading to them. I wanted to speak to the parlourmaid, and I rang the bell for her when the door opened, and on looking up I saw a figure of a woman come in and walk up to the side of the table, stand there a second or two, and then turn to go out again, but *before* reaching the door she seemed to dissolve away. She was a grey, short-looking woman, apparently dressed in grey muslin. I hardly saw the face, which seemed scarcely to be defined at all. None of the children saw her, and I did not mention the circumstances to them nor to the servants, lest they should get frightened and leave. I only told my husband. I was in perfect health at the time.

During the next two months, a figure, described exactly like the one I had seen, was seen by two different servants, during the absence of the family. One of them saw it in the afternoon in daylight, and the other at 10 o'clock at night; one saw it on the little staircase, and one in the day nursery. Neither of these servants had by any possibility heard of my having seen anything of the sort. They were both in good health, and, having been with me for some time, had long grown accustomed to the noises; but one of them was so upset and frightened by the apparition that she sent word to us at once that she must leave us.

The following summer, in July, I was awoke in the night by a frantic scream of terror from my little girl (then six years old), who slept in a tiny room opening out of ours. Her father ran to her, when she said, 'Oh! I awoke and saw a little wicked-looking old grey woman standing at the foot of the bed, looking at me with a horrid face, and then suddenly she went down through the floor with a loud noise, and I screamed out.' The child was in good health and had never heard any talk of the apparition.

In the autumn of 1876 I was awoke one night, and felt an icy wind blowing through my room, and heard loud sobs; the curtains of the bed were pulled back and my hair was pulled. Another night I was awoke by a brilliant light in my room and the same cold wind. Previously to this, my husband, on one occasion, heard his name distinctly called in his studio, as he sat at work. Since all this [1876] only occasional rappings have been heard, and I have not felt that feeling of being watched, which used to come over me when sitting in my room, the feeling which I had for years before I saw any apparition.

Mrs Sidgwick considered that the appearance to the child was not important, as it may have been merely a bad dream, but there could hardly be a mistake, she said, as to the servants having seen independently a figure very much like that seen by Mrs Richmond. Mrs Sidgwick also commented on the mysterious noises, and a detailed account of a disturbed night in which loud noises were heard is contained in a letter which Mrs Richmond wrote to Edmund Gurney on 11 March 1884:

I was, as far as I can remember, awoke by the dog barking about 12 o'clock. The barking stopped, but I heard what sounded like steps downstairs. Very soon the old noises began in our little library: jumping about, the window rattling, the whole place shaking, till my windows rattled too. The dog whined incessantly, and the banging and jumping seemed to grow more and more boisterous. I got up and made some noise with the furniture in my room, lighted my candles, and went on to the landing to listen if there were noises in the other part of the house, but all was perfectly quiet there, though in the little room downstairs the dog seemed to grow more and more distressed, and the noises continued more violently than ever. I listened to them till 3 o'clock, and as there seemed no chance of their stopping, I left my room and passed the rest of the night in Helen's. The dog evidently was still afraid of the room when the morning came. I called to him to go into it with me, and he crouched down with his tail beneath his legs, and seemed to fear entering it. That was all that disturbed me, but I found it enough as I was alone in the house with only Helen and the maid. [Helen was the child who had been frightened by the appearance of a figure when she was six.]

Referring to his wife's experience of the apparition, Richmond claimed that no trick of light 'could account for this appearance seen thus and studied leisurely in broad daylight. It remained standing in front of my wife for an appreciable time, and appeared to be solid, yet in a sense vague and incomplete. Its hand was under the drapery which was raised above its mouth and partially concealed its face. My wife was peculiarly veracious, and the last person to be led away by imagination.'

Meanwhile, on several occasions, Mrs Richmond heard a voice call 'Clara! Clara!' and on going to her husband under the impression he had called her she found that he had not done so; while he on his part distinctly heard someone crying 'Willie! Willie' only to find that his wife had never spoken.

Richmond personally did not pay serious attention to the haunting until he himself had a strange experience. One autumn he was alone at Beavor Lodge while his family was away in the country. The house was shut up save for two sitting-rooms, and only one servant, the cook, was left in charge. Enjoying the unwonted quiet one evening after a hard day's work, Richmond drew up his chair to the fire, lit his pipe and settled down to read. By his side was his collie, Nelson, and on a table nearby was a reading lamp which shed a subdued light through the comfortable room with its dark walls and blazing fire.

Richmond was absorbed in his book and Nelson curled up on the rug at his feet was fast asleep, when the dog suddenly woke up and gave a low growl of warning. Simultaneously the handle of the door shook, but the door itself did not appear to open, yet; when Richmond glanced round, in the doorway, about twelve feet away from where he sat, stood a figure. It was that of a woman of nun-like appearance, clad in long flowing grey draperies; the face invisible, shrouded in a filmy veil. The dog shrank terrified beside his master, making no attempt to attack the intruder. The apparition remained standing in the doorway for a few seconds before disappearing or dissolving – which, it was impossible to say.

The moment the figure vanished, Richmond sprang up and hurried through the passage to the kitchen, where the cook was busy sewing. 'Is there anyone in the house?' he asked. The answer was in the negative. 'Did you come into the drawing-room just now?' 'I have never left the kitchen!' was the reply. The whole house was promptly and thoroughly searched, but there were no signs of an intruder.

About this date Richmond's father, George Richmond, then a celebrated portrait painter, travelling by train, heard two men talking about haunted houses. At length, joining in the conversation, he observed, 'My son lives in what is said to be a haunted house in Hammersmith!' 'Ah,' replied one of the men, 'I wonder if that is the house where the coiners lived, and where they sewed up a woman who had spied on them in a sack and threw her over the wall into the Thames!' 'That explains the sound which is heard,' said George Richmond, much interested, 'the stitching and the sound of a woman sobbing!' In consequence, he would never sleep in the house again.

According to the author of *Ghosts Vivisected*, the grey lady was seen in the garden at Beavor Lodge as well as in the house; and Bishop Brown used to vouch for the following story which he had direct from William Richmond. One day Richmond, going into the garden, saw a woman sitting under a tree opposite the house in an attitude of grief. At the same moment his attention was distracted by the opening of the door which led into the garden from Beavor Lane and the entry of a friend; and when he looked round the woman was gone. After the usual greetings had been exchanged his friend remarked, 'When I came in, there was a woman sitting under that pear tree – a lady in grey. Where has she gone?'

'That is precisely what is puzzling me!' said Richmond.

Thus two people simultaneously, and from different points of vantage, had both received the impression that a third person was present; and each, as it proved upon comparing notes, had seen the same figure, a sorrowful woman in grey, seated under the same tree.

John Ruskin was deeply interested in the story, and professed himself anxious that they should dig under the pear tree and see if any bones were reposing there. Subsequently Gurney, G. F. Myers [the painter is probably referring to F. W. H. Myers] and Mrs Augustus De Morgan held a séance to try to discover the cause of the visitation, and reported that they had secured information which differed from the explanation given to George Richmond by the men in the train. Their tale was that a girl belonging to some Sisterhood, or convent, had committed an indiscretion, and in order to conceal her guilt, she murdered her child, and 'buried it in the field' – a field then adjoining Beavor Lodge. She stood in need of prayer in order to release her earthbound soul from painful wandering.

'Mrs Augustus De Morgan, mother of the artist and novelist,' wrote Richmond concerning this explanation, 'was an extremely sensible lady of exceptional accomplishments which, by their nature, were directly opposed to undue credulity. She was a good scholar, the daughter of a hard thinker, the wife of a great mathematician, deeply religious in her own way, and a great friend of Carlyle. A lady of strong, independent judgement, she quite satisfied herself as to the truth of this story.'

Some light on the haunting is given by Sir Arthur Richmond, son of Sir William, who was born in Beavor Lodge in 1879 and died in 1968. He carried on the family's artistic traditions, being Deputy Director of the Victoria and Albert Museum, London, between 1907 and 1910, and a member of the Fine Art Commission; and before his retirement he was chairman of the Land Settlement Association. In his memoirs (72), Sir Arthur said that when his parents first went to live at Beavor Lodge they used to be disturbed night after night by a strange uncanny sound as of someone weeping her heart out. At the same time it seemed as though whoever it was who was weeping was also sewing some thick material, for the sound of a needle passing through it was quite distinguishable. 'Nothing could explain rationally this strange phenomenon. It was so disturbing that at one time my parents seriously considered leaving the house.'

Sir Arthur heard that at one time a gang of false coiners operated in Hammersmith. Someone 'peached' on them; they were arrested and served a long sentence. On their release they came to live in Beavor Lodge, lured there the woman who was believed to have betrayed them, and condemned her to be drowned in the Thames in a sack which she was ordered to sew for herself.

Sir Arthur said, 'Although I never saw anything alarming, it was impossible for me not to hear about the grey lady . . . My mother never had any fear of the grey lady. She believed her to be an unhappy spirit and wanted to comfort her. Over and over again on meeting her she would speak to her and hope for a reply. No response ever came beyond the fixed glare from the large eyes that peered over the shawl concealing her face.'

Helen Richmond, who was frightened by the appearance of the 'little wicked-looking old grey woman' when she was six, was to recall how when she was about thirteen, and spending a few days alone with her mother in Beavor Lodge, she was awakened one night by her coming into her room, which was next to hers, and dragging a chair-bedstead on which she slept. She fastened the door and explained that she had been disturbed by a great noise in the library below her room; 'it was as if a number of people were fighting and throwing things about, while the collie dog barked violently. She thought thieves had got in under the impression that the house was empty; but on going into the room next morning, there was no sign of any disturbance; only the dog still seemed nervous.'

Another who had a strange experience in the house was young Herbert Richmond (1871–1946), who rose in the Royal Navy to become Admiral Sir Herbert Richmond, and who subsequently was Master of Downing College, Cambridge. When he was thirteen he heard someone sobbing in the corner of a room: 'it went on for a long time, and I was very frightened.' In 1894, when he was home from the Mediterranean with Malta fever, he had 'a curious experience' as he described it to his sister.

I woke up with the knowledge that someone was about, and I felt strangely afraid. The door opened and someone came in and stood by my bed. I can see it very clearly in my mind's eye now, standing there for a short time, then turning towards the window at the back, whither it went and disappeared. A large dog appeared to run across the room at the time . . . It is a curious feeling, that of intense fear – so intense that one can't even speak.

Mrs Stirling interviewed several people who said that they had experienced strange happenings at Beavor Lodge. One was Miss Perceval Clark, Richmond's niece and a daughter of a well-known QC, who wrote an account at Mrs Stirling's request.

It was three o'clock on a sunny afternoon when I went into my uncle's little room beyond the studio to fetch a book. On turning to go out, I felt as if there was something behind me, and thinking it was the cat, I glanced round. To my intense surprise, I saw a thin figure in light grey, chiffony, flimsy stuff, standing in profile against some armour that was hung over an unused door, which led into the tool house and furnace place. As I stood looking at it, it moved slowly behind the armour and disappeared.

I felt nothing but interest and wonder, till afterwards when I went into the garden to get rid of the uncanny feeling the incident had given me.

A few nights afterwards the same figure came and stood beside me in the drawing-room and I felt as if she wanted something from me.

Miss Perceval Clark's sister also had a strange experience. She was staying at Beavor Lodge one hot August night when there was a full moon pouring its light through her bedroom window. About midnight she was disturbed by a loud banging of doors and general clatter downstairs, and she wondered why it was that a household usually so quiet should be making so much noise.

After a time, the row ceased, but still I could not sleep; I heard the clock strike each hour, and two o'clock had just ceased to chime through the house when I heard another sound which I first thought was a little breeze in the trees outside. The night was stifling and had been deadly still, as I lay listening to the welcome stir of the fresher air, I became aware that it was no breeze that I heard but the sound of *skirts*, as though some woman was moving swiftly along the passage outside my room. Right up to my door she came, then paused, as though she were listening outside.

Promptly, and with shame I say it, under the bedclothes went my head! How long I kept it there I do not know, but when I ventured to peep out again it was only for a second; an indescribable feeling of terror which I could not conquer impelled me to cover it up again. *Five times I did this!* At the fifth nervous peep, I distinctly saw a dim figure standing in the corner by the door. The head was veiled, I merely saw the outline of a woman's figure, dressed in pale grey, standing there in the bright moonlight. The next instance it had vanished without a sound.

On mentioning to my aunt the next morning about the visit of the Grey Lady, I asked what could have caused the banging noise at midnight. 'Oh, that was what we call the Roystering Beavorites,' she said; 'often before a visit of the Grey Lady they are heard roystering.'

Mrs Stirling had an account of somewhat similar phenomena from a woman whom she does not name. At midnight she was aroused by a sound as though a number of carriages were driving up the lane outside the garden, and it seemed as though these drew up at the garden door. Surprised, as there was usually little traffic along the lane after dark, she sat up in bed to listen. Next she heard the noise of voices and the tramp of footsteps, as though a great company of people were coming through the garden laughing and talking; then it seemed as though they entered the studio beneath her window, for she heard the window opened, and the laughing and voices were now indoors.

From twelve to three in the morning, the noise continued, the sound of talking and laughter, ceaseless footsteps and the banging of doors, as though a party were taking place downstairs. Too frightened to investigate personally, she tried to get the collie to go down, but he resisted all her attempts and trembled visibly, till at last, with the approach of morning, the inexplicable row subsided and silence once more reigned in the house.

Yet the next day, instead of finding the windows open to the garden and confusion in the room below, all was in normal condition. The windows were tightly fastened from without; the furniture was unmoved, and there was no sign of any disturbance having taken place . . .

An account of yet another apparition was given by Gaetano Meo, an artist's model who later became an artist. Meo, who came from Italy, was a much-prized model for Rosetti, Burne-Jones, Ford Madox Brown, and Sir William Richmond, for whom he afterwards worked as an assistant. It was as an old man that he told Mrs Stirling of his strange experience on the first occasion when he sat for Richmond at Beavor Lodge. She gives it in his own words.

Do you believe in ghosts? I do not! and yet I once had a strange experience for which I cannot account. Eccolo! I was to sit to Mr William Richmond for the first time. Now when there are two doors to a house, I always choose the humbler one, so I went round to the back door and rang the bell. Almost immediately the door was opened, and there stood before me a very pretty dark-haired lady, who welcomed me graciously, and, to my surprise, addressed me in faultless Italian.

'Why do you come to this door?' she asked me in that language. 'Go round to the other side.' And I went.

Afterwards I explained to Mr Richmond why I had come to the front door, and I asked him why was the pretty lady who had spoken to me in such perfect Italian. He looked perplexed and said he could think of no one in the house answering my description; his wife was out at the time and no one else knew my native language. Enquiries were made but the mystery could not be solved.

I never saw the lady again or discovered who she could have been; but some time after, I saw a painting of Mr Richmond's first wife, who had died many years before. *And there I recognized the face of the pretty lady who had first welcomed me to Beavor Lodge.*

Mrs Stirling said that Richmond's first wife, a most beautiful woman, had died of consumption soon after their marriage, leaving the young bridegroom, for a time, broken-hearted and affected with the same complaint. 'Why the lovely but hapless lady should, many years afterwards, have taken a special interest in a new model arriving for her husband and have answered the door on that occasion is incomprehensible, but as Gaetano told me the story, his recollection of the incident was as vivid and his description as circumstantial as if it had just happened.'

Details of Sir William's first marriage are given neither in his entry in the *Dictionary of National Biography* nor in *Who Was Who 1916–28.* His bride was Charlotte Foster, whom he had met as a child. They were married in 1864, and she died two years later, the effect on Richmond being 'to sear brain and soul'. There is no indication in *The Richmond Papers* that the first Mrs Richmond could speak Italian.

According to Mrs Stirling, after the death of Sir William

Richmond in 1921 she and her husband discussed for some time whether to purchase Beavor Lodge as a site for the De Morgan collection. Although they eventually decided against it, owing to its proximity to Hammersmith Broadway, while the matter was under discussion Sir Willam's solicitor informed her, 'We cannot *legally* advertise the house as a "desirable residence" because it is so haunted'. In some surprise she remarked, 'I did not know that the Law took cognizance of a Ghost!'; but rightly or wrongly, he insisted that the case was as he had stated.

Commenting on the case in his article in the *Journal*, G. W. Lambert said that the earliest and most persistent phenomena consisted of inarticulate noises in the lower part of the house which suggested that they might have originated underground. Beavor Lodge stood on the east side of Beavor Lane, at the bottom of which there were some oil mills, worked partly by flood water coming from the land, and partly by tidal water penned up at high tide and released at low tide.

It is therefore likely that there was a channel under or near Beavor Lane, reaching inland certainly as far as Beavor Lodge. About ¼ mile to the west along British Grove, Stamford Brook discharges into the river, and less than that distance to the east another stream, coming down the line of Dalling Road, does the same. When both these streams were in flood, there was probably an overflow down Beavor Lane, which provided a short cut from Ravenscourt Park to the river [see map at the end of *The Lost Rivers of London* by Dr N. Barton] (7). As to the likelihood of there having been serious floods in the 'seventies', that was a notoriously wet decade. In 1872, 1875 and 1877–9 rainfall was above average. Both topography and rainfall data point to the mysterious noises at Beavor Lodge having been of subterranean origin.

Lambert considered that the incidents said to have happened there no doubt did happen as described, but it was a reasonable assumption that they were purely physical events, due to conditions all too common at the time. 'The prevalent belief that they were "ghostly" events led to a search for causes in the past history of the place.' He said in conclusion that 'It is perhaps worth observing that the "grey lady" of Beavor Lodge "walked" at just about the same time as the "widow" of Garden Reach, Cheltenham, better known as the Morton Ghost. Perhaps they were made of the same kind of "stuff" as both were seen by several different observers.'

There were indeed points in common in accounts of the two apparitions. Both covered the lower part of the face, both frightened the dogs of the households concerned, both were seen indoors and in the open air, neither was able to speak – it is instructive to compare Rosina Despard's account of her efforts to communicate with the apparition with Sir Arthur Richmond's statement that his mother made many efforts to get a reply to her questions from the 'grey lady', but without success – both figures were seen at times in an attitude of grief, and neither figure was visible to all members of the household. Captain and Mrs Despard did not see the figure at Cheltenham and Sir Arthur said he 'never saw anything alarming' at Hammersmith.

The previous history of the house does not throw light on the strange happenings there. Beavor Lodge was named after Samuel 'Bever' or 'Beaver', of St Paul's, Covent Garden, a woollen draper, who was probably the builder of the house. He was a man of substance who owned a site of two and a half acres which included Linden House and Grafton House in addition to the Lodge. The earliest reference to Beavor Lodge is contained in a lease dated 13 April 1757. Samuel Bever also gave his name to Beavor Lane, which, significantly in view of Lambert's theory of the effects of water on the occupants of the house, was called the 'Washway' in a deed of 1758.

In 1773 the house was in the occupation of Joshua Adam, a wax chandler. According to Mrs Stirling, 'its successive residents appear to have been harmless and respectable citizens.' The local vicar, the Reverend Francis Thomas Attwood, purchased the house shortly after the birth of his son in 1835 and it passed into the hands of the son on the death of his father in 1856. It was eventually sold to the Richmond family. Before their occupation it had housed the large family of Mr Seaton, a horse trainer. Richmond believed it was this Mr Seaton who had built a large room in which his girls could dance: the artist converted this into a temporary studio.

*   *   *

The time has now come for us to draw some conclusions from this interesting case. I feel we should not attach too much importance to the story about the coiners and the unfortunate woman who was said to be their victim. No evidence has been produced for the truth of this story and I was unable to get proof that Beavor Lodge was ever used as a 'hideout' by coiners when I made enquiries about the history of the house at the Hammersmith Central Library. Likewise, we should not place too much reliance on the story about a girl who murdered her child and buried it in a field then adjoining Beavor Lodge. Material produced at séances can be very unreliable. It is natural that people should want an explanation for a haunting, but often there is none.

The inhabitants of Beavor Lodge did not, apparently, consider that the noises at Beavor Lodge might have a physical cause, but I feel that this factor should be taken into account. It is significant that Beavor Lodge stood near a tidal river. Sounds interpreted as 'sobbing' and 'stitching' might well have been caused by underground water. On the other hand, we should bear in mind that phenomena with a physical cause could be expected to happen at different times when there was a high tide or heavy rainfall, but Mrs Richmond, in her earliest account, said that 'windows would be violently shaken every night between 2 and 4 o'clock, and steps were heard apparently going about the house.' The regularity of sounds heard at the same time *every* night is puzzling. Such a phenomenon is also very rare.

Lambert considered that there was a physical explanation for what he regarded as the shadowy figure seen at Beavor Lodge, but we must take account of the fact that the figure was invariably described as being that of a woman and also that it was seen more distinctly by some than by others. Sir William Richmond, who saw the figure at a distance of twelve feet, was so convinced of the reality of his experience that, unable to accept that he had seen an apparition, he hurried to the kitchen to ask the cook, the only other person in the house, if she had come into the drawing-room.

It would help in the assessment of this case if we could know precisely when some of the visitors had the experiences they described, but this information was not given by Mrs Stirling. However, the evidence came from people who seemed to her to be reliable. Some of the phenomena described – the sounds of talking, laughing, the arrival of people, 'ceaseless footsteps and the banging of doors, as though a party were taking place downstairs' – are characteristic of a certain type of haunting (a more recent example is given in Chapter 14).

Although some of the phenomena at Beavor Lodge probably had a physical origin, other happenings there remain unexplained by any such hypothesis, and, in the true sense of the word the house may, in my opinion, be said to have been haunted: certainly the solicitor, entrusted with the sale of the house, thought so. As is usual in so many hauntings, the phenomena gradually ceased. It is possible that this was due to the increasing industrialization of the neighbourhood.

When you visit Hammersmith today it is difficult to visualize what it was like even sixty years ago. The site of Beavor Lodge and its pleasant garden is occupied by a massive building owned by the Whitworth Electric Company. As the house stood only two hundred yards from the Thames it is possible that water from the river once flowed through a hidden channel beneath or near the building at high tide, and an overflow of water down Beavor Lane ('Washway') at times of flooding of nearby streams could have affected inhabitants of the Lodge when it was diverted below it, but as the district was developed such water would have been contained to allow for foundations to be laid on firm ground.

There have been other changes. In the Richmonds' time it was possible to stroll from the Lodge down Beavor Lane, past the larger grounds of Linden House, to the river. Such a walk is today impossible. The Great West Road separates the end of Beavor Lane from the river, and the rush of traffic banishes any attempt to evoke the spirit of the past.

7   A White Rose from the Grave

The narrative given here, which opens with the appearance of apparitions in a haunted house in Clifton, Bristol, and ends in a visit to a country church in Norfolk, is one of the strangest, if not the strangest, in the annals of psychical research. Although nearly all hauntings seem to be aimless and to defy analysis, the apparitions in this case were, in Andrew Lang's words, 'ghosts with a purpose' and this is extremely rare.

The case was first published by F. W. H. Myers in a long paper on 'The subliminal self' in Proceedings *in 1895 (60e pp. 547–59). Pseudonyms were used: the principal person involved, Mrs Goodeve, is 'Mrs Claughton' in* Proceedings, *and she was told by an apparition to go to 'Meresby', which, in fact, is the village of Snettisham in Norfolk, four miles south of the seaside resort of Hunstanton. Lang, who had personal knowledge of the case, used the same pseudonyms in his account of it in his book* Dreams and Ghosts *(46b). The real names were first revealed by the Rev. Rowland W. Maitland in a booklet* The Snettisham Ghost *(52). Maitland was allowed access to the case notes in the archives of the SPR by the then honorary secretary, W. H. Salter, and through his research at Snettisham managed to throw new light on what happened there. I have drawn on these three sources for the account that follows. In many respects it reads like a ghost story taken from fiction, but readers may be assured that those parts of it that could be verified were verified at the time. Other parts, mainly for family and legal reasons, remain obscure.*

This case provides a useful opportunity for discussion of purported communications from apparitions.

The haunting of 5 Rodney Place, Clifton, began after the death there of a Mrs Seagrim at 5.0 a.m. on 22 December 1878. She had moved there only a few days previously; according to her physician, Dr Marshall, who was a trustee of the house, the cause of death was chronic diarrhoea of long standing. Rodney Place was one of the earliest examples of the many terraces which adorned Clifton as it grew into a fashionable watering place about the year 1800. The house in which Mrs Seagrim died was at one time the home of a celebrated physician, Dr Beddoes, who frequently entertained Coleridge and Southey. Her children stayed on in the house until the eldest girl married in 1880. The eldest son told Dr Marshall that the family often heard strange noises in the night, and evidence from another source mentions Miss Seagrim as having seen her mother on one occasion.

The house was empty for a time, then tenanted for five years, during which no noises were reported. The house again was empty until Lady Day, 1888, when a Mr Ackland took possession. His mother and two sisters were much alarmed by sounds as if of heavy steps on the stone staircase. This lasted for about three years, but the sounds were never heard by Ackland. Water was carried up by servants only to the first floor; but two years after the family took up residence Miss Ackland was in the attic kneeling by a trunk when she felt some water swished at her. She thought it was a practical joke carried out by her brother, but he was not in the room. A small pool of water was on the floor where she stood, and the wall beyond was sprinkled. Soon after, as Mr Ackland went upstairs in the dark, carrying an ink bottle and some pens, he found his hand wet. He thought it must be ink, but on getting to the light found it was clean water; there was a little pool of water on the stairs where this occurred, but no sign of damp on the ceiling above.

In October 1893, Mrs L. A. Goodeve, widow of a barrister, came to stay in the house. According to Myers, Mrs Goodeve was 'a widow lady, moving in good society, with children growing up, and known to many persons as a cheerful, capable, active woman, who has seen much of the world, and has plenty of business of her own to attend to: and who is by no means given to dwelling on things morbid or mysterious. She has, indeed, had some previous experience of apparitions, which all appear to have been veridical, but she has paid but little attention to them, and has never sought to encourage such visitations in any way.' Mrs Goodeve lived in very comfortable circumstances in London, in a house in Collingham Road off Cromwell Road.

Mrs Goodeve had heard that the house was haunted and admitted that she may have heard that the ghost was that of Mrs Seagrim. I will give her own account of her experiences in a statement she made, in the third person, to the Marquis of Bute, a wealthy landowner prominent in psychical research at that time.

About 1.15 a.m., Monday, October 9th, Mrs Goodeve was in bed with one of her children, the other sleeping in the room. Mrs Goodeve had offered to be of any use she could to Miss Ackland, who had arrived from London unwell on the Saturday. She had been asleep, and was awakened by the footsteps of a person coming downstairs, whom she supposed to be a servant coming to tell her to call her to Miss Ackland. The steps stopped at the door. The sounds were repeated twice more at the interval of a few moments. Mrs Goodeve rose, lit the candle, and opened the door. There was no one there. She noticed the clock outside was at 1.20.

She shut the door, got into bed, read, and leaving the candle burning, went to sleep. Woke up, finding the candle spluttering out. Heard a sound like a sigh. Saw a woman standing by the bed. She had a soft white shawl round the shoulders, held by the right hand towards the left shoulder, bending slightly forwards. Mrs Goodeve thinks the hair was lightish brown, and the shawl partly over the head, but does not remember distinctly, and has no impression of the rest of the dress: it was not grave clothes. She said, 'Follow me.' Mrs Goodeve rose, took the candle, and followed her out of the room, across the passage, and into the drawing-room. She had no recollection as to the opening of the doors. The housemaid next day declared that the drawing-room door had been locked by her. On entering the drawing-room Mrs Goodeve, finding the candle on the point of extinction, replaced it with a pink one from the chiffonier near the door. The figure went nearly to the end of the room, turned three-quarters round, said 'tomorrow', and disappeared. Mrs Goodeve returned to the bedroom, where she found the elder child (not the one in the bed) sitting up. It asked, 'Who is the lady in white?' Mrs Goodeve thinks she answered the child, 'It's only me – Mother; go to sleep,' or the like words, and hushed her to sleep in her arms. The baby remained fast asleep. She lit the gas and remained awake for some two hours, then put out the lights and went to sleep. Had no fear while seeing the figure, but was upset after seeing it. Would not be prepared to swear that she might not have walked in her sleep. Pink candle, partly burnt, in her room in morning. Does not know if she took it burnt or new.

In the morning she spoke to Mr Ackland, on whose advice she went to ask Dr Marshall as to the figure about 3 p.m. He and his wife said the description was like that of Mrs Seagrim, whom Mrs Goodeve suspected it to be. Thinks

Dr Marshall told her that Miss Seagrim ... had seen her mother in the same house. Mrs Goodeve cannot recognize the photograph of Mrs Seagrim shown to her ... She says the figure seemed smaller, and the features much more pinched and attenuated, like those of a person in the last stage of consumption, which was also the general appearance. By his advice, Mr Ackland put an electric bell under Mrs Goodeve's pillow, communicating with Miss Ackland's room, as Mrs Goodeve determined to sit up that evening and watch.

That night Mrs Goodeve sat up dressed, with the gas burning. About 12 she partly undressed, put on dressing-gown, and lay down outside bed, gas still burning, and fell asleep reading. Woke up and found the same woman as before, but the expression was even more agitated. She bent over Mrs Goodeve and said: 'I have come. Listen!' She then made a certain statement and asked Mrs Goodeve to do certain things. Mrs Goodeve said, 'Am I dreaming, or is it true?'

In the interests of clarity I will paraphrase the rest of Mrs Goodeve's statement. The figure then said something like this: 'If you doubt me you will find that the date of my marriage was 26 September 1860.' This was the date of Mrs Seagrim's marriage in India to Major Seagrim, who was still alive and had married again (Mrs Goodeve learned the corroboration of the date from Dr Marshall on the following Thursday). After this, Mrs Goodeve saw a man standing at Mrs Seagrim's left hand – tall, dark, well-made, healthy, sixty years old or more, dressed in a man's ordinary day clothes, kind, good expression. A conversation ensued between the three, in the course of which the man stated that he was Henry Barnard and that he was buried in Snettisham churchyard. He also gave the dates of his marriage and death. Mrs Goodeve had never heard of Henry Barnard or of Snettisham.

The apparition of Henry Barnard then asked Mrs Goodeve to go to Snettisham and verify these dates in the register. If she found they were correct, she was to go to the church at the ensuing 1.15 a.m. and wait in the south-west corner of the south aisle at the grave of Robert Cobb, who died on 15 May 1743, aged 67. The outgoing half of her railway ticket, she was informed, would not be taken; she was to send it along with a white rose from the grave to Dr Marshall. The apparition forbade her to have any earlier communication with the place and also told her not to go in her own name (this last injunction she disregarded). The apparition further said that John Bishop, a dark man, would help her, and that she would lodge with a woman who would tell her that she had a drowned child buried in the same churchyard. When Mrs Goodeve had done all this she would hear the rest of the history.

Towards the end of the conversation Mrs Goodeve saw a third phantom – that of a man whose name she was not free to give – in great trouble, standing with his hands on his face – these he afterwards lowered, so that his face was shown – behind Mrs Seagrim on her right. The three disappeared. Mrs Goodeve rose and went to the door to look out at the clock, but was seized with faintness, returned, and rang the electric bell. Ackland found her on the ground. She was able to ask the time, which was about 1.20. Mrs Goodeve then fainted, and the Acklands undressed her and put her to bed.

By great good fortune the well-known writer Andrew Lang, who was to become President of the SPR in 1911, was staying in Clifton at the time and heard the story of the haunting, and what had just happened to Mrs Goodeve, from Dr Marshall. Mrs Goodeve went to the post office to inquire if there was a village called Snettisham in Norfolk: there was. She asked Dr Marshall if he could help her to obtain the date of Mrs Seagrim's marriage, which he did by writing to her married daughter. When the answer arrived he showed it to Mrs Goodeve, who at once showed Ackland and Dr Marshall that date noted in her diary.

Armed with this confirmation, Mrs Goodeve returned to London before making preparations for her journey to Snettisham. There were strange happenings in Mrs Goodeve's home; an account of them, by the governess, Marie Giraud, was published in *Proceedings* in 1895.

I was sitting at needlework in the schoolroom last night (Friday, October 13th) at about 11 o'clock. Mrs Goodeve was in her room, the door was shut, the servants all in bed. I heard someone crying or rather sobbing, very low but *very* distinctly, as if their heart would break. I immediately thought of Hilda and went half-way downstairs when I found her door wide open and all perfectly still. I returned to my work, the sobbing continued, like a woman's or a girl's voice. I thought it strange that one could hear so distinctly through the walls, but determined it must be from next door and thought no more about it.

I was awakened from my first sleep by loud moans which seemed to fill the room and come from every part. As soon as I was awake they ceased. Oddly enough, I did not feel a bit frightened, but made up my mind that it was a sudden gust of wind. I sat up in bed and listened. All was perfectly still, till I heard a very odd sound overhead like some electric battery gone wrong and broken. I thought of thieves, then remembered that the telegraph wires are fixed to this house, but thought it odd I should hear them, having the nurseries over my room. I hesitated whether I should go round the house and see if all were well, but determined to go to sleep again, as the sound was certainly not that of housebreakers. I also thought of a supernatural cause and could fine none. I was *wide* awake and sitting up in bed when I heard this strange sound, and not being able to account for it satisfactorily, lay back and went to sleep again. All was so perfectly still in the street and everywhere I should imagine it must have been between the hours of one and two.

I slept soundly and was awakened at least three times more always with these fearful moans, which filled the room, always feeling wide awake and each time attributing it to the wind, although when one awoke the sounds ceased and there was not a breath of wind to be heard. Towards morning I *distinctly* heard a very, very heavy footstep overhead and a heavy *thud* as of somebody moving something very cumbersome and heavy. I thought of Richardson [presumably a servant] and wondered if she had returned without any one knowing. As I knew the nurseries to be locked and the keys (as I *then* thought) in *her* keeping, I sat up again and listened. All was perfectly still. I knew I had *not* been dreaming, and yet could not account for the noises all being so perfectly still.

I slept again and heard the servants going down, some hours later, and thought no more about my dreams until I saw Mrs Goodeve after breakfast. Mrs Goodeve had talked of Spiritualism during breakfast, yet this did not bring my night's experience to my memory. It only came back link by link when I saw Mrs Goodeve and told her.

The governess's statement is important because it provides independent evidence that something very strange was happening at the time. The sound of heavy footsteps without apparent physical cause, and an unexplained thud in a locked room, are typical of hauntings.

On the night of the governess's strange experiences Mrs Goodeve dreamt that she arrived at Snettisham at five o'clock, after dusk; that a fair was going on; and that she had to go to place after place to get lodgings. Also, she and her eldest daughter dreamt that she would fail if she did not go alone. She made a note of these expected happenings in her diary which was afterwards inspected by Myers.

Mrs Goodeve set out for Snettisham on Sunday morning. She went to the refreshment room at the station for luncheon, telling the porter to call her in time, but he went by mistake to the waiting room, with the result that she missed her train. As there was a long wait for the next train Mrs Goodeve visited the British Museum, where she wrote her name in the register in the jewel room. She duly caught a later train, reached Snettisham to find there was a fair in progress, and had great difficulty in finding accommodation. At the suggestion of the porter who carried her luggage, she took lodgings at the home of a certain John Bishop, who, as predicted in the ghostly experience at Clifton, was dark. Bishop, as it happened, was the parish clerk. Mrs Goodeve explained that she wished to examine the church registers, and asked if the curate would be willing to come to the house. Bishop thought he would, so a note asking him to call was sent by a porter. However, the curate was just going out to dinner and did not come to Bishop's house until half-past eleven, by which time Mrs Goodeve was in bed. He left a message that he would be happy to show Mrs Goodeve the register on Sunday morning after the service.

On the Sunday morning Mrs Bishop spoke to Mrs Goodeve about her drowned child buried in the churchyard. Mrs Goodeve attended the morning service and examined the register from which she was able to verify the marriage and death of Henry Barnard exactly as it had been told to her at Clifton. (He was married on 7 November 1839 and was buried on 7 August 1878, aged 72.) Mrs Goodeve gave a description of Henry Barnard which, the parish clerk said, was 'quite correct'. She also verified the reference to the death of Robert Cobb in the register. Bishop took her to the graves of Cobb and Barnard. 'On the latter,' said Mrs Goodeve in her statement, 'there is no stone, but three mounds surrounded by a railing overgrown with white roses.' She picked a rose for Dr Marshall, 'as had been directed. Walk and talk with the curate, who was not sympathetic.'

Henry Barnard had been the owner of Cobb Hall, a country house in a park, and after luncheon Mrs Goodeve walked there with Mrs Bishop. Now the evening was approaching, with the prospect of a lonely vigil in a church by the grave of a man who had died 150 years earlier. First of all, she had to have permission, and this proved difficult. The curate at first refused, but eventually told the clerk that he could do as he liked. The vicar was not consulted.

Mrs Goodeve attended the evening service; afterwards, while watching the lights put out and the church furniture covered up, she wondered if she would have the nerve to go on. 'Back to supper; afterwards slept and had dreams of a terrorizing character . . . Dark night, hardly any moon, a few stars. To church with John Bishop at 1.0 a.m., with whom searched interior and found it empty. At 1.20 was locked in alone, having no light; had been told to take Bible, but had only Church-service . . . Waited near grave of Robert Cobb. Felt no fear. Received communication, but does not feel free to give any detail. No light. History begun at Rodney Place then completed. Was directed to take another white rose from Henry Barnard's grave, and give it personally to his daughter (unmarried – living at Cobb Hall), and to remark her likeness to him.'

About 1.45 John Bishop knocked and let Mrs Goodeve out. She went to Henry Barnard's grave and gathered a rose for Miss Barnard, as she had been directed. Mrs Goodeve then went home and slept well for the first time since seeing the apparition of Mrs Seagrim.

The next day Mrs Goodeve sketched the church and identified the grave of 'Mrs Rowe' on whose grave, she had been told in church, she would find a message for herself. She then called on Miss Barnard and recognized the strong likeness to her father – 'carried out all things desired by the dead to the full, as had been requested. Has had no communication from any of them since. Nothing since has appeared in Rodney Place.'

Mrs Goodeve considered that the wishes expressed to her 'were not illogical or unreasonable, as the ratiocination of dreams often appears, but perfectly rational, reasonable, and of natural importance.'

Myers, in the introduction to this case, considered that 'the kernel of the case must be kept secret for reasons affecting survivors.' By the time Maitland took up the trail all those concerned with the happenings at Clifton and Snettisham were dead, but some reticence still had to be observed for legal reasons.

The inscription on the grave of 'Mrs Rowe' – the pseudonym used in *Proceedings* – is 'To teach self-sacrifice and simple faith', and it closes with the line, 'And flights of angels sing thee to thy rest.' In reality the grave is that of Kunnigunda (Olive), the wife of Charles Neville Rolfe, born 2 May 1851, died 17 January 1891. According to Maitland, there was a connection between the Cobbs and the Neville Rolfes, for a Robert Cobb, presumably the Robert Cobb of this story, married a Catherine Rolfe, daughter of Edmund Rolfe, of King's Lynn, and the Rolfes subsequently became the Neville Rolfes. Mrs Seagrim, it may be noted, was Marian Elizabeth Cobb before her marriage.

Maitland, helped in his research by members of the Neville Rolfe family, added considerably to the story told in *Proceedings*. Henry Barnard, he ascertained, was a well-to-do farmer who, about 1860, had acquired the property of Cobb Hall, now better known as Park House. Before he bought it, however, it had been in Chancery for many years, and according to local gossip, 'and perhaps more than local gossip, some sort of title had to be patched up before he was able to buy it . . . Now Mrs Seagrim was a Cobb, in other words, one of the family which had given its name to Cobb Hall. What relationship she bore to the last of the Cobbs living at Cobb Hall we do not know, not a very near one, probably, as according to rumour or gossip, or whatever else you like to call it, the one who would have inherited Cobb Hall, if Henry Barnard had not bought it, would have been a Neville Rolfe . . . When we put all these facts together and remember that rumour is not always a lying jade, we see that there might be some truth in the gossip that the title to the Cobb property which Henry Barnard had obtained was not altogether a sound one.'

This, then, is the end of the extraordinary story of the Snettisham ghost or ghosts. What are we to make of it?

Myers said in his paper in the SPR *Proceedings*:

The whole story is no doubt very different from the usual tenor of our narratives, and much more resembles some of the figments of romance. On the other hand the evidence for the external facts of the narrative is absolutely conclusive. There is (as will be seen) no doubt whatever that Mrs Goodeve did make the journey to Snettisham, giving as her reason some message conveyed to her on an occasion when she undoubtedly was found fainting in the middle of the night. There is no doubt that at Snettisham she obtained admission to the church at a similar hour of the night; nor that after so visiting the church she paid certain other visits to persons previously strangers to her. Nor has any explanation due to self-interest or to insanity been suggested, so far as I can discover, by any of the persons concerned. The whole expedition was a source merely of trouble and embarrassment to Mrs Goodeve, who left a sick child to attend to the alleged injunction, under circumstances of much inconvenience, and with no possible advantage to herself. An explanation from insanity or hysterical desire of notoriety is equally untenable . . .

After reviewing the case in *Dreams and Ghosts*, Andrew Lang commented:

Of this story the only conceivable natural explanation is that Mrs Goodeve, to serve her private ends, paid secret preliminary visits to Snettisham, 'got up' there a number of minute facts, chose a haunted house at the other end of England as a first scene in her little drama, and made the rest of the troublesome journeys, not to mention the uncomfortable visit to a dark church at midnight, and did all this from a hysterical love of notoriety. This desirable boon she would probably never have obtained, even as far as it is consistent with a pseudonym, if I had not chanced to dine with Dr Marshall while the adventure was only beginning. As there seemed to be a chance of taking a ghost 'on the half volley', I at once communicated the first part of the tale to the Psychical Society (using pseudonyms, as here, throughout) and two years later Mrs Goodeve consented to tell the Society as much as she thinks it fair to reveal.

This, it will be confessed, is a round-about way of obtaining fame, and an ordinary person in Mrs Goodeve's position would have gone to the Psychical Society at once, as Mark Twain meant to do when he saw the ghost which turned out to be a very ordinary person.

There I leave the ghosts, my mind being in a just balance of agnosticism. If ghosts at all, they were ghosts with a purpose. The species is now very rare.

The written evidence, Myers suggested, could be divided into three parts:

1. Mrs Goodeve's own diary, written mainly in pencil, during

and after the Snettisham journey. This diary bore the marks of hasty writing and was dated from day to day and in parts from hour to hour during the events which interested the Society. It contained the secret matter, and had not been entrusted by Mrs Goodeve to anyone; but Lord Bute and Myers had been allowed to read portions of it, and to observe the dates of the important entries there.

Along with this diary must be classed a document which Myers was allowed to reproduce almost *in toto*: the sheet of memoranda made by Mrs Goodeve before her Snettisham visit, about what would happen to her there, and what she was to do. (I have incorporated the main evidential points in his narrative, as reproduction in full, with pseudonyms and initials, could be confusing.)

Myers said that he became possessed of this document in the following manner. Mrs Goodeve had stated that she was told beforehand by the phantom that her tickets (the outward half of a return ticket) would not be asked for on her arrival at Snettisham. In fact it was not asked for; Mrs Goodeve sent it to Dr Marshall, who testified to having possessed it, and to having seen a letter from the Railway Company stating that no other ticket had been issued from London for Snettisham by the train in question. As Mrs Goodeve had not mentioned the prediction as to the ticket to Dr Marshall *before* her journey, Myers asked her whether she had herself made any note about the ticket before that journey. She at once brought her packet of private papers connected with the case; searched among them in his presence, and found the paper with the instructions as to what she was to do and to expect on the journey, written before starting. Cutting off a part of that paper which dealt with the secret matters, she gave him the rest. 'The porter's omission to take the ticket is therefore predicted in writing before the event, along with many other particulars as to the Snettisham visit.'

2. The second main piece of evidence was an account, written by Andrew Lang, and sent by him to the SPR, embodying the written and oral statements of Dr Marshall (and of another friend) communicated verbally while Mrs Goodeve was

actually on her journey, and in writing before the incidents and results of that journey were known.

3. The third main document, according to Myers, was the account dictated by Mrs Goodeve to Lord Bute on 17 May 1895, giving for the first time her history of the journey to Snettisham. She had kept 'this present adventure' as quiet as she could, but other people had heard vaguely of it, and she was annoyed by distorted versions; so she had eventually consented to give it to Lord Bute, and through him to the SPR.

This case, therefore, provides a good example of the care taken by investigators from the SPR in checking details. Letters in confirmation of Mrs Goodeve's statement were obtained from the Parish Clerk of Snettisham, John Bishop; from the curate; and from Dr Marshall and Lang, whose conclusion was: 'There is now no doubt that Mrs Goodeve did all she says.'

One of the most surprising features of this case, and one which has escaped the attention of commentators on it, has been the apparent ability of the apparitions to convey information. Although there are many examples of apparitions which speak in the early cases published by the SPR, there are very few today. Tyrrell, discussing the characteristics of an apparition in the book of that title, remarked that an apparition might speak to us, and possibly it might go so far as to answer a question; but we should not be able to engage it in any long conversation (91d p. 78). Yet we find in the case under discussion apparitions which are able to give such information as names and dates and specific details about a journey. Does this seeming departure from the commonly observed behaviour of apparitions invalidate much of the other evidence in this case?

My first reaction was that it did, but on reflection it seems to me that what is interpreted as speech from an apparition is often a communication received telepathically and converted by the recipient into language. In such circumstances knowledge of a language presumably 'spoken' by an apparition is not necessary. In my anthology *A Gallery of Ghosts*, I discuss the very strange case of a Swede who received repeated visits from an apparition claiming to be that of Harry Price, the well-known 'ghost

Professor Henry Sidgwick, President, 1882-4 and 1888-92.

William James, the great American psychologist; President, 1894-5. (*By courtesy of the Mary Evans Picture Library*)

Mrs Henrietta Sidgwick, President, 1908-9 and President of Honour, 1932.

FWH Myers, President, 1900.

(*left*) Edmund Gurney, co-author with Myers and Podmore of the famous book *Phantasms of the Living*.

(*right*) GNM Tyrrell, President, 1945-6.

(*above*) Professor HH Price, President, 1939-41, 1960-1.

(*below*) WH Salter, President, 1947-8.

(*below*) GW Lambert, President, 1956-8.

Johnnie Minney aged three, before the onset of his illness.

Johnnie Minney's grave.

(*below*) Vicarage Farm, Waresley. The arrow shows the window of the room in which Mrs Herbert saw the apparition (*see* Chapter Two).

The haunted mill house at Willington, now demolished, with the adjacent mill which still stands (*see* Chapter Four).

The church at Snettisham, Norfolk, where Mrs Goodeve kept her vigil and received a communication from the dead (*see* Chapter Seven).

The Petit Trianon, c. 1900 (*see* Chapter Nine. *By courtesy of the Mary Evans Picture Library*)

(*below*) A sketch of the circular kiosk at Le Petit Trianon, seen by Miss Moberley in 1901 and drawn by her from memory in 1904.

The late Lady Carson with her spaniels at Cleve Court (*see* Chapter Twelve).

(*below*) Abbey House, Cambridge (*see* Chapter Thirteen).

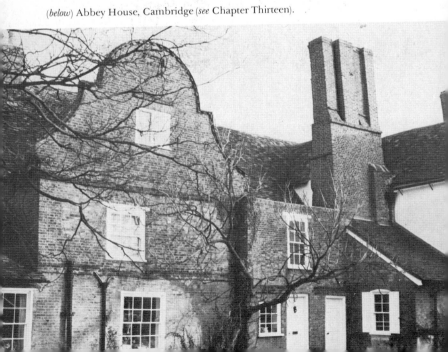

hunter', and although the Swede could not speak English, and Price, presumably, could not speak Swedish, they managed to converse.

'Price' explained that he had just died and when alive had studied ghosts and similar objects. Erson (pseudonym) found increasingly that he could understand 'Price' and in a peculiar way started to talk to him, although he had studied English so little. Conversation took place in a way which the patient could not explain, so it seemed quite natural when 'Price' appeared (pp. 150–60).

Erson had reported his experiences to a well-known Swedish scholar, the late Dr John Björkham, from whom he received treatment for his emaciated condition. The key passage in the quotation I have just given is 'Conversation took place in a way which the patient could not explain.' This suggests to me that the exchange was telepathic rather than verbal.

Other factors could be involved in such experiences. Dr Louisa E. Rhine has pointed out in the *Journal of Parapsychology* (70c p. 161) that 'the apparitions in my collection are almost always mute. But those in earlier collections, I note, often talked, sometimes at some length. Is this, too, the result of a change in general culture? If so, and if apparitions are figments produced by percipients to express unconscious ESP material, it would mean that the more sceptical, materialistic present-day outlook affects even such unconsciously produced imagery as that of hallucinatory experiences. This would not be too surprising.'

When we look back on this case we realize there is much that is obscure and, with all the principals long since dead, it will remain obscure. I have examined the case notes in the archives and it is obvious from them that efforts to obtain information from Miss Barnard, described as 'a middle-aged woman of whom people seem to be a little afraid', were fruitless. Likewise, Mrs Goodeve refused to give information on what took place in her interview with Miss Barnard. What remains in the mind, surely, is the courage of Mrs Goodeve, a 'little fragile woman, richly dressed', in allowing herself to be shut in a church in the early hours of the morning, there to receive messages from the dead. There must have been powerful compulsions for such an act. What weaknesses there are in the case are concerned with episodes in which corroboration was not possible, such as when Mrs Goodeve was alone in the church.

Snettisham was a small village when it was visited by Mrs Goodeve, and today the population is only 1,443. It is most unlikely that Mrs Goodeve could have carried out enquiries into the history of local families prior to her recorded visit without the fact being noted. Cobb Hall, now known as Park House, is divided into flats, but one thing is unchanged: white roses still grow around the grave of Henry Barnard, as they did in 1893 when Mrs Goodeve plucked blooms from the grave. I find it pleasing to think that some physical features attached to a ghost story do not change with the passing years.

The three chapters that follow are studies in retrocognition.

8   A Haunted Road

It is rare for an account of a haunting to be published in two issues of the SPR Journal separated by an interval of seven years – and rare also for the haunting to be associated with a stretch of road. The apparition in this case was that of a tall old man in the costume of an eighteenth-century Scottish clergyman. The principal witnesses were three sisters of a family named Scott who lived at Lessudden House in the little village of St Boswells, Roxburghshire. The case was brought to the notice of the Society by Miss E. E. Guthrie, Orme Square, London, who enclosed a letter from Miss M. W. Scott which gave details of her first experience of the apparition. The figure was mistaken by her, and by others, for that of a living person seen in broad daylight. Miss Scott later corresponded direct with the Society, and one account was written on the day after her experience with the apparition. Some of the evidence is secondhand because the witnesses concerned were unable, or unwilling, to commit their evidence to writing; and the earliest witnesses, some boys who were reported to have seen the apparition in the early morning, had left the country. However, enough firsthand evidence, some of it very detailed, was obtained to make the case one of good evidential standard. The haunting lasted ten years. The narrative that follows is taken from the SPR Journal for November 1893 (82h pp. 146–50) and that for October 1900 (82i pp. 298–306). It also includes some hitherto unpublished material from the Society's archives.

Miss Scott's first experience of the apparition was on 7 May 1892 between five and six in the afternoon:

Having gone for a walk, I was returning homewards by a road in the vicinity of St Boswells. The greater portion of the way is quite level, but at one part a short incline terminates with a sharp corner at the end. From the top of this eminence the whole road is conspicuous, with a hedge and bank on either side. Upon reaching the specified point, and finding time limited, I thought

I would expedite matters by running, and had not gone many steps when I came to a sudden halt, for just a few yards beyond I perceived a tall man dressed in black, and who walked along at a moderate pace. Fancying he would think mine an extraordinary proceeding, I finally stopped altogether to permit of his getting on further, while at the same time watching him turn the corner and pass on where his figure was still distinctly defined between the hedges referred to. He was gone in a second – there being no exit anywhere – without my having become aware of it. Greatly surprised, I then myself passed the same corner where I had seen the man vanish a few seconds before, and here, a short space onward, I saw one of my sisters standing and looking about everywhere in a bewildered manner. When I came up to her I said: 'Wherever has that man disappeared to?' and upon our comparing notes together it became evident that we had both experienced a similar sensation regarding the stranger, the only difference being that I had seen the apparition on in front, while she says he came facing her, and she, too, had noticed he vanished almost immediately.

But here the strangest part of it all is that we found that when the man became *invisible to her,* he *appeared to me between the part of the road where she and I were standing.* I may also here add that at the time we saw the apparition neither sister knew the other was so near.

Louisa Scott gave her own account of this incident. She said that it was in the 'broad daylight' and at a quarter before six on 7 May 1892.

As I was walking homewards, I saw advancing towards me at an ordinary pace a tall man dressed in black, whom I believed to be a clergyman. I removed my gaze but for a second, when great was my surprise when looking up again to find that he had gone from my sight. The hedge on either side of the road is very thick, with wide fields on either side, so that the man could not possibly have sprung over it without my having seen him. I felt extremely mystified, and stood for several minutes, looking backwards and forwards into the fields and in all directions, when I was much surprised by seeing my sister turn the corner of a little incline higher up the road and commence running down it, almost immediately coming to a sudden halt, and I saw her acting in the same way as I had done about five minutes before. Soon she walked onwards again, and finally turned the same sharp angle of the road and came hurriedly towards me, looking very much excited. (I had no idea that she was behind, nor did she know that I should be likely to be found in front of her.) Upon coming up to me she said, 'Where on earth is that man who was standing only about ten feet from you?' And here, what makes it still more striking is that I was facing the tall spectre, *yet could not see him when my sister did.* She was more fortunate than I, for she saw the entire dress of the man, while I only noticed his long black coat, the lower part of his body to me being invisible; while she had the

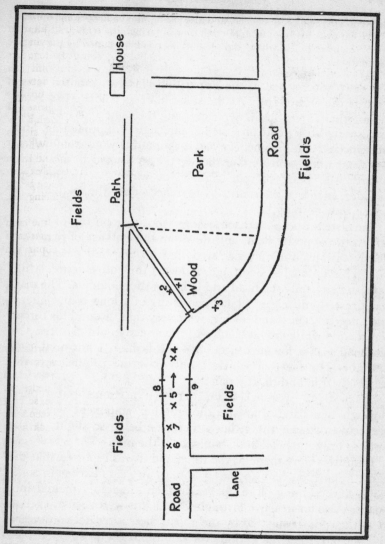

Plan of the locality where the Scott sisters first saw the apparition of the clergyman. 1, 2, and 3 are respectively the positions of Miss M. Scott, Miss L. Scott, and the clergyman in 1892. 4–9 indicate positions on 16 August 1900: 4, Miss Scott; 5, apparition; 6, man on road; 7, his pony and trap; 8 and 9, gates into the fields.

satisfaction of seeing him entirely and also seeing him vanish, as she did not remove her eyes, as I did, from the first time of seeing him. This is all I have seen of the man, but to what I did see nothing has been added by the aid of imagination.

The next appearance of the apparition was two months later, towards the end of July. At the same hour as before Miss Scott and another sister, Susan, were crossing the same spot when, not far distant, Miss Scott observed a dark figure approaching, and exclaimed: "'Oh, I do believe *that* is *our* man. I won't remove my eyes from him!" and neither did we till he seemed to *fade* away towards the bank on our right. Not waiting a moment to consider, each rushed frantically to either side of the road, but, of course, saw nothing.'

The sisters questioned some boys who were on top of a hay-cart in the opposite field, and to whom the expanse of road was clearly visible, but they declared that no one had passed that way. This time Miss Scott again viewed the entire figure, while her sister saw only the head and to below the shoulders. The man was dressed entirely in black, consisting of a long coat, gaiters, and knee-breeches, and his legs were very thin. 'Round his throat was a wide white cravat, such as I have seen in old pictures. On his head was a low-crowned hat – the fashion I am unable to describe. His face, of which I only saw the profile, was ex-ceedingly thin and deadly pale.'

Susan Scott was asked for her own account, but replied through her sister that she thought her statement would be scarcely worth anything, her experience being so slight, as she noticed only the head and shoulders of the man.

Enquiries were made at the time, and it was reported that the same apparition had appeared about two years earlier to some boys, and, coming close up beside them, instantly melted into space. 'Also for nearly a fortnight blue lights were seen after dark near the spot frequented by the ghost; these were not stationary, but moved about in various directions. Many people followed them, but all attempts to solve the mystery have proved fruitless. No cause can be suggested for the strange proceedings, though legend hath it that a child was murdered close by, but this fact is quite beyond the recollection of the oldest inhabitant of the neighbourhood. The apparition has been visible to many, and few care to traverse his haunts after dark.'

Miss Scott added that two girls from the village were attracted near the haunted walk by some wild strawberries growing on the bank. They stopped to gather them, and while thus employed they heard a thud or thump upon the ground beside them, but seeing no one they again continued their occupation. The sound was repeated. 'Looking up, they then saw a tall man gazing intently, and they, being almost paralysed with fright at the awful expression of his countenance, clutched one another convulsively and fled precipitately, but after a time, venturing to look back, they saw the figure still standing, and while they looked he *gradually faded away*. These girls affirm that the man was dressed exactly as I have before described, that his face was white as death, and a white filmy sheet or vapour now enveloped his raiment.'

Miss Scott asked the girls to give statements in writing, but they failed to do so. 'Perhaps the reason is that being so young they may feel themselves unable to commit their experiences to paper,' she explained.

The next time Miss Scott saw the apparition was on Sunday 12 June 1893. The account that follows is dated 14 June. At a few minutes before 10.0 a.m. she was walking on the stretch of road she had described previously when she saw far in front a dark figure who, at that distance, could have been a man or a woman. Thinking that it might be a woman she knew, and one who could be there at that hour, Miss Scott determined to hurry on and overtake her.

I had not gone far, however, when I discovered it to be none other than the apparition we had looked for and failed to see for so many months. I did not then feel at all afraid, and, hoping to get a nearer inspection, boldly followed, running in close pursuit; but here the strangest part of it all is that, though he was apparently walking slowly, I never could get any closer than within a few yards, for in a moment he seemed to *float or skim away*. Presently he suddenly came to a standstill, and I began to feel very much afraid, and stopped also. There he was! – the tall spectre dressed as I have described before. He turned round and gazed at me with a vacant expression and the same ghastly, pallid features. I can liken him to no one I have ever seen. While I stood, he still looked intently at me for a few seconds, then resumed his former position. Moving on a few steps he again stood and looked back for the second time, finally *fading from view* at his usual spot by the hedge to the right.

There was no one else on the road but myself, and here I solemnly state that what I have written is not at all traded upon by imagination, as I was not thinking of the apparition at the time, he not having been seen for months previous to this visitation. With this strange experience I now felt really terribly frightened, so much so that I beat a hasty retreat homewards, when further on I met a woman coming along who knew of the bad reputation of the road, and to her I related my adventure. She, too, was terrified, and declared she would go no further alone, so at last I agreed to accompany her onwards to see if we could perceive anything more of the man. We, however, reached our destination in safety, without the ghost becoming visible.

All I can say in conclusion is that I will never voluntarily pass along the same place alone . . .

In a letter of 28 June 1893 to Miss Guthrie, Miss Scott added: 'I have had a splendid inspection of his appearance this time. He wears what is likely to be black silk stockings and shoe-buckles, short knee-breeches, and a long black coat. The hat I cannot describe. The man is certainly dressed as a clergyman of the last century, and we have an old picture in the house for which he might have sat.'

As to the costume in which the apparition was seen, Miss Guthrie said: 'The dress worn, as regards the knee-breeches and silk stockings, I can vouch for as having been formerly a part of clerical attire, as my aunt had an engraving of Dr Rankine, minister of St David's Parish, Glasgow, in which he wears these and, I think, buckles in his shoes. The Moderator of the Scottish Church also wears this dress.'

Miss Guthrie, who had visited the locality, told the Society that so thick was the beech hedge and so open the fields that no man could penetrate the one or conceal himself in the other.

The story of the apparition of the tall man in black is continued in the SPR *Journal* in 1900. Louisa Scott wrote on 14 August 1894 to her friend Miss Guthrie to describe the experience of a young lady, Miss Irvine, who was a governess in the neighbourhood, in the spring of that year.

was returning home along the haunted road at about 4.15 hen she was attracted by seeing in front of her a rather tall old man dressed in a long black cloak, with one cape which came to a little below his shoulders; his hat was low-crowned, and the brim slouched over his eyes.

My informant was much interested in this peculiar-looking person, and did not take her eyes off him, whilst she watched him walk backward and forward between the turn of the road and a heap of stones about a hundred yards lower down; he repeated this six times, the last time stopping as if he were speaking to a man who was cutting the hedge at the time. What struck Miss Irvine as peculiar was that the man who was hedge-cutting did not look round, and seemed quite unconscious of the other's presence. Miss Irvine walked on, and was going to pass the old man, when, to her astonishment, he vanished when she was only about three yards from him. I know that you will think it foolish of Miss Irvine not questioning the hedger to whom the apparition looked as if he were speaking. I asked her why she had not, and she answered that she had not liked doing so, as the labourer would undoubtedly have thought her mad, as he clearly did not see any one.

This evidence was, of course, secondhand, so Miss Irvine was asked to send her own account to the Society. 'By an unfortunate accident' the first sheet of her letter was lost, but the second page was printed in the *Journal*. Miss Irvine said:

This seemed to me stranger than ever and I wondered what I had seen, for he was nowhere in the field. On returning home I described the old gentleman to some friends who were likely to know if a person answering my description lived in the neighbourhood, but was told, 'No.' He was dressed rather like a clergyman, wore a long black cloak with cape and slouched hat, his hands in his coat pockets. I had never seen anything of the kind before, though I had frequently walked the same road and at all hours. This happened about four o'clock in the afternoon. I have not again seen him . . . Mary Blamire Irvine.

In a letter to Myers, Miss M. W. Scott said that Miss Irvine was 'so much upset by the incident that she went into the house not far off and took hysterics.'

In August 1898 Miss Scott wrote to Myers to say the apparition was still being seen:

My latest experience was about a fortnight ago, when coming down the haunted road in the dusk I distinctly heard footsteps walking beside me, but could see nothing, though I am sure there must have been an unseen presence around from the state of nervous terror which generally makes itself felt on such occasions.

Last autumn, and again in the dusk, I was walking down the little wood adjacent to the road with my sister [Louisa]. We were both talking upon different subjects and putting the ghost as far from our thoughts as possible, when suddenly I was carried spell-bound by distinctly seeing the apparition walking alongside of us on the other side of the hedge. My sister saw me gazing vacantly on space when I suddenly exclaimed 'The man!' When we came to the gate which divides the wood from the road there was no one to be seen either way, though 'he' had walked within three feet of me the whole time; he was invisible to my sister. It is a strange phenomenon altogether. He had the same countenace we have always seen, but I did not seem to have the power to look beyond his face. This ghost always appears when our thoughts are bound up in something else, but if the opposite, then we are sure not to see him, and many persons who have accompanied us up [and] down the road in hopes of seeing him have, like ourselves, failed to do so . . .

On 17 August 1900 Miss Scott wrote to say that she had recently seen the apparition twice, the most recent occasion having been 'only last night'. Her description is as follows:

. . . The locality has been described before so that it is not necessary for me to enter into further details regarding it. On the evening of July 24th I was standing speaking to a friend, exactly upon the part known as the property of that 'mysterious he'. I had forgotten the very existence of our supernatural neighbour, and while we conversed upon different subjects, I inadvertently glanced carelessly down the expanse beyond, when I perceived the tall black figure walking on in advance with his back towards us. How he came to be there I had not the faintest idea, not having remarked his advent. I made no comment to my companion, but, wishing her a hasty adieu, hurried away as quickly as possible to try and make up upon him, but he instantly vanished: – there was no one to be seen either high or low. It was just eight o'clock in the evening, as I heard the hour chime in the village almost at the same time. He was dressed in the same way, namely, all in black, and only proceeding twenty yards away.

I have not since ascertained if my companion at the moment saw any one, as she is an unbeliever in such manifestations, and says it is all imagination, and often laughed me to scorn when I said anything about the ghost on the road; but, believing or not believing, it is certainly an unpleasant sensation to see a long figure clad in sable raiment appear and so quickly vanish again without apparent reason on a lonely thoroughfare.

My second illustration of last night, August 16th, 1900, can tell you something more definite than the previous one, for I certainly believe the man to be a clergyman of the ancient school, but why this 'Father of the Church' frequents *that* road is an unexplained mystery. On this occasion the outline of his head and shoulders were completely visible – all black, with a wide white muffler-looking thing wound round his throat; his hair seems light;

face clean-shaven and very pale, but he was not quite near enough for the features to become clearly defined; the hat looked like an ordinary clerical wide-awake, only the crown seemed much higher than those used in the present day. The lower part of his body [was] overshadowed, as he was advancing towards me up the incline, while I was on the level above.

There was a man with a pony and trap cutting grass by the roadside, within a few feet of where I saw the apparition appear, who had his back to the worker; yet, the most wonderful part of it all is that when I questioned the man, he declared he had seen 'no one'. 'But,' I said, 'he was close beside you.' He still declared he saw 'no person there', so I let the matter end, though I expect that he, like the whole village, knows well the reputation of the road, for he looked slightly nervous and remarked 'it was not a safe place to come down alone'.

The Society sent some questions to Miss Scott, and she replied on 26 August:

... Last evening I went down the road with my two sisters and some friends, but the 'ghost' did not make his presence apparent; neither did he upon our return; so I had time to make a few more definite observations which will form the answer to your question. The apparition and I were walking *towards one another*. I was too much taken up watching the proceedings of the supernatural to notice the operations of the working man, until the vision of the other had died away, when I turned my attention to the real subject, who was then *facing the road* and actually *looking* at the place where the spectre had disappeared a few seconds before. The pony and trap had evidently moved on a little from the part where the owner was occupied and afterwards stood still; the movements of all being such that the entire expanse beyond was an unobstructed view to any person coming or going upon it; thus, the animal was really nearest the apparition, whose back was close to its head as he advanced. It may only have been a coincidence, but the pony gave itself a violent shake in its harness just at the time. Horses have been known to exhibit signs of fear on such occasions, but as they frequently go through such antics for other causes, this fact can be no criterion for judging the point ... We have interrogated different persons employed on the road, and one in particular who had occasion to pass along that way every morning and evening and to the village in all seasons, but he has never noticed any one answering to the description given ...

This ends the report in the *Journal*; but in a letter dated 10 October 1900, acknowledging copies of the *Journal* sent to her, Miss Scott said she had heard of two other occasions of the ghost having been seen by two stepsisters. 'They are both old Scotchwomen and speak the broad dialect and quite illiterate so that nothing could be gained in writing.'

One, the lodge keeper at Lessudden House, told Miss Scott that about six years earlier she got 'a terrible fright' with a man all dressed in black whom she had seen 'beyond the church' and who had suddenly vanished. She added, 'I waited, expecting him to pass me but he never did.' This woman spoke of the figure as 'the devil or black man'.

The other woman had seen the figure as recently as August of that year. She was returning home from a mothers' meeting in Maxton, a neighbouring village, at an hour when it was rather dark but light enough to distinguish figures. When she got to the haunted road she saw the tall figure just in front of her. They walked almost together for some time and eventually she passed the man; 'he was so light of foot he made no sound in walking.' She was so much frightened and upset by the incident that she took an ignominious flight through the fields to her home as quickly as possible, and nothing would now induce either woman to go that way after dark.

The previous week, 'by the merest chance', Miss Scott's letter concluded, she had heard the story of this apparition. 'The ghost is believed to be that of a clergyman in St Boswell's who murdered his servant. It must have taken place quite 150 years ago as we can trace the ministers of the parish back to a certain date without any apparent blot on their escutcheons. I am now using every effort to find out more about it, as *everyone* is so certain on the point of the apparition being a clergyman it seems almost conclusive that the above story is perfectly correct.'

The story related by Miss Scott may be correct, but the evidence is far from being conclusive. Who was this clergyman, who was his victim, and when did the murder take place? Such information is necessary before any reliance can be placed on the story. Miss Scott assumes that the appearances of the apparition were associated with some tragedy, or crime, but this does not follow.

The apparition could have been that of a clergyman of the parish who was accustomed to walking on that stretch of the road while pondering on the sermon he was to give the following Sunday or other spiritual matters.

In this case we have the firsthand evidence of the three Scott sisters, the governess, Miss Irvine, and the two Scotswomen interviewed by Miss Scott; she was asked by the Society to prepare a statement and get them to sign it, but this, apparently, was not done: as the women were 'quite illiterate' it is possible that they could not write their names. We must also bear in mind that when one woman saw, as she claimed, the figure, the light was not good and the effects of suggestion may have added to her fright.

Miss Scott also interviewed the mother of Carrie Miller, aged 13, one of the two girls who were disturbed by the apparition while picking wild strawberries. Her companion, a girl called Anderson, was at the time on a visit to St Boswells. Unfortunately Miss Scott had not prepared a statement for the girls to sign; it is interesting that the apparition should have drawn the girls' attention to his presence by a thump or thud.

Miss Scott's determined pursuit of the figure reminds me of that of Miss Despard in the Cheltenham case. Neither woman was able to grasp the apparition, which always remained just out of reach; both saw the figure disappear suddenly; both were unable to communicate with the apparition; both were unable to point it out to others – Miss Despard to her father and Miss Scott to the man with the pony and trap. Miss Irvine saw the figure stop as if to speak to a man cutting a hedge but, as she pointed out, 'he clearly did not see anyone'; another example of the way that some people are unable to see apparitions.

It is significant in this case, and the Cheltenham one, that conscious efforts to see the apparition were always unsuccessful – a point I will deal with in the closing chapter.

9　The Ghosts of Versailles

One of the most famous, and almost certainly the most controversial, ghost stories of this century concerns the figures seen by Miss Annie Moberly and Miss Eleanor Jourdain, two English academics – Miss Moberly, the daughter of a Bishop of Salisbury, was to become the first principal of St Hugh's College, Oxford, and Miss Jourdain, the daughter of a vicar in Derbyshire, the second principal of that college – in the park of the Petit Trianon, Versailles, on 10 August 1901. The two women carried out intermittent research for ten years before publishing the results of it, in relation to the events in the park, in An Adventure *(55).*

It had an unfavourable review by Mrs Sidgwick in Proceedings *in 1911 (81e). Officers of the Society knew about the case because the 'adventure' had been brought to Mrs Sidgwick's attention in 1902. After the book was published Miss Moberly was again in touch with the Society, and some rather acrimonious correspondence took place with Miss Alice Johnson, the research officer and editor, mainly concerning the dates on which the accounts by Miss Moberly and Miss Jourdain were compiled. Despite the Society's doubts about the case, the reading public greeted the book with enthusiasm. Five editions of* An Adventure *were published between 1911 and 1955, with numerous reprints, and the book would undoubtedly be still in print today but for the decision by the late Dame Joan Evans, owner of the copyright, not to allow a new edition to be printed in English because she had reached the conclusion that there was a natural explanation for what the two women saw: that the figures which they assumed were apparitions were those of Count Robert de Montesquiou and his companions, who had access to the park at the time, and, wearing eighteenth-century costume, gave poetry readings there.*

If this were all, I would not devote a chapter to the case in this book, but over the years fresh reports of visitors to the park who have seen there figures in the clothes of a bygone age have come in and research by G. W. Lambert and others has shown that some of the features in the park mentioned by the

*authors which had not been physically there in 1901 had actually existed –
not in 1789, the year of Queen Marie Antoinette's last visit to the park,
round which the two Englishwomen had based their research, but in 1770–
71, a period which had not come into their calculations. The American
parapsychologist, Professor Ian Stevenson, once said that 'when an
investigator attempts to probe reports of spontaneous cases, a very considerable number of them simply melt away or prove worthless' (85a p. 144).
What is so unusual about the Versailles 'adventure' is that what at first
seemed a very doubtful case, contained in an account compiled as a result of
muddled research, turned out to be much stronger than it had seemed.*

Mrs Sidgwick's unsigned review of An Adventure *in* Proceedings
*was accompanied by a sketch, reproduced on p. 143, which shows the
probable route taken by the two women. I will quote at length from this
review because of the guidance it gives to readers who want, with the help
of the map, to retrace the steps taken by Miss Moberly and Miss Jourdain
eighty years ago. The review also has the advantage of combining in one
narrative the separate accounts of the two women.*

The first edition of An Adventure *appeared as the work of a 'Miss
Morison' (Miss Moberly) and 'Miss Lamont' (Miss Jourdain). The
identity of the authors was not revealed until the publication of the fourth
edition of* An Adventure, *by Faber, in 1931. In order to avoid
confusion, I have substituted the real names of the authors for the
pseudonyms used in the early editions of the book and in Mrs Sidgwick's
review. If we accept the accounts of Miss Moberly and Miss
Jourdain – and it is up to the reader, as always, to make up his or her
own mind on the evidence presented here – the case may be considered to
provide an outstanding example of retrocognition. The Versailles case,
considered as a whole, is also noteworthy for the unusually large number
of collective experiences in one area, the park of the Petit Trianon, between
1901 and 1955. I have been careful to give both favourable and unfavourable views of the case.*

*If there is a lesson to be learned from the Versailles 'adventure' it is
that the researcher must set about his or her task with an open mind, and
not try to interpret the evidence to suit one particular theory. Miss
Moberly's belief that she and Miss Jourdain might have 'inadvertently
entered within an act of the Queen's memory when alive' – the Tuileries
were sacked on 10 August 1892 – misled them in their research and invited
the mockery of some commentators on the case. However, Miss Moberly
and Miss Jourdain did make careful enquiries to ensure that a fête had not*

taken place on the date of their first visit to the Petit Trianon, nor were
preparations for a film being made.

In the summer of 1900 Miss Jourdain stayed in Paris for the first time and in the following year asked Miss Moberly, who was seventeen years her senior, to visit her there. 'We decided to go to Versailles one day, though rather reluctantly, as we felt it was diverging from our plan [to see the historic part of Paris in something like chronological order] to go there too soon. I did not know what to expect, as my ignorance of the place and its significance was extreme,' Miss Jourdain said in her contribution to *An Adventure*. Miss Moberly's knowledge of the Petit Trianon was, she said, derived from a magazine read as a girl from which she received a general impression that it was a farmhouse where the Queen had amused herself.

The two women first visited the Palace of Versailles and, as there was time to spare, decided to go to the two Trianons. 'By not asking the way we went an unnecessarily long way round – by the great flights of steps from the fountains and down the central avenue as far as the head of the long pond,' said Miss Moberly. 'The weather had been very hot all the week, but on this day the sky was a little overcast and the sun shaded. There was a lively wind blowing, the woods were looking their best, and we both felt particularly vigorous. It was a most enjoyable walk.'

Readers of the review of *An Adventure* in *Proceedings* in 1911 were able to consult a map drawn by a friend of the Society, M. Sage, who lived in Paris and who had walked over the ground with the accounts of Miss Moberly and Miss Jourdain before him. M. Sage's sketch gave an enlarged representation of a portion of a map of the palaces and gardens of Versailles by M. Marcel Lambert, Architecte des Domaines de Versailles et des Trianons. The line and letters on the plan explained M. Sage's view of the route taken by Miss Moberly and Miss Jourdain. It should be observed that the plans in their book did not profess to be more than diagrammatic.

Mrs Sidgwick wrote as follows:

The two ladies having reached – by a route which their description leaves doubtful, but which is unimportant – the intersection of the Allée de la

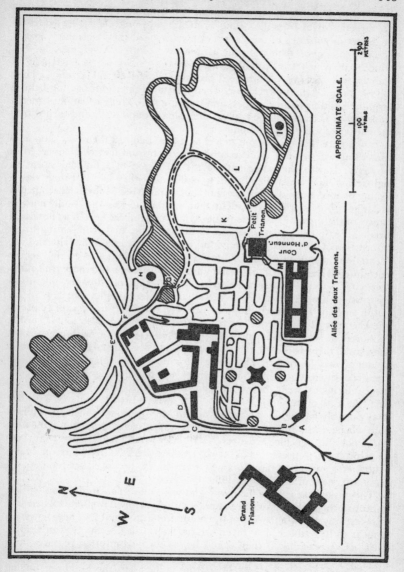

This sketch of part of the Petit Trianon accompanied Mrs Sidgwick's review of *An Adventure* in 1911.

Reine with the Allée des deux Trianons, should have followed the latter in the direction away from the Grand Trianon, and would shortly have arrived at the main entrance of the Petit Trianon. Instead they took the 'Chemin Creux', passing on their right the Musée des Voitures, A, on map, out of a window of which (the dwelling-house of the *gardien* forms part of it) a woman was shaking a cloth, and on their left the Grand Trianon. They followed the Chemin Creux to C, then turned to the right, passing behind farmlike buildings and cottages, and noticing farm and garden implements probably at D, reached the crest of the rising ground at E, and turned into the garden of the Petit Trianon.

It was here that they began to feel as if they had lost their way, and as if something was wrong. 'An extraordinary depression had come over' Miss Moberly. It was the latter part of the afternoon of a hot day spent in sightseeing, and when they began to realize that they had lost their way a feeling of oppression was perhaps not unnatural. Miss Moberly attributed it to fatigue, but afterwards thought that the fatigue was the result, not the cause, of the uncomfortable sensations, and remembers herself as not at all tired. Miss Jourdain describes the feeling as eerie, and culminating in an impression of something uncanny, but is careful to explain that she 'did not mean that she had the least idea at the time that any of the people encountered were unreal or ghostly', and that 'this was still more true of the scenery.' Nevertheless, remembering this feeling of 'dreamy unnatural oppression' a week later, they agreed that the place was haunted.

On entering the garden they saw two men (probably at F, a spot close to the entrance of a gardener's yard, and where M. Sage also found garden labourers at work) whom they describe as dressed in 'greyish-green coats with small three-cornered hats' (Miss Moberly), 'in official dress greenish in colour' (Miss Jourdain). This description does not seem to correspond to the dress of either officials or gardeners at Trianon now. The former, M. Sage informs us, wear cocked hats, and the latter have by way of uniform a *képi* (the kind of cap French soldiers wear) with a broad red band. This last may possibly have given an impression to Miss Jourdain which crystallized into official dress. But whatever the dress was, it seems clear that at the time they took the men for gardeners ... In later years they decided that these men probably represented ... two brothers Bersy, attendants on Marie Antoinette, who, research shows, were likely to have been on guard somewhere about that spot in 1789.

They asked these men their way and were told to go straight on. If that meant by the path marked on our plan with an arrow it would have been the shortest way to the entrance of the house from the point F. They, however, appear to have taken it to mean the path towards G – the Rocher bridge. Just before reaching G they would be, as their description requires, at a point where their path ended, being crossed by another. They would then have a kiosk, (the Belvédère, H), in front to their left (this building, judging from postcards and map, seems to be called indifferently by the names 'Belvédère', 'Pavillon de Musique', and 'Kiosque'), and a rustic bridge (the Rocher Bridge, G) to their right.

The ladies do not admit, however, that either the bridge or the kiosk have any resemblance to those they saw, and further conclude from researches made in 1908 and 1907 that besides these and not far from them there were in 1789 another kiosk and another rustic bridge, now no longer existing, which may have resembled what they remember. Much stress is laid on these two items as evidence of supernormal vision. It is unfortunate for their theory that neither lady saw more than one kiosk or one bridge in that region on their first visit, nor does Miss Jourdain appear to have done so on the subsequent one when she regarded her experience as supernormal ... That no more kiosks or bridges were seen than now exist goes to confirm our conjecture that it was the existing ones which they saw.

It is true, however, that the descriptions of the kiosk in the book, 'A light garden kiosk, circular and like a small bandstand' (in Miss Moberly's account); or 'A building consisting of some columns roofed in' (in Miss Jourdain's account) – do not correspond well to the Belvédère, and are more like the Temple de l'Amour. On the other hand, Miss Jourdain in January, 1902, went to see the Temple de l'Amour, and decided it was not the building they had seen in 1901, and on the same occasion took for granted that the Belvédère was that building, 'for coming upon it from behind, all the water was hidden from' her. Is it possible that they saw both buildings in 1901 and retained a kind of composite mental picture of them? We understand from M. Sage that the Temple de l'Amour (I on the map) is visible from the points – among others – marked K and L on the map, and if the ladies made a *détour* through either of these points in approaching the house, which there is some reason to think they did, they would have had a view of it in front and to the left, which might have merged itself in memory with that of the Belvédère. It must be remembered that the grounds are not large (the distance as the crow flies from the Belvédère to the Temple de l'Amour is only about 300 yards), but they are carefully laid out, and – except in the formal French garden – planted with trees and shrubs so as to give an idea of size and distance and prevent the plan of the grounds from being obvious from any one point. That, in fact, is the meaning of Jardin Anglais (English garden).

Near the kiosk sat a man in slouched hat and cloak whose appearance the ladies disliked, and who they afterwards thought might be the Comte de Vaudreuil, well known at the Court of Marie Antoinette.

At the junction of the paths a man ran up to them from behind and directed them to the right as the way to the house. They heard but did not see his approach. This running man may, as Miss Moberly at first supposed, have been one of the gardeners they had spoken to, who, observing that they still did not realize the way, pursued them to put them right. This would accord well with his curious smile, for most of us are slightly amused when others lose their way in a place familiar to ourselves ... The sudden appearance and disappearance of this man is easily accounted for, M. Sage thinks, as the paths are narrow and tortuous and the shrubs thickly planted, Miss Moberly speaks of 'rock (or whatever it was) that shut out the view at the junction of the paths' and over or through which she supposes the man to have come. Neither any mysteriousness in the man's appearance and disappearance, nor any strangeness in his costume seems to have struck the ladies at the moment. It was only a week later, on talking it over, that they 'realized, for the first time, the theatrical appearance of the man who spoke to [them], the inappropriateness of the wrapped cloak on a warm summer afternoon, the unaccountableness of his coming and going'. His accent puzzled them somewhat. It is suggested . . . that it may have been Austrian pronunciation of French or Breton, but M. Sage remarks '*il y a de bizarres accents en Seine-et-Oise*', and much cannot be based on that.

It is interesting to note that 'the rock or whatever it was that shut out the view at the junction of the paths' (pp. 5–6) becomes definitely an 'isolated rock standing up as we saw it behind the running man' on p. 71, to correspond with what the authors regard as the aspect of the garden in 1789 . . . After the rustic bridge, the way by which the ladies approached the house is too vaguely indicated to be securely traced. M. Sage thinks it most likely that they followed the dotted line (see map). Miss Moberly says the 'pathway led under trees; it skirted a narrow meadow of long grass, bounded on the further side by trees, and very much overshadowed by trees growing in it. This . . . shut out the view of the house until we were close to it.' Miss Jourdain says: 'We then followed a narrow path till almost immediately we came upon the English garden front of the Petit Trianon.' Near the house Miss Moberly saw a lady, unnoticed by Miss Jourdain, wearing a pale green fichu and sitting on a seat on the grass. She took her at the time for a tourist, but now supposes it may have been a vision of Marie Antoinette, who they find possessed in 1789 green bodices and white fichus. A green bodice with a white muslin fichu over it would look greenish. The idea seems to have been suggested by a report heard by Miss Jourdain in November, 1901, 'that on a certain day in August Marie Antoinette is regularly seen sitting outside the garden front at the Petit Trianon, with a light flapping hat and a pink dress.' This legend, however, they tell us, 'is of course incapable of proof.'

The Petit Trianon has terraces on its north and west sides – the west one fitting in architecturally with the French garden. From this terrace the ladies looked over into the Cour d'Honneur on the south (the only way into the house for visitors), inaccessible from where they were, and then moved towards one of the long windows, which was unshuttered. These movements seem sufficient to suggest to any one watching them that they wished to get into the house and did not know how to proceed, and probably account for a young man politely coming to them and showing them the way round. He 'looked inquisitively amused' as he did so, like the running man.

There are, however, two mysteries connected with this man. In the first place the ladies thought he came out of a door which he banged behind him, and four years later identified the building from which he came as the disused chapel (M on the map) from which no openable door on the terrace has existed for many years. A door now inaccessible from inside once opened on to what is now a small terrace or balcony, and they make out to their satisfaction that there was once a connection on a level between this terrace and the one on which they stood. We do not profess to be able to follow their reconstruction of the altered terrace with complete conviction, but assuming them to be right about this, their suggestion is that they were approached by a ghostly man walking along a ghostly terrace. The chapel door in question is only partially visible now from the terrace on which they remember standing, and another door observed by M. Sage about 10 ft. further west and suggested by him as a more plausible alternative is not visible from the terrace at all. On the whole our own suggestion would be that a noise as of a banging door occurred simultaneously with the approach of the man, and suggested to them in recollection that he came through a door.

The other mystery we have already referred to. It is that, as the ladies neither remember walking so far round as is necessary in order to get from the west side of the house to the Court of Honour, nor entering the Avenue des Deux Trianons by so narrow a path as the present one, they think they may, in order to reach their destination, have been transported by a roadway that existed through the buildings in Marie Antoinette's time where there is now solid building with no gates! We may remark that in the incident of 'the chapel man' the ladies themselves played in the supposed act of memory the part of intruders observed by the Queen while sitting in front of the house, while in the incident of the running man their part was that of the Queen herself. This, however, may be what happens in 'acts of memory'.

These are the principal incidents of the 'Adventure'. In others there seems even less solid foundation for a supernormal explanation. We ought perhaps to refer to supposed hallucinatory music heard by Miss Jourdain on a subsequent visit in 1902, and believed by her to have been of the date of Marie Antoinette – 'faint music as of a band, not far off'. She ascertained that no band was playing in the grounds for the public benefit on that day. She wrote down from memory about 12 bars, but these are not reproduced in the book, and have not been found consecutively in any music examined. They may of course be so characteristic as to be convincing, but even in that case may have been an appropriately hallucinatory reproduction of Miss Jourdain's general recollection of eighteenth-century music. On the other hand, a more realistic explanation may be afforded by the fact that a good deal of exercising of soldiers goes on constantly in the neighbourhood of Versailles and the Trianons, and that snatches of military band music might well be heard, M. Sage tells us. It is true that in a later part of the book the sounds are said to be 'of a band of violins', but as they were faint and intermittent it seems not impossible that there was some uncertainty about the instruments.

In conclusion, while gladly admitting that Miss Moberly and Miss Jourdain have produced a very readable book and have taken praiseworthy trouble in looking up historical facts and traditions, we cannot honestly say that they appear to us to have added anything of interest on the positive side of Psychical Research. The foundations on which the supernormal claims of the 'Adventure' are built are too slight, and too little allowance is made for the weakness of human memory both in adding to and subtracting from facts – weaknesses from which there is no reason to think the writers of this book suffer less than the rest of the world.

The opening passages of the review are equally cool and critical.

It does not seem to us that, on the evidence before us, there is sufficient ground for supposing anything supernormal to have occurred at all. The persons and things seen were, we should judge, the real persons and things the seers supposed them to be at the time, probably decked out by tricks of memory (and after the idea of haunting had occurred to them), with some additional details of costume suitable to the time of Marie Antoinette. No detailed account of the experiences was apparently written till three months later, Nov., 1901, and it is unusual to be able to rely on one's memory of things seen after even a much shorter interval of time. Vagueness of memory is the more likely to have occurred in this case, as the ladies, who at best do not seem to be very good at topography, were not apparently attending closely to their surroundings . . .

If there is a fault in the review it is that it does not convey adequately the flavour of the narrative. For instance, Miss Moberly, in describing the moment when she saw the circular kiosk, by which a man was sitting, said, 'Everything suddenly looked unnatural, therefore unpleasant; even the trees behind the building seemed to have become flat and lifeless, *like a wood worked in tapestry*. There were no effects of light and shade, and no wind stirred the trees. It was all intensely still.' And later, 'I was beginning to feel as though we were walking in a dream – the stillness and oppressiveness were so unnatural.' Miss Jourdain recalled, after leaving the two men in green, 'I began to feel as if I were walking in my sleep; the heavy dreaminess was oppressive.'

Miss Jourdain paid a second visit to the Petit Trianon on 2 January 1902. She did not retrace the old route but went along a path leading to the Hameau, a little village where Marie Antoinette, with the ladies of her court, played at being a dairymaid. There had not been any of the eerie feeling she had experienced with her friend the previous August, 'but, on crossing a bridge to go to the Hameau, the old feeling returned in full force; it was as if I had crossed a line and was suddenly in a circle of influence. To the left I saw a tract of park-like ground, the trees bare and very scanty. I noticed a cart being filled with sticks by two labourers, and thought I could go to them for directions if I lost my way. The men wore tunics and capes with pointed hoods of bright colours, a sort of terracotta red and deep blue; one man wore red, the other blue; the colours were not mixed. I turned aside for an instant – not more – to look at the Hameau, and when I looked back men and cart were completely out of sight, and this surprised me, for I could see a long way in every direction and their total disappearance in so short a time seemed unaccountable. And though I had seen the men in the act of loading the cart with sticks, I could not see any trace of them on the ground either at the time or afterwards.' Then followed the incident, referred to in the review, of hearing music when lost in the wood.

Miss Moberly paid her second visit to the Petit Trianon on 4 July 1904, with Miss Jourdain and a Frenchwoman who had not heard their story; and again on 9 July, when they were unaccompanied. They went up the lane as before, and turned to the right on reaching the building which they now knew had once been the quarters of the Corps of Guards. From this point everything was changed. The gardener's house was quite different in appearance from the cottage described by Miss Jourdain in 1901. Beyond the gardener's house was a *parterre* with flowerbeds, and a smooth lawn of many years' careful attention. It did not seem to be the place where they had met the garden officials. They spent a long time looking for the old paths. Not only was there no trace of them, but the distances were contracted, and all was on a smaller scale than Miss Moberly recollected. The kiosk was gone; so was the ravine and the little cascade which had fallen from a height above their heads and the little bridge over the ravine was, of course, gone too. The trees were quite natural, and seemed to have been a good deal cleared out, making that part of the garden much less wooded and picturesque.

The English garden in front of the house was not shaded by many trees, and they could see the house and the Hameau from almost every point. Instead of a much-shaded rough meadow continuing up to the wall of the terrace, there was now a broad gravel sweep beneath it, and the trees on the grass were gone. Exactly where the 'lady' was sitting they found a large rhododendron bush of, apparently, many years' growth. They did not recognize the present staircase, which led up to the northwest end of the terrace, nor the extension of wall round which one then had to go in order to reach the staircase. They thought that they went up to the terrace from some point nearer to the house from the English garden. The present exit from the French garden to the avenue was not as near the house as they expected, nor was it as broad as they remembered it. According to Miss Moberly:

To add to the impossibility of recalling our first visit, in every corner we came across groups of noisy merry people walking or sitting in the shade. Garden seats placed everywhere and stalls for fruit and lemonade took away from any idea of desolation. The commonplace, unhistorical atmosphere was totally inconsistent with the air of silent mystery by which we had been so much oppressed. Though for several years Miss Jourdain has assured me of the change, I had not expected such complete disillusion.

It was all very confusing and disappointing. However, over the years reports of other strange experiences in the park at Versailles came to light. The fourth edition of *An Adventure*, published by Faber in 1931, contained for the last time an appendix which told of the meeting of Mr and Mrs John Crooke, and their son, Stephen Crooke, with the two authors on 14 May 1914. The full names of the family concerned are not given in this edition but they are contained in the September 1916 *Journal* of the American SPR.

The Crooke family, who were English, lived in a flat in the Rue Maurepas at Versailles in 1907 and 1908, their rooms looking on the park by the Bassin de Neptune. They had been interested in *An Adventure* because, in 1908, they had – all three persons together – twice seen the 'sketching lady'. Both times it had been in July and at the Grand Trianon. The first time she was sitting in the garden, close to the glass colonnade, on a low stool on a green bank where there was no green bank, but only gravel and flowerbeds. The second time she was sitting below the balustrade, over which one can look from the Grand Trianon to the canal below. On both occasions she was dressed in a light cream-coloured skirt, white fichu, and a white untrimmed flapping hat. The skirt was full and much gathered, and the lady spread it round her. Both times she appeared to be sketching. Being an artist himself, and supposing that she was sketching, Mr Crooke had looked with curiosity at her paper and, though the lady did not seem to notice him, she at once quietly turned her paper aside from his observation with a rapid movement of her wrist. They never doubted that she was ghostly because of the peculiar way in which she appeared and disappeared, 'seeming to grow out of, and to retire into, the scenery with a little quiver of adjustment.' Her hair was fair. On one occasion the lady sat down, settled her dress, moved, and sat down again, giving them the impression that she resented their intrusion. As artists they had carefully noticed the lady and had observed that though she seemed quite real, all the contours of her figure and her general bearing were not what they were accustomed to then. 'Not only her dress, but she herself, belonged to another century.' The second time they saw her some of the party wished to stay longer, but Mr Crooke was overcome 'with such terrible fatigue' that they all went home.

On one occasion, Mrs Crooke had met a man in eighteenth-century costume with the small three-cornered hat, different from what was worn now, but such as described by the two authors. Mr and Mrs Crooke had seen a woman in the grounds in an old-fashioned dress picking up sticks. They had noticed the flattened appearance of the trees. One day, when he was alone, Mr Crooke had heard music coming over the water from the Belvédère, where certainly none was going on. It was a stringed band playing old music, and he enjoyed listening to it for nearly a quarter of an hour, but he did not identify it or write any of it down. At the time he was standing on low ground near the stream in the English garden.

The Crooke family mentioned a curious hissing sound that sometimes came when things were about to appear, possibly suggesting some electrical condition, and they also spoke of the vibration in the air which accompanied vision. On hearing this in 1914, Miss Moberly and Miss Jourdain immediately looked in the Almanack, and found that 10 August 1901 had been remarkable for an electrical storm all over Europe.

It will be noted that the Crooke family had their experiences three years *before* the publication of *An Adventure*, but critics could argue that their recollection of what they had observed, particularly in respect of the 'sketching lady', had been aided by what they had read.

Another 'adventure' came to light in the correspondence columns of the magazine *John o' London's Weekly* on 19 November 1932, and it was reproduced, with his comments, by G. W. Lambert in the *Journal* (44d pp. 12–18). The percipients were Miss Clare M. Burrow, at the time a mistress in a school for girls at Haslemere (Surrey), and a former pupil, Miss Ann Lambert, (no relation to G. W. Lambert), later Lady Hay. Early in October 1928 they were staying for a few days in Paris and, with no expectation of seeing anything uncanny – both were sure they had not previously heard of Miss Moberly and Miss Jourdain's 'adventure' – they visited Versailles one afternoon. Miss Burrow wrote:

After exploring the great palace we set out to find the Trianons. Although we were in the company of many other visitors after leaving the Grand Trianon we found ourselves practically alone when we turned into the long green statued avenue which we hoped led to the Petit Trianon. We soon came upon a deserted building hemmed in by nettles, and a strange feeling of depression came over me – we ceased to talk, and hurried on till the ruined 'Hameau' came into sight, and from the window of a farmhouse near the lake a woman looked down on us. On turning to look for the Temple of Love among the trees we saw an old man whom we judged to be an official as he was clad in an old green and silver uniform, approaching down a side avenue. I called to him, seeking information about the elusive Petit Trianon; he replied by shouting sentence after sentence in hoarse and unintelligible French as if in great haste. Something sinister in his face caused us to hurry on, and looking back we saw he had completely vanished. The strange feeling of depression increased and it was with relief we saw the Petit Trianon among the trees.

That winter my friend's mother sent me *An Adventure* – and on reading the first pages I was astonished to find that our experience was very similar to that of Miss Moberly and her friend. The sight of that old official in the uniform of the ill-fated Bourbons – the strange feeling of depression – the fact that we took the long and wrong way to the left when a short path to the right leads to the Petit Trianon – all were similar. It was the more strange because, before our visit to Versailles, I had never heard of the experiences recorded in *An Adventure*.

This case was brought to Lambert's attention by Monsieur M. Dayet, a French member of the Society who, in 1946, having heard of it through a private channel, got in touch with Miss Burrow. As a result he was able to correct two errors in her account. The reference to the Hameau should be to the farm

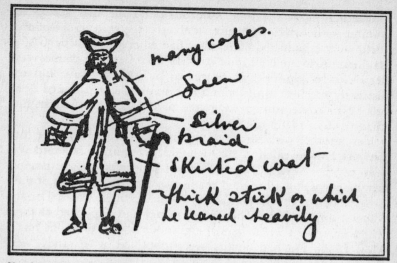

many capes.

Green

Silver braid

skirted coat

thick stick on which he leaned heavily

Sketch made by Clare Burrow of the man she 'saw' during a visit to the Petit Trianon in October 1928: 'many capes, silver braid, skirted coat, thick stick on which he leaned heavily'.

buildings near the Gardener's Gate, and the reference to the Temple of Love should be to the Belvédère. With the aid of a map M. Dayet worked out with Miss Burrow the route she and her companion took, and it was clear that the man in green was encountered quite soon after they had entered the garden near the Belvédère.

Miss Burrow added some details: the woman who looked down from the farmhouse window was wearing 'a type of high muslin mob cap'; the man in livery (she enclosed a sketch) was wearing a long green skirted coat, with multiple collars edged with silver braid, large cuffs, stockings which she thought were white, buckled shoes, and was carrying a stick with knob and tassel. As described, Lambert noted after interviewing Miss Burrow and Lady Hay, the man was clearly wearing a 'reding-ote', a kind of overcoat with multiple collars and wide cuffs, which was a good deal worn in France and England during the last thirty years of the eighteenth century.

Lady Hay generally corroborated Miss Burrow's account. She shared the feeling of depression, not attributable to any personal

circumstances at the time. She did not remember seeing the
woman at the window, but certainly saw the man in out-of-date
costume at a point soon after they had entered the garden. After
all these years she could not confirm from her own memory the
details of his clothing, as described by Miss Burrow; but she
distinctly recollected the sound of his voice, as he seemed to be
talking in some strange language or patois. She thought him
'queer', but was not frightened.

Yet another 'adventure' at Versailles, also involving two
persons, was revealed in 1957 when a large bundle of letters was
sent to the SPR by a well-known journalist on a national
newspaper who had invited readers to send in accounts of their
experiences of the 'supernatural'. Among them was a London
solicitor and his wife. They related what had happened to them
when they went walking in the grounds of the Trianons on 21
May 1955. Further details were obtained when they were
questioned by an official of the Society.

The 'adventure' started when the solicitor and his wife were
proceeding along a path leading to the Hameau. On the left there
was a wall with gaps in it and beyond the wall a deep and muddy
ditch; on their right, open parkland dotted with trees, chiefly
conifers. The weather was very close and oppressive after a heavy
thunderstorm. There was an extraordinary feeling of tenseness in
the air; the solicitor's wife felt unaccountably depressed. They
had seen no one since leaving the Grand Trianon to pass through
the grounds of the Petit Trianon on the way to Marie Antoinette's village. Suddenly the sun came out and she saw, coming
towards them down a long grassy avenue on the right which
joined their path ahead, a woman between two men.

They were then between ninety and one hundred yards away.
As they came closer she was attracted by the colour of the
woman's dress: it was yellow of an unusual brilliance. The dress
was fluffed out at the waist, very full and to the ground.

'What a lovely colour,' the solicitor's wife thought. 'I must
look at it closely when these people pass on.' The men appeared
to be in black but she did not notice details of their clothing.

The solicitor, on the other hand, did observe what the men
were wearing. He had first seen the group when it was directly
ahead of them on the same path and about fifty or sixty yards

away; the woman, in the long yellow dress, and the two men in black, strolling along and talking quietly among themselves. As they approached he saw that the men were wearing long coats, open in front and nearly down to their knees at the back. They had black breeches, black stockings, black shoes with silver buckles, and black hats (but when interviewed, he could not recall their shape). He felt no surprise when he saw these figures; in fact, he took no more notice than he would of any persons seen casually walking in a public park. His wife was on his right and he continued talking to her, mostly about the trees in the park.

Suddenly he became aware that the little group approaching them had vanished. It was impossible, he reasoned to himself, that they could have gone from the path to his left because of the wall and the ditch.

'That's odd,' he said to his wife. 'Where have those persons gone?'

She agreed with him that it was strange that the group had disappeared.

The solicitor's wife, in her account of the disappearance, said, 'Then a peculiar thing happened. It was as though a curtain were drawn across my mind, obliterating the vision, and I entirely forgot them till we reached the spot where I had seen them, when my husband suddenly said: "That's odd. Did you see a lady with two gentlemen walking towards us? What's happened to them? They've vanished!"'

When the route taken by the solicitor and his wife was studied, it appeared that the junction of the paths marked what was once a corner of the old wood of Les Onze Arpents, laid down during the reign of Louis XIV. The wood contained a hexagon with diagonals of formal broad avenues. A possibility considered later was that the apparitions were following the course of one of the diagonals, and they then disappeared into a corner of the wood. These formal avenues were swept away by the time Richard Mique, architect to Marie Antoinette, had finished the replanning of this part of the grounds in 1786 (51a pp. 58–60).

The solicitor, then in early middle age, had read *An Adventure* in 1954, but had never seen an apparition prior to his walk in the park at Versailles the following year. His wife, however, before her marriage had several times seen what she thought to be an apparition. One of these experiences, told here for the first time, concerned the apparition of an Irish wolfhound named Megan which, she said, was seen by a number of people, including children, in a school at Nonington, near Dover, Kent, before World War II. She herself saw the dog three times: once in daylight and twice at night. On two occasions the animal was only a foot away. 'It was in view only a few moments, seemingly solid, but I remember no shadows. I was taken utterly by surprise – it was there and then it was not! I was alone on all occasions. I had the impression that Megan liked company.' The apparition is believed to be that of an animal which was lost on the downs in the early part of the century when the building at Nonington was a private residence (it was destroyed by fire in 1945).

The solicitor's wife sent me her account of the apparition of an animal after reading my book *Apparitions and Ghosts* (51c pp. 136–44), which contained reports of other strange experiences at Versailles. One concerned the visit of Mr Jack Wilkinson, a poultry farmer, of Levens, near Kendal, Westmorland, with his wife, Mrs Clara Wilkinson, and their four-year-old son to Versailles in 1949. On 10 October, which was a fine sunny day, they entered the park by the statue of Neptune and approached the Grand Trianon by way of the cottages and garden nurseries. As they came out of the woods at 11.0 a.m. they saw a woman standing on top of the steps of the Trianon about fifty yards away. What impressed them immediately was her costume. She was wearing a light gold-coloured crinoline-type dress reaching to the ground, a large picture hat, and was carrying a stick or parasol. She was of medium height, with dark ringlets to her shoulders, and according to Mrs Wilkinson was aged between twenty-five and thirty. There was nothing ghostlike about her. Their son also saw the figure.

Mr and Mrs Wilkinson felt astonished at seeing someone dressed like this in the park and wondered how she had entered it without attracting attention. As they walked towards the building the woman moved to the balustrade overlooking the arm of the Grand Canal. Not wishing to watch her all the time, they turned their attention to the building, and when they looked in her direction after a few moments she had disappeared. They went at once to the balustrade, feeling 'a bit queer', in Mr Wilkinson's words, but could see no sign of the figure, which had been in view for two or three minutes.

The Wilkinsons had not seen anyone else since entering the park. In reply to a question about their mood, Mr Wilkinson said, 'We cannot remember being in any special mood, except that there was a noticeable quiet and stillness about the place.' He had not, he said, read *An Adventure*.

Another strange experience was that of Mrs Elizabeth Hatton, a former resident of Oxford. Early in September 1938, she was walking down an avenue in the park of the Petit Trianon towards Marie Antoinette's village when suddenly, about six feet from her, two figures appeared. 'I could see by their dress they were peasants,' Mrs Hatton wrote to me. 'The woman was wearing a brown sort of fustian dress with white kerchief across her shoulders and the white frilly cap, the man in fustian clothes. They were drawing along a little wooden trundle cart, with logs of wood on it. They passed quite close without saying a word. I was completely baffled and turned to watch where they were going . . . as I watched them they seemed gradually to vanish.'

The time was about midday, the sun was shining, and Mrs Hatton was alone. She claimed to have been in her usual mood, and enjoying her holiday in Paris. The two figures showed not the slightest awareness of her. As the cart passed it made no sound.

I asked Mrs Hatton if she had read *An Adventure*, or heard the Versailles case discussed *before* she had her experience, and she replied that she had not.

A pessimistic view of the value of the evidence for anything paranormal in *An Adventure* was taken by W. H. Salter in a paper in the *Journal* in 1950 (76c pp. 178–87). He based his comments on (a) the various editions of the book; (b) letters and notes of interviews in the SPR archives; and (c) such of the documents concerning the case in the Bodleian Library, Oxford, as he was able to see on a visit in 1935, and others inspected later by a friend at his request.

Salter pointed out that the Versailles 'adventure' lacked what should be the starting point in any case of paranormal perception, namely an unambiguous description of what had been experienced recorded in such a way as to exclude faults of memory. Also, it had long been recognized that the possibilities of a normal explanation were much greater when a supposedly paranormal perception occurs out of doors than when it takes place in a room. 'A public park is, evidentially, about the worst setting for a ghost-story, especially if the supposed ghosts can only be identified from descriptions made months, or possibly years, later. No one can say what persons, beside the authors, were in the gardens of the Petit Trianon on 10 August 1901 during the time of their visit . . . By 1911 all that was possible was to consider whether the persons described were the sort of persons who might naturally have been met in the Versailles of 1901.'

For instance, the uniform worn by the 'gardeners' could have been that of minor functionaries on a visit. France was full of all sorts of uniforms and Versailles attracted visitors from all over the country. The cloaks and sombreros (or slouch hats) of the sitting and running men were an attire much affected by contemporary artists. M. Sage, who knew Versailles well, gave it as his opinion in 1911 that all the supposed eighteenth-century persons described in the book might well have been met in the flesh in the Versailles of 1901.

In Salter's opinion, the two ladies 'recorded, investigated, and published their experience in such a way as to leave the whole affair in an impenetrable fog of uncertainty . . . As the book still attracts attention, the time has come when it can without offence be pointed out how two extremely able women, starting out with the best intentions, muddled their case at an early stage so completely as to make all their later labours useless: and all because they had not joined the SPR!'

However, during the past thirty years Salter's 'impenetrable fog of uncertainty' has begun to lift from the landscape of Versailles, thanks to Lambert's researches, published in a series of papers in the *Journal*, and to Mr and Mrs Gibbons in *The Trianon Adventure, a Symposium*, to which Lambert and Joan Evans contributed (24).

It is helpful for the understanding of this case to begin with the history of the Petit Trianon. The house was intended by Louis XV to be the home of his mistress, the Marquise de Pompadour. It was designed by Gabriel, the Royal Architect; work was started in 1762, but two years later the Marquise died. Madame Dubarry became the next Royal mistress and occasionally lived in the house when it was taken over by the King on 9 September 1770.

The house, as finally planned, required a large kitchen block, and the original one was finished in 1770. However, additions were necessary to this block, and the work of providing them was carried out in the next two years. The King had a small menagerie and home farm in the grounds, and a plan by Gabriel shows a carriageway leading to the Allée de la Ménagerie, as the broad way out was called. Gabriel's plan was to scale and the width between the gate posts was nearly sixteen feet.

The carriageway was not to stay open very long. The King decided that the house should have a chapel, and this was finished in 1773. As the chapel was to replace certain kitchen and service premises, these had to be provided elsewhere, and it was in the course of the extensions that the carriageway was closed. Arnold Gibbons maintained that it could be established irrefutably that the southern end of the Allée de la Ménagerie was obliterated by 1771 at the latest.

Gabriel's kitchen block, before the kitchen was built, provided a door at the top of some steps, which then went westwards into the garden. These steps were replaced by the present steps descending northwards into the garden, serving both the chapel doors and the present service door.

Miss Moberly and Miss Jourdain said in the section of their book devoted to the results of research that 'In 1905 we found that the building out of which the man came was the old chapel, which is in a ruinous condition.' It did not occur to them that the 'man' could have come out of a kitchen; and in the light of this Miss Moberly's description of their arrival at the building takes on a new significance. The terrace, she wrote, 'was prolonged at right angles in front of what seemed to be a second house. The door of it suddenly opened, and a young man stepped out on to the terrace, banging the door behind him. He had the jaunty manner of a footman, but no livery, and called to us, saying that the way into the house was by the *cour d'honneur*, and offered to show us the way round.'

Discussing the incident in my book *The Unexplained*, I asked what would a man dressed like this, and with the air of a footman, be doing in a chapel, unless he were sweeping the floor? He was dressed for work in a kitchen; and in 1770–71, the door out of which he stepped was a kitchen door. Some doors at that time were equipped with a rope, pulley and weight so that they would close behind the person who had pulled the door open; the fact that a door constantly being opened and shut as servants hurried about with refreshments for the King's guests could have such a piece of equipment would account for the slamming sound heard by the two ladies.

Two important figures would be found in the gardens in 1770: the Royal gardeners, who were Claude Richard, then aged sixty-five, and his son Antoine, aged thirty-five. Claude's father was of Irish stock and had followed the British King James II into exile in France. Such was Claude's fame as a gardener that Louis XV, having decided to develop the park and gardens of the Petit Trianon, offered him the post of gardener. He did not want to accept, but did so eventually on condition that he took orders from none but the King himself.

The two royal gardeners lived in houses near the gardeners' gate. In his paper on Antoine Richard's Garden in 1955 (44d pp. 15–16), Lambert produced for the first time conclusive evidence that in 1775 or 1776 the Richards (father and son) wore a green livery, a conclusion based on a document in the National Archives discovered by M. Léon Rey which set out Queen Marie Antoinette's wishes for her Petit Trianon. It includes the phrase, 'It is thought that as the Richards are in green, they ought to be in red with blue velvet facings.' In the margin, near the end of the document, in a different hand, is written, *Oui partout*, endorsement clearly signifying Louis XV's approval of the proposals.

Lambert asked Miss Burrow how old the man she saw in 1928 appeared to be and her answer was 'sixtyish'. This would accord with the age of Claude Richard in 1770. In his later paper on Richard's Garden Revisited, Lambert gave the results of further research into the costume of the man seen by Miss Burrow. The type of coat which had three capes, large cuffs, and skirts down to just below the knee was attributed to the period 1715–73, and was called a 'Roquelaure' after its designer, the Duc de Roquelaure. Rather outré in style, it was the predecessor of the redingote, which was somewhat more restrained. The change to the latter seems to have taken place about 1775. Lambert remarked that 'it is curious that in 1928, long before anyone had suggested that a date as early as 1770 should be attributed to the visions seen in 1901, Miss Burrow should have described a man dressed in livery so much more appropriate in cut and colour to that earlier period than to 1789' (44e p. 291).

Of all the people seen during the 'adventure' of Miss Moberly and Miss Jourdain in the park and gardens of the Petit Trianon on 10 August 1901, Claude and Antoine Richard are the only ones to have been identified with any degree of probability.

While Miss Moberly and Miss Jourdain were talking to the two men in green the latter saw to the right of them 'a detached solidly built cottage, with stone steps at the door. A woman and a girl were standing at the doorway, and I particularly noticed their unusual dress; both wore white kerchiefs tucked into the bodice, and the girl's dress, though she looked thirteen or fourteen only, was down to her ankles. The woman was passing a jug to the girl, who wore a close white cap.' This cottage no longer existed in 1901, but Arnold Gibbons proved that one had once stood on the site indicated by Miss Jourdain by buying a 'utility grade kitchen poker' in a hardware shop with which to trace the foundations of it through the soft loamy soil.

There has been much speculation about the kiosk seen by Miss Moberly and Miss Jourdain and sketched by the former from memory in 1904. If there was one it could not have stood very long because it is not shown in any map of the grounds before the Revolution – that is, at the time of Marie Antoinette – or after the Revolution. Marie Antoinette took little interest in horticulture, but Louis XV did. The old king often walked with Claude Richard among the nursery beds in the northern parts of the ground. Possibly musicians played for him in a nearby kiosk, but a more likely reason for the existence of a kiosk would be to afford him shelter from a sudden shower.

The first evidence found that a circular pavilion existed in that part of the garden where the two ladies said they saw one is provided by Mr and Mrs Gibbons in their contribution to *The Trianon Adventure*. They found in a box in the National Archives an account 'for work done in clearing ground to form terraces' in that part of the gardens where the Belvédère, the *rocher* and part of the lake now stand. The accounts seem to be in the handwriting of Antoine Richard, who was responsible for the payment and indeed the engagement of the labourers. The second document, dated 1776, a much more detailed account dealing with the same area, has the arresting item: 'Digging out and freeing from stones another part adjoining the circular pavilion – 27 X 15 toises'. A toise equalled approximately 6.4 feet.

'Moreover this evidence does confine the date of [the ladies'] vision, for the little kiosk cannot have survived after 1776, by which date it must of necessity have been swept away by the general transformations in the area,' Mr and Mrs Gibbons stated (24 p. 41).

King Louis XV died in May 1774. The new King, his grandson, Louis XVI, gave the Petit Trianon and its grounds to his Queen, Marie Antoinette, who immediately planned changes in the park. Claude Richard appears to have chosen this moment to pass into virtual retirement, although he continued to live at the Petit Trianon and to interest himself in the work of his son, the new royal gardener. Antoine Richard was asked to prepare a project for a new garden, and we know from his plan, made in 1774, that there was a tall rock in the middle of a path near the gardeners' gate. Yet another piece of the puzzle has fallen into place. However, Antoine Richard's plan was rejected as mediocre, and the redesigning of the gardens was undertaken by a gifted amateur gardener, the Comte de Caraman. Changes ordered by the Queen were put into effect in 1775–6.

The indications are, therefore, that Miss Moberly and Miss Jourdain 'saw' the park as it was between 1770 and 1774. As the southern end of the Allée de la Ménagerie was obliterated by 1771 at the latest, and it is unlikely that the house would be shuttered, and the gardens deserted, after the King had taken over the house in September 1770, the two ladies may have seen the scenery of the park as it was in August 1770. At this time Marie Antoinette had been married to the Dauphin for only a few months and was not yet fifteen. This disposes of Miss Moberly's suggestion that the 'sketching lady' she saw was the apparition of the ill-fated Queen.

It still has to be explained how the two ladies made their way to the avenue. In their 'Results of Research' they said that 'The road from the garden to the avenue (through which the man ushered us) was not far from the chapel and was broad enough to admit a coach. The present one is narrower and farther to the west.'

It is highly significant that the women saw this carriageway, but it is quite obvious that they could not have gone out that way in 1901 because this would have meant passing through several solid walls. As Mrs Sidgwick remarked in her review of the book in 1911, 'a good deal of evidence would be required before a phenomenon of this kind could be accepted as fact.' A possible explanation is that Miss Moberly and Miss Jourdain were passing out of their trancelike state of mind as they went towards the avenue, took the usual gate which was there in 1901 as their point of exit, and did not register the fact. My comment on this aspect of the case in *The Unexplained* is that 'Mediums often experience a period of confusion as they come out of trance and, although they would hate to be described as mediums, Miss Moberly and Miss Jourdain were, I believe, in a confused state of mind as they left the gardens to enter the house, but this is not to say that they were in a confused state of mind earlier as they walked through the grounds.' It may be argued, of course, that there is little difference between being confused and being hallucinated, but it has been established that some hallucinations convey information which can be confirmed.

In his summing-up of the Versailles case in the SPR *Journal* (44e p. 281), Lambert said that taking only the visit of 10 August 1901, eight features could be listed which were quite inconsistent with the 1901 scene.

1. Two gardeners (or dignified officials) in greenish clothing and small three-cornered hats;
2. a tall rock blocking the view up a path near the gardeners' gate;
3. a temple or kiosk, of light construction, circular like a small bandstand, having pillars and a low surrounding wall;
4. a narrow meadow of long grass, bounded on farther side by trees, and very much overshadowed by trees, a barrier on the right shutting out the view of the house, till they were close to

it. [The plan of the garden as it was in Louis XV's time shows that anyone approaching the house from the north would have to pass along a narrow headland, presumably with grass underfoot, a thick hedge on the right, ensuring the privacy of the small garden on the north front and numerous trees on the left, in what was a nursery garden of trees. In the notice advertising the latter for sale at the end of 1774, the trees were described as 'fully grown'. As this part of the garden was cleared of most trees in the 1776 upheaval, here, too, a date before that year is indicated];

5. a feeling of loneliness, and hardly anyone about;

6. a shuttered house. On 10 August 1901 the garden was not deserted and the house was not shuttered;

7. a servant coming out of a garden doorway, opening out of the kitchen block (later called the Chapel door). In 1901 the floors behind the Chapel door and the service door next to it were ruinous, and an ordinary man could not have come out of either door;

8. a way out of the French garden, not far from the house, wide enough for a coach – the best clue of all, in Lambert's opinion, to the date to which the visions refer.

If the idea that the visions were retrocognitive was wholly misconceived, Lambert concluded, he could not believe that they would have thrown up anything like eight features consistent with the situation in about 1770, yet quite inconsistent with the scene in 1901. And in the two narratives there were some twenty distinguishable features in all. Besides the eight already mentioned, there were twelve, *viz.*: a plough, a rustic bridge, a small ravine, a cascade, two cottages, three women and three men (other than the gardeners). Two, the plough and one cottage, were distinctly relevant to 1770, but were not there in 1901. The rest were not inconsistent with that dating.

Mr Lambert said:

The eight 'verified' features form forty per cent of the whole, a much higher proportion than one would expect to find in the circumstances. Attempts to verify historical descriptions, purporting to be retrocognitive, given by sensitives as visions of the past, are usually fruitless. Often the details given are too unimportant to have been recorded anywhere, and not infrequently names of persons and places are discovered to be fictitious, and events to be false, the whole dramatization turning out to be pure fantasy. A very detailed and life-like description is no more likely to be veridical than a vague one. It is therefore very surprising to find any 'hits' at all in this case.

Further, if the effect is merely accidental, one would expect to find that a more careful ascertainment of facts on the historical side would soon lead to a divergence between vision and past fact that would soon dispose of any link between them. Here, on the contrary, the discoveries about the circular pavilion and the broad way out have led to a closer approximation of the visions to the facts than was at one time thought possible . . .

This review of the visionary material in *An Adventure* suggests that, if related to the year 1770, it kept closely to actual scenery, and that there is no need to interpret any details as symbolic. Attempts to explain the whole episode away, as having been due to temporary indisposition, bad memory, wishful thinking, possible manipulation of the data after the event, so as to produce spurious effects, and so on, would be more telling if the material was utterly confused, or else warped in the direction of the prejudices of the authors, i.e. towards the years 1789–92. But we find that the data point to a year which was not canvassed by either author . . .

Nor is it relevant to decry their academic qualifications or their behaviour long after the event. In cases where percipients see, out of doors, visions of houses, etc. which are believed to be 'non-existent' they are allowed to pass without being subjected to the kind of attacks made against the authors of *An Adventure*. The reason appears to be that in the latter case there was a suggestion that the visions in some way reflected the historic past. Nature has geared us so closely to the present that a direct intrusion from the past usually causes a feeling of acute embarrassment, and an instinctive urge to explain it away at once as an impossibility. The history of science furnishes so many examples of supposed impossibilities which have later been realized that it is hardly safe to trust to instinctive guidance in matters of this kind.

The whole question of the validity of the 'adventure' by Miss Moberly and Miss Jourdain in 1901 was revived in 1965 by the publication of Philippe Jullian's book *Un Prince 1900 – Robert de Montesquiou* (42) in which the author suggested that there was a natural explanation for the experience of the two ladies: they had wandered into the park when the poet and his friends were rehearsing, in eighteenth-century costume, a *tableau-vivant* for a fête. The relevant passage in the English translation of the book is as follows:

Montesquiou and Yturri [the poet's Peruvian secretary] would spend whole days in the park of the Trianon, attracting to it both poets and elegant women who came to listen to Nolhac [Pierre de Nolhac, a writer who had keys to the park] or to Montesquiou himself. Mme Greffulhe [a friend of the poet] organized a fancy-dress party for charity in the Dairy. The two friends were so very much at home there that it is possible to suggest an explanation for the strange encounter which two extremely rational English women dons at an Oxford college experienced in the park. These ladies published, under the title of *An Adventure*, an account of how they both witnessed the apparitions of people in bygone costumes and heard mysterious music. Perhaps, however, the 'ghosts' which they took for Marie Antoinette and her courtiers were, quite simply, Mme Greffulhe, dressed as a shepherdess, rehearsing an entertainment with some friends. Or 'Marie-Antoinette' may have been Mme d'Hervey de Saint-Denis, of whom Montesquiou possessed several photographs in the costume of the queen. The description of one of the apparitions by Miss Moberly [the running man seen by the rock] exactly corresponds to Yturri . . . Did the visitors intrude upon one of those re-enactments of the past that the poet devised for a rigidly exclusive circle of chosen friends? That would explain the panic of the more or less disguised participants and the manner in which a short young man slammed a door in their faces . . . It is extremely rare in the whole history of apparitions for two people to see the same images and to hear the sounds at exactly the same time . . .

One who was convinced by M. Jullian's explanation for the events of 10 August 1901 was Dr Joan Evans, to whom Miss Moberly and Miss Jourdain had bequeathed the copyright of the book. Dr Evans had always been a most loyal supporter of the two ladies, and had contributed a preface to the fifth and final edition of *An Adventure* in 1955 (Faber). Now, convinced that there was a natural explanation for the 'adventure', she decided that the case should be decently buried and that there should be no further editions of the book, at least in English. As she explained in her article 'An end to An Adventure' in the literary magazine *Encounter*, 'New evidence has come to light, which in my view provides a rational explanation of the story, with no supernatural element remaining. At the same time the integrity of the ladies is completely vindicated and the accuracy of their observations in great measure confirmed. The justification of maintaining the book in print was that it should be available to those interested in psychical research. In my view the reason is no longer valid, and I do not propose to authorize a reprint or fresh edition of *An Adventure*' (21b).

I had been aware of Dr Evans's decision not to allow the reprinting of the book since 1969, and have in my files a copy of a letter I sent her pointing out the significance of the research which revealed the existence, in 1770–71, of features in the park which were not there in 1901, and of the experiences of the Crooke family, Miss Burrow and Miss Lambert, and the solicitor and his wife. However, Dr Evans, as she was then, would have none of it. She replied that her decision not to reprint *An Adventure* was 'irrevocable' and I was invited to 'kindly consider the matter closed.'

Dame Joan – she was made a DBE in 1976 – was a noted historian of French and English medieval art. She died on 14 July 1977 at the age of eighty-four. In her last years she changed her mind and allowed a new edition of *An Adventure* to be published, but it was in French: *Les Fantômes de Trianon* (1) was produced with her approval, and she was quoted on the jacket as stating that the present French edition was superior to all others.

The author, M. Amadou, a scholar who has made a special study of the Versailles case, gave details of some experiences in the park of the Petit Trianon that were new to me.

One which I quoted in my review of the book in the *Journal* (51g pp. 187–9) concerned Robert Philippe, a cabinet maker and teacher of drawing and the history of art, who, after seeing a TV programme in 1968 about the phantoms of the Trianon, wrote to describe his own adventure there one June morning several years before the outbreak of war in 1939. He went with his parents to visit the dairy in Marie Antoinette's 'village' in the park. The place was otherwise deserted. He went behind a tree (it is not necessary to expand on the reason), and on the way to rejoin his parents, who had gone on ahead, he had the impression of a presence at his side: it was that of a woman. Embarrassed at having been surprised, he lit a cigarette. The woman entered into conversation with him. She had a foreign accent. Did she live in Paris? No, she lived at the Trianon. He did not think that the Trianon was inhabited. 'But it is for me.' The cigarette had gone out and M. Philippe relit it. When he turned his head the 'woman' had disappeared. His parents had not seen the figure and had heard him talking, they believed, to himself.

If this proves anything it is that the British are not the only people to have strange experiences in the park of the Petit Trianon; some French commentators on the case have derived amusement from what they regard as the British fondness for ghost stories which they carried with them across the Channel and placed in a new setting at Versailles.

When we look back on this case we see that it has been viewed differently by influential members of the SPR, not surprisingly, as the Society does not hold a corporate opinion. Mrs Sidgwick took an unfavourable view; understandably, because all she had available to her was the results of the poor research by Miss Moberly and Miss Jourdain. As Dr Evans pointed out in her foreword to *The Trianon Adventure*, 'they planned and tackled their researches in an amateurish way, with little sense of the relative value of primary and secondary evidence, and a very sketchy idea of such fundamentals as the organization of the French household.' Salter, too, was irritated by the muddled presentation of the evidence.

Still, as Dr Evans pointed out, Miss Jourdain had 'learned enough to go to the original archives, even if she sometimes got lost in their intricacies; and at least she discovered enough to make the strangeness of the story notable.'

As for Lambert, he was set on the trail of the Versailles 'adventure' by an article he read in the *Revue de Paris* of December 1952 under the title of 'Une Promenade hors du Temps', by Léon Rey, whose book *Le Petit Trianon et le Hameau de Marie-Antoinette* (69) attracted much attention. M. Rey discussed the kiosk 'seen' by the two ladies, and in following up the research to date of this feature of the visionary scene Lambert was led to a conclusion which was 'both extraordinary and unexpected', as he expressed it in the first of the series of articles on the case he contributed to the Society's *Journal* (44b p. 123).

Lambert's finding that the eight 'verified' features in the two narratives form forty per cent of the whole demands respect. If we add another verified feature, the foundations of the walls of the cottage traced by Arnold Gibbons with a poker, the total becomes nine, or forty-five per cent. Dame Joan Evans, on the other hand, offered no evidence whatsoever for her conclusion that Count Robert de Montesquiou and his friends were in the park on 10 August 1901. 'I am myself quite sure that what the ladies saw was a Dress Rehearsal for one of the Montesquiou parties,' she wrote to me; but how could she be sure?

Others have shared my doubts about her 'explanation'. Brian Inglis wrote in the London *Evening Standard* on 9 March 1977 that 'Joan Evans, who edited one of the editions of *An Adventure*, thinks that she has solved the mystery: what the ladies saw was a rehearsal for a *tableau-vivant* to be given by Robert de Montesquiou . . . It is possible, but it is certainly not yet the explanation, as she seems to imagine . . . the theory is still merely speculation.' Lady Gladwyn, wife of a former British ambassador to France, said in a letter to *Encounter* in March 1977, 'With the greatest respect, Dame Joan Evans is too categorical in declaring that a full explanation has at last been found for *An Adventure*. She bases her discovery on suggestions made by Philippe Jullian in his biography of Robert de Montesquiou, but she produces no hard evidence.'

It seemed obvious to me that, before the theory of de Montesquiou and his friends being the figures seen by the two English-women could be accepted, it had to be reasonably certain that the Count was a resident of Versailles at the time of the 'adventure', August 1901. It was known that he had lived in Versailles in the 1890s, but was he still there in 1901? For years I had been trying without success to find the solution to this problem, and received it only when this book was in the final stages of revision. For this I have to thank M. François Chapon, Conservator of the University of Paris's Bibliothèque Littéraire Jacques Doucet. He wrote in January 1981, to say that in the library they had visiting cards and letters from Montesquiou to the poet Mallarmé, in 1896, with the address 80 rue de l'Université, Paris, 7 ème. So the Count was not in Versailles in 1901; and the theory, advanced by Philippe Jullian and embraced by Joan Evans, collapses.

It may be argued, of course, that Montesquiou and his friends could have gone to Versailles for the day or the weekend, and at the house of a friend donned costumes appropriate to the time of Marie Antoinette, but this is unconvincing, particularly when the distance between Paris and Versailles is taken into account.

For an explanation of Dame Joan's attitude to the 'adventure' in the closing years of a long life we must look to its controversial aspects. She had presumably become tired of defending the intellectual honesty of two women she greatly respected; when she saw a way out with honour she took it. It is significant that she was unwilling to discuss with me the experiences of others in the park of the Petit Trianon because, once they were admitted, they could not be attributed to Robert de Montesquiou and his friends.

In my opinion, too little attention has been paid to the experiences of the Crooke family, Miss Burrow and Miss Lambert, Mrs Hatton, the Wilkinson family and the solicitor and his wife in assessing the Versailles 'adventure'. I also have in my records accounts of other experiences at Versailles that have still to be assessed; and I have little doubt that after the publication of this book I will receive still more. Still, it will continue to be argued that when people have had strange experiences at Versailles it is the result of suggestion after reading *An Adventure*; and even the assertion of some people who have had such experiences that they had not read the book or heard about the case does not deter determined critics, who point out that the people concerned could have heard about the 'adventure' but forgotten that they had done so.

For this reason the Society has been anxious to hear of experiences which pre-date those of Miss Moberly and Miss Jourdain. There were high hopes that one had come to light when a letter written on 14 January 1957 by Mrs Dorothy Wright, of Thornton Stewart, Ripon, Yorkshire, reached the Society. It ran:

In view of the publicity that has been given both in the Press and on the wireless lately to the 'Ghosts of Versailles' I thought this might be of interest to you. About 1870 my grandmother Lady [Julia] Smith Dodsworth took her three children – my Uncle Fred, Matt, and my mother, Nina – to France for a year to a house they rented close to Versailles. One day my Uncle Fred aged about eleven went to play in the gardens of Versailles and came back to my grandmother full of the people, etc., he had seen in the gardens, describing them and their clothes, etc., in great detail – he had a great gift for description as shown by some of his letters and 'Journals'. My grandmother, realizing that what he described to her was not of that day but of a past age, wrote his account down, and my mother used often to tell me of his 'Adventure' (as it was known) when I was a child and it was always one of my favourite stories. After I grew up I picked up the book called 'The Adventure' (*sic*) in a house where I was staying and to my great astonishment found it to be the same story as told me by my mother in about 1900 – in the broad sense identical but of course not so much detail as in the book: my grandmother died in 1893 (?) and my Uncle Fred about 1905. My grandmother never published any of her 'Journals' and never had any connection in any way with the authors of 'The Adventure'. But in view of the fact that the story has been brought before the public eye and so discussed, I thought this might be of interest to you. I could give you exact dates, etc., if you should think it worthwhile.

I travelled to Yorkshire to interview Mrs Wright. The family had a flat in the Rue Maurepas, she told me; and one day the boy came home with a story about having seen a hunt come through the trees in the gardens, with the huntsmen wearing jackets of green velvet, with gold braid, and three-cornered hats. He also saw 'a lovely lady with a beautiful dress'. I brought the evidence to the SPR; enquiries were made in Paris, and it was learned that hunting still took place in the woods of Versailles in 1870, the time of Napoleon III. The boy, therefore, could have seen one of the last meetings of the Imperial Hunt before the outbreak of the Franco-Prussian war. If there is a lesson to be learned from this it is that a natural explanation for an event must always be sought before it is assumed that it is paranormal.

Discussion on the Versailles case has centred almost exclusively on the experiences of Miss Moberly and Miss Jourdain, with particular emphasis on whether the features they saw in the park could have been those that were there at the time or whether the 'apparitions' could have been figures of flesh and blood, i.e. Robert de Montesquiou and his friends. In my opinion, the discussion should be widened to include other reported experiences in the park. When this is done the case will be seen in an entirely new light.

Miss Moberly, for instance, saw a 'sketching lady'. The same figure was seen in 1908 by three members of the artistic Crooke family, and as it seemed to grow out of the scenery 'with a little quiver of adjustment' it could hardly have been that of a living person. Miss Moberly and Miss Jourdain saw two figures in green uniforms. A figure also in a green uniform of a bygone age was seen in the park in 1928 by Miss Burrow and Miss Lambert. Something sinister in his face caused the two women to hurry on, and, looking back, they saw that he had completely vanished. Where did he go? This experience suggests that the figure seen was not a living one. The figures in the clothes of peasants seen pulling a trundle cart with logs of wood on it by Mrs Hatton in the park in 1938 were in view for a few seconds and, as she watched, 'seemed gradually to vanish.' The woman wearing a light gold crinoline-type dress seen by the Wilkinson family at the Grand Trianon in 1949 disappeared when they glanced away for a few moments. The three figures seen by the solicitor and his wife in the park in 1955 vanished while in full view. The two men who escorted the woman in a yellow dress of unusual brilliance wore black breeches, black stockings and black shoes with silver buckles. This is not the costume of the present day.

If we accept the above accounts it should be obvious that the figures seen were not those of living persons. M. Jullian remarked in his book on Robert de Montesquiou, 'It is extremely rare in the whole history of apparitions for two people to see the same images and to hear the sounds at exactly the same time.' In this he is mistaken. With the exception of Mrs Hatton's experience, all those given here were collective (I do not include Miss Jourdain's accounts of her visits when she was alone).

Some commentators on the case have shown little awareness of what is involved in retrocognitive and hallucinatory experiences. First of all, let us consider the hallucinatory aspects of the case. According to Miss Jourdain, the two men in green answered her question about the way, 'in a seemingly casual and mechanical way.' The woman and the girl at the cottage, 'seemed to pause for an instant, as in a *tableau vivant*.' Miss Jourdain herself began to feel as if she were walking in her sleep; the heavy dreaminess was oppressive. When she came across the man sitting on the steps of the kiosk 'the eerie feeling which had begun in the garden culminated in a definite impression of something uncanny and fear-inspiring'. Miss Moberly also felt that she and her friend were walking in a dream – 'the stillness and oppressiveness were so unnatural.' From these few extracts from the two narratives it should be obvious that the two women were far from being in a normal state of mind during the walk.

It should be understood that during a retrocognitive experience the scenery is hallucinated while the person who has the vision, which may concern the landscape as it was in the past, remains in the present: he or she is not transported bodily to a former age. During some such experiences the landscape of the present day disappears. If we accept that the experience of Miss Moberly and Miss Jourdain related to the period of 1770–71 it is understandable that they did not see the Belvédère, the Temple de l'Amour, or the Jeu de Bague. These were built at a later date. There has been much discussion on whether the visitors could have mistaken the Belvédère, or the Temple de l'Amour, both of which still stand, for the kiosk they could not afterwards find; but it should be kept in mind that the Jeu de Bague, a kind of merry-go-round, built for the Queen in 1776, was swept away during the Revolution, and it is a fact that a circular pavilion once stood in the part of the park where they said they had seen it.

What was so unusual about the experience of Miss Moberly and Miss Jourdain during their first visit to the Petit Trianon was the length of time during which, to varying degrees, they hallucinated. The walk could easily have lasted thirty minutes. I do not know of any other reported experience in which a landscape of a bygone age, with figures appropriate to the period in it, was hallucinated for such a long time. Salter, though he did not accept the conclusions of Miss Moberly and Miss Jourdain, admitted that if they were sound, 'the authors had indeed had a most remarkable experience, much the most striking instance of paranormal retrocognition on record.'

When we take into consideration all the experiences outlined here, it will be seen that they fit into the pattern of an aimless haunting. There were no dramatic events at the Petit Trianon in the period 1770–71. The old King was still alive; the garden was as he wanted it to be; and the emotion that was to be engendered in the Court by the new Queen's plans for her garden was still a few years away. The rumblings that preceded the Revolution of 1789 had yet to be heard. Miss Moberly wondered whether she and Miss Jourdain 'had inadvertently entered within an act of the Queen's memory when alive', a statement which afterwards aroused a certain amount of derision. I think that we may speculate that some members of the Court felt that an era was drawing to an end, that the old order was passing, and in wandering around the grounds, soon to be so changed when the new Queen's plans for the gardens were put into effect, they pondered on these things with emotion. Beyond this we cannot go. A few days before writing this passage I read an interview in which Andrew Wyeth, the noted American painter, told William Feaver, art critic of the *Observer* newspaper, that 'There are places that have emotional power.' The Petit Trianon seems to be one such place. People who wander there on certain occasions seem to be able to activate scenes from the past.

Lambert ended his review of the case with the remark that Miss Moberly would not have accepted the view that her visions, either at Versailles or elsewhere, were of pathological origin. Her own psychological assessment of them is on record in a letter she wrote to Sir William Barrett from the Hôtel des Réservoirs, Versailles, on 15 August 1913, now in the archives of the SPR.

And now we have come to the stage of theorizing about them psychologically. Three principles seem to run through them all.

1. They come absolutely unexpectedly. The ordinary imaginative expectations which must accompany the first sight or still more the second or third sight of historic places do not of themselves produce the phenomena. We have experimented on this over and over again. Whatever has come has in every case been off the lines of ordinary expectation or knowledge and has presented itself as entirely natural; therefore the work of research into its historical significance has to be done independently of previous knowledge either on our part or of anyone else.

2. It is necessary to be in complete health and enjoyment, and full of living interest in *something else*. On every occasion our minds and conversation have been directed to quite different topics, and there has seemed to be no room for more than ordinary unexaggerated observation of what has passed round us; but that observation has been clear and definite to a point which has been unusual when compared with other recollections.

3. The meditative dreaminess, which is so often supposed to be the starting ground of visions, is not so with us. We cannot remember any personal occasions when poetic imaginations in half light, or appreciations of beauty in historic places, or nervous trepidation, have produced any pictorial images. To us – and we know such things well – such things tend rather to generalizations of thought. (44e pp. 291–2)

An important lesson from this case is that to reach a conclusion about subjects as complex as those dealt with here it is necessary to consider the evidence in detail, and not to come to a conclusion based on some hastily formed opinion that 'it must have been like this' or 'it must have been like that.' 'Must' does not come into our consideration of the evidence: at best we are dealing with probabilities, not certainties, and often the production of fresh evidence can show a case in a completely new light. We view the world in what we like to think is a commonsense way, but, as Dr R. H. Thouless pointed out in his preface to my book *Riddle of the Future*, 'there is nothing sacred about "commonsense"; it may only be the name for our firmly established habits of thought.'

Nor, I may add, should belief in the paranormal be attributed, as a matter of course, to the wish, or will, to believe, as is so often argued. Equally powerful may be the wish to disbelieve. I remember well the views of Rosalind Heywood on this subject. In a discussion we had on the repeated attacks on parapsychology by certain writers, she said that if the subject were 'all nonsense' it should be disregarded, and nothing more said, but the way in which some critics kept returning to the attack indicated, deep down, anxiety that the claims made for parapsychology might be true. I agree.

Two modern examples of ostensible retrocognition are given in this chapter. Although retrocognition is not the principal factor to be taken into consideration in studies of haunting, clearly it is a significant one in some cases. In Chapter 8 we had an example of a recurrent localized apparition, the figure of a Scottish clergyman of the old school, seen by three sisters and by some others; in Chapter 9 an account of figures of the past seen at Versailles. In this chapter the experiences described, although apparently retrocognitive, have not been reported by other people; so, strictly speaking, they cannot be advanced as examples of haunting. The Dieppe Raid Case is well known, but Miss Smith's experience of the aftermath of the battle of Nechtanesmere is less so. Perhaps publication will bring to light other experiences connected with this battle between the Picts and the Northumbrians.

When two English ladies in their early thirties, Mrs Dorothy Norton and her sister-in-law Miss Agnes Norton (pseudonyms have been provided for both), went on a summer holiday to Puys (Puits) near Dieppe, in France, in 1951 they were not to know that they would be involved in a most remarkable experience, apparently involving retrocognition. The sounds they heard on 4 August suggested those made during a raid on Dieppe, which is about one and a half miles from Puys, on 19 August 1942, during which Canadian forces sustained heavy casualties.

At Puys Dorothy and Agnes Norton shared a bedroom on the second floor of a three-storey house facing the sea, which was about a quarter of a mile away, down a steep path. The house, they were informed, had been used as quarters for German troops during the war. Mrs Norton's two children and their nurse, who heard nothing unusual, were in another bedroom on the same floor, two doors away. The times mentioned in the statements made afterwards to the SPR were taken from the two ladies' wristwatches. Both watches were set to 'Single Summer Time' (one hour ahead of GMT), which was also in use on 19 August 1942 for service purposes in the Allied Forces and for civil purposes in France. Agnes Norton was in the Women's Royal Naval Service during the war, and became accustomed to the accurate recording of time.

Dorothy Norton's statement about the events on Saturday 4 August 1951 is as follows:

At 4.20 a.m. A. got up and went out of the room. I said, 'Would you like to put the light on?', but she didn't. She came back in a few minutes. She said, 'Do you hear that noise?' I had in fact been listening to it for about 20 minutes. I woke up before it started. It started suddenly and sounded like a storm getting up at sea. A. said she had also been listening to it for about 20 minutes. We lay in the dark for a little listening to the sound. It sounded like a roar that ebbed and flowed, and we could distinctly hear the sounds of cries and shouts and gunfire. We put the light on and it continued. We went out on the balcony where we could look down towards the beach, though we could not actually see the sea. The noise came from that direction and became very intense, it came in rolls of sounds and the separate sounds of cries, guns and dive bombing were very distinct. Many times we heard the sound of a shell at the same moment. The roaring became very loud. At 4.50 it suddenly stopped. At 5.5 a.m. it started again and once more became very intense, so much so that as we stood on our balcony, we were amazed that it did not wake other people in the house. By now it was getting light, cocks were crowing and birds were singing. We heard a rifle shot on the hill above the beach.

The sounds became more distinctly those of dive bombers rather than the cries and shouts we had heard earlier, although we could still hear them. The noise was very loud and came in waves as before. It stopped abruptly at 5.40.

At 5.50 it started again but was not so loud and sounded more like planes. This died away at 6 a.m. At 6.20 a.m. the sound became audible again but it was fainter than before, and I fell asleep as I was very tired.

I was woken by a similar sound on Monday, July 30th, it sounded exactly the same only fainter and not so intense. At the end I seemed to hear a lot of men singing. It ended when the cocks started crowing and I went to sleep. My sister-in-law did not waken.

Agnes Norton also provided a statement:

I woke in what I realized was very early morning, although not yet dawn as no birds were singing. I was immediately aware of a most unusual series of sounds coming from the direction of the beach which were cries of men heard as if above a storm.

After listening for about 15 minutes I got up to leave the room and D. spoke to me and asked if I would like to put on the light which I did not in fact do. On my return I asked D. if she heard the noise too, and she said 'Yes', whereupon we put on the light and checked the time as 4.20 a.m. Our next move was out on to the balcony where the sounds intensified and appeared to me to be a mixture of gunfire, shellfire, dive bombers, landing craft and men's cries. All the sounds gave the impression of coming from a very long distance, i.e. like a broadcast from America in unmistakable waves of sound. At 4.50 a.m. all noises ceased abruptly and recommenced equally abruptly at 5.07 a.m. At 5.50 a.m. planes distinctly heard in large numbers and other fainter sounds dying away at 6 a.m. At 6.25 men's cries heard again gradually growing fainter and nothing at all heard after 6.55 a.m.

The statements were based on notes taken during the experience which lasted nearly three hours, from 4.0 a.m. to 7.0 a.m. They were prepared partly on the same day (4 August) and partly on the following day, before the two ladies left for England. They were posted to the Society by Mrs Norton with a covering letter dated 9 August, written after her return, describing the circumstances in which the experiences took place, and enquiring whether the Society had had any other reports of this kind.

Commenting on the experiences of the two ladies in an article in the *Journal* (44j pp. 607–18), G. W. Lambert and the late Honourable Mrs Kathleen Gay, a keen worker who had investigated a number of important cases, said that the remarkable feature of this case was the close correspondence between the times of the 'battle sounds' heard on 4 August 1951 and the times of the actual battle sounds resulting from the operations on 19 August 1942, a correspondence which was brought out in tabular form in the *Journal*. The only account of the raid which was in the hands of the two ladies at the time was in a French guidebook entitled *Dieppe*; and although they knew of its existence, they had not read it before the experience started. After the noise had begun, they read it on the balcony at about the middle of the third phase of the raid. Examination of the guidebook by Lambert indicated that the percipients' timetable could not have been obtained from the French account, except perhaps the time 5.50 for the sound of aircraft at the fifth phase of the raid. Agnes Norton assured the investigators that during her service in the service in the Women's Royal Naval Service she was not in a position to see unpublished naval reports of operations. Between 4 and 9 August, when Mrs Norton wrote to the Society, neither percipient appeared to have attempted to correlate the times given in her notes with actual battle times.

Pointing out that many supposed auditory hallucinations turned out on investigation to be cases in which the same ordinary noise had been misinterpreted, Lambert said it was necessary to emphasize that this explanation would not serve here. The percipients had enquired during the day (4 August) of several persons whether they had been disturbed during the night by any unusual noise, and received negative answers. In particular, they had asked a fellow visitor who had repeatedly complained of being disturbed at night by casual noises, as they had seen her bedroom light on when they were standing on the balcony listening to noises of 'amazing' loudness. She said she had not heard anything unusual. On the other hand, Lambert and Mrs Gay warned, 'it would, in our opinion, be rash to assume that the sounds heard were a sort of "sound track" repetition of the sounds of the Raid. The various kinds of sounds heard, gunfire, divebombing, planes, a rifle shot, shouts and cries, are all appropriate, but there is not enough detailed information available as to when the several different kinds of sound first occurred to enable one to judge whether they were "phased in" correctly . . .'

The percipients, said the investigators, seemed to be well-balanced individuals, with no tendency to add colour to their accounts. Neither of them had shown any concern whatever to 'prove' by the experience any preconceived theory of its cause, which would have been likely to determine the form it took. 'Both as regards form and content we think the experience must be rated as a genuine *psi* phenomenon, of which little or nothing was derived from previous normally acquired knowledge.'

But were the noises hallucinatory? This point was raised in 1968 in a letter to the *Journal* for September 1968, by R. A. Eades, who described how, towards the end of August 1951, he was returning with his family from a camping holiday in France and spent one night camping just outside Dieppe (to the east). 'During the night we were awakened by an indescribable noise which continued for several hours. Talking about it among ourselves we said it sounded like a zoo gone mad, like a fair, or like an amplified distant school playground, though, naturally, we did not think it was any of these things. The next morning I asked about this in the town and was told that it was the dredger which was then inactive in the harbour.'

Eades added that his party also heard the sound in waves: 'this is normal when hearing distant sounds.' Although the noise was that of a loud sound far away, 'I don't suppose the sound level was high where we were and it is not surprising that most people slept through it.' He had written to the Dieppe Port Authorities about the dredging service and was informed that the dredger operated from 00.15 hours to 08.15 hours on 4 August 1951.

Lambert also consulted the Harbour Master at Dieppe, who furnished the times of working of the dredger there between 30 July and 5 August. On 30 July the dredger was worked between 10.0 and 11.30 a.m. and between 9.30 p.m. and midnight. On 4 August the hours of working were from fifteen minutes after midnight until 8.15 a.m.

'It will be seen,' said Lambert, 'that on 30th July, when D. [Mrs Norton] alone heard faintly some strange noises, in the early morning "before cockcrow" the dredger was not working; and on 4th August the dredger started about 3¾ hours before the "battle noises" started, and stopped about 1¼ hours after the "battle noises" had stopped. Quite apart from the differences in the character of the two sets of noises, I find it hard to believe that the dredger, even if it had been only subconsciously heard, could have acted as a subliminal stimulus to cause the experience.'

Robert J. Hastings, a member of the Society keenly interested in spontaneous cases and a very thorough and pertinacious investigator, now joined in the controversy. In a paper in the *Journal* (32b pp. 55–66), he made the interesting point that in one important respect the Dieppe Raid case stood as an 'odd man out' among all other cases of paranormal visual or auditory experiences associated with particular places or localities. In other well-authenticated cases with which he was acquainted, including the Versailles Case, the percipients had not realized *at the time of the experience* that what they were seeing or hearing was paranormal, whereas in the Dieppe Raid case, which lasted about three hours, the percipients were in a sufficiently normal state to be critical of their experience during the whole of that time. Miss Norton had claimed among other things to have heard the sound of 'landing craft and men's cries' about 4.20 a.m., or shortly after. This would be about three-quarters of an hour before the time the first landing craft had touched down in the actual raids. He suggested that real aircraft might have been responsible for the sounds of aircraft reported by the two ladies, as Puys lies in the path of aircraft flying from London to Paris. He also suggested that much of what the two ladies heard might be attributable to the sound of the sea, distorted perhaps by the surrounding cliffs which were generally about 250 feet high.

Hastings considered that, by itself, the sound of the dredger might not be quite a perfect explanation for what occurred, for the times it was known to have been working did not correspond exactly to the times mentioned in the percipients' statements; but the sound of the dredger coming from a distance, together with the sound of the sea nearby, distorted perhaps by acoustic effects due to the conformation of the cliffs, might well have produced a pandemonium which visitors to Puys could be forgiven for failing to identify. Also, evidence that the ladies were acquainted with the sounds that were normal at night at Puys, which was needed as a basis for comparison before paranormality could be postulated, was missing.

Answering the argument about aircraft, Lambert pointed out that, according to the official report, there was no air activity at Puys. Just before the landing craft touched down there was no doubt a heavy sound of RAF planes attacking Dieppe, which was being 'prepared' for the main landing, but the plan required the RAF to keep clear of the beaches selected for the flank landings, where it was hoped to get ashore by surprise. Both percipients had had war service and must be assumed to be well able to distinguish between the occasional sound of civil aircraft passing steadily overhead on a recognized route from the sound of RAF planes flying in mass formation and dive-bombing at their objectives. 'If the whole experience was due to ordinary noises heard in an unfamiliar environment', Lambert argued – 'and some of them were described as "very loud" – why did no one else hear them?'

I have given the details of this case at some length because it provides an excellent example of critical standards within the Society, where critics are as active as are believers. Before the end of the last century William James said that 'According to the newspaper and drawing-room myth, soft-headedness and idiotic credulity are the bond of sympathy in this Society, and general wondersickness its dynamic principle. A glance at the membership fails, however, to corroborate this view. The president is Professor Henry Sidgwick, known by his other deeds as the most incorrigibly and exasperatingly critical and sceptical mind in England . . . through the catalogue of membership are sprinkled names honoured throughout the world for their scientific capacity. In fact, were I asked to point to a scientific journal where hard-headedness and never-sleeping suspicion of sources of error might be seen in their full bloom, I think I should have to fall back on the *Proceedings of the Society for Psychical Research*' (40b pp. 28–9).

The sounds heard by the two ladies at Dieppe suggested those made during a raid nine years earlier, but very occasionally one comes across an account of a seemingly retrocognitive experience of a battle fought in the remote past. One such account, concerning a vision of the aftermath of the Battle of Nechtanesmere, in Scotland, in the year AD 685, was published in the SPR *Journal* (50) by Dr James McHarg, of Dundee. The interval of 1,265 years between the date of the battle and the vision of the aftermath of it by the percipient, the late Miss E. F. Smith, of Lethan, in Angus, in 1950 is an extraordinarily long one.

Dr McHarg said that 'In recording this experience, no *evidential* significance is implied. It was merely thought desirable to record the incident, despite the interval of time since its occurrence, before the experiment became too old – and without regard to possible explanations for the apparition.'

After a preliminary talk with Miss Smith who was in her seventies, Dr McHarg arrived at her house on 22 September 1971 with Malcolm McFadyen, clinical psychologist, and Alex Bell, technician, who supervised the tape-recording to which

Miss Smith had agreed. After the initial recording the team took Miss Smith slowly, in a car, over the route she had been walking during the experience, and she pointed out, from different points along the road, the sites and distances of the successive components of the apparitional happening twenty-one years earlier. Then they returned to Miss Smith's home and recorded some further, clarifying, discussion.

It was assumed that the scene Miss Smith described concerned the aftermath of the Battle of Nechtanesmere – generally regarded, in the late seventh century, as one of the outstanding events of the age. It took place on the afternoon of Saturday 20 May AD 685; and in it the Northumbrians, under their King, Ecgfrith, were decisively beaten by the Picts, under their king, Brude mac Beli. The battle marked the end of an aggressive expedition by Ecgfrith undertaken against the advice of St Cuthbert and other Northumbrian notables.

Little is known for certain about the expedition prior to the battle, but it has been suggested that the Northumbrians, already in control in the Lothians, crossed the Forth near Stirling, and the Tay near Perth. Of the two alternative routes after that – south or north of the Sidlaw Hills – it is thought more probable that they took the northern route through Strathmore as far as Dunnichen Hill. The suggestion is that Ecgfrith was there drawn off his route by a feigned Pictish retreat through the cleft in that hill and that the Northumbrians, bursting through the cleft, realized too late that the Pictish fortress on the south side, invisible from the north, lay only 300–400 yards to their left. It is presumed that, with Pictish reinforcements from the fortress, pursuit by the Northumbrians was quickly turned into flight – flight downhill towards the mere, or loch, at the bottom.

What is certain is that Ecgfrith himself was slain, and his whole royal bodyguard around him. Most of the Northumbrian army was killed – the few who survived no doubt saved themselves by flight. Ecgfrith's body was carried off to the royal burial ground at Iona.

At the time of her strange experience Miss Smith, who was already in her late fifties, was living in Letham, a village near the fields of Dunnichen, now believed to have been the original site of the 'mere' of Nechtan. She had never before or since then had any apparitional experience. On 2 January 1950 she attended a cocktail party at a friend's house at Brechin, ten miles to the north of Letham, and stayed on for dinner. It was late at night when she set off for home in her car. A fall of snow had been followed by rain and, two miles outside Brechin, the car skidded into a ditch. There was no question of the skid having been due to her fainting, or other lapse of consciousness; nor of Miss Smith having been injured in any way, or concussed. She had to abandon her car, however, and continue her journey on foot – a distance of about eight miles. Her walk was along deserted country roads in a countryside with a few scattered farms. She had her little dog with her but, for the last two miles of the journey, she had to carry him on her shoulder; and as she neared Letham, she must have felt fairly exhausted. She had also felt 'nervous' immediately prior to the onset of the apparitional experience, for she had deliberately refrained from taking a commonly used, and normally welcome, short-cut, because it would have taken her out of the open country and alongside a dark, wooded area.

The apparitional experience began when Miss Smith was about half a mile from the first houses of Letham village and it continued until she reached them. The time was getting on for 2.0 a.m. The first phase (see plan) started as Miss Smith approached a crest of the road over which, by daylight, the top of Dunnichen Hill would first have come into sight, and then its base, straight ahead of her, about a mile away, at which she first saw moving torches.

Continuing her journey she made, at a T junction, a turn to the left towards Letham so that the distant lights were on her right. The second phase of the experience began a little lower down the winding road as she watched, on her right, in the middle distance, about a third of a mile away, further figures carrying torches. The third phase followed quickly upon this as she watched figures even closer to her, in the field on the right, about fifty yards away, in the direction of some farm buildings, which, however, were not visible in the darkness.

At this stage, the dog started to growl. Miss Smith said, 'He was sitting on my left shoulder and he turned and looked at the lights and started growling and I thought now next he's going to

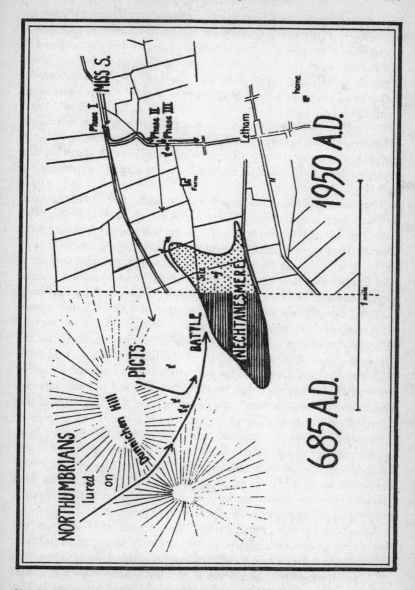

Sketch map, prepared by Dr McHarg, showing on the right the phases of Miss Smith's experience and, on the left, a plan of the battlefield of AD 685.

bark.' She was anxious that the dog should not bark and wake up the village. The experience, which lasted, Dr McHarg estimated, about twelve minutes, ended when Miss Smith left the scene with the figures and torches behind her as she entered the village through which she continued her walk to her own home – a distance of perhaps a further quarter of a mile – where she went straight to bed.

'It had been an exclusively visual experience,' said McHarg. 'There had been no preceding auditory or olfactory experience to suggest a temporal lobe disturbance. Only on waking in the morning, she said, had she realized what a strange experience it had been.'

The mere, or loch, no longer exists, and, indeed, its original site was long a matter of conjecture. A patchwork of fields, with their fences and boundaries, effectively camouflages it; and, as viewed from the surrounding roads, there is at present nothing to indicate its original outline or even to suggest that a loch was ever there. The late Dr F. T. Wainwright, one-time head of the Department of History at Queen's College, Dundee, had noticed, in 1947, how floods following the winter of 1946–7 had temporarily restored at least part of the old loch and how, in the following summer, as a result of faint colour changes in the growing grasses, the flood marks in the fields could still be seen. Wainwright determined to try to indicate on a map the extent of the vanished loch and this he did with the aid of photography and a field survey to determine contour lines. On the basis of this survey he published a paper in 1948 in the journal *Antiquity* (92). This paper included a reproduction of an Ordnance Survey Map of the district on which he had been able to superimpose the boundaries of the loch as deduced from his observations and measurements. This showed, in particular, a finger of the loch projecting in a north-easterly direction, round which people moving towards the east would have had to skirt.

Asked about her experience, Miss Smith said that at the beginning of the first phase, in the distance straight ahead, she saw 'people who looked as if they were carrying flaming torches . . . and there were quite a lot of torches.' Miss Smith felt that what she was seeing had not suddenly started but that it had already been going on when she came upon it. Her recalled reaction was to say to herself, 'Well, that's an incredible thing.' The nearer figures carrying torches which she saw during the second phase were, she said, 'quite obviously skirting the mere, because they didn't walk, from where I was looking, straight across to the far corner of the field, they *came round* . . .' Speaking about the nearest figures of all, which she watched during the third stage of her experience, Miss Smith said, 'They were obviously looking for their own dead . . . the one I was watching, the one nearest the roadside, would bend down and turn a body over and, if he didn't like the look of it, he just turned it back on its face and went on to the next one . . . There were several of them . . . I *supposed* they were going to bury them.'

When asked about clothing, Miss Smith said '. . . they looked as if they were in – well, I would have said brown, but that was merely the light – anyway, dark tights, the whole way up . . . a

Tracing of an incised picture of a Pictish warrior on a stone at Golspie.

sort of overall, with a roll-collar, and at the end of their tunics there was a larger roll round them too. And it simply went on looking like tights until it reached their feet. I did not see what was on their feet. But they weren't long boots . . .'

A tracing from an incised picture of a Pictish warrior on a stone at Golspie shows a bootless figure, gives the impression of tights, and also of a roll-neck tunic with what could be a 'roll' at the bottom of it.

When asked specifically about headgear, Miss Smith said that the figures she saw were wearing '. . . the kind of thing a baker's boy used to wear . . . Just like a hard roll, round, stuck on the top of their heads . . . excellent for carrying things on top of the head with.' The bearded Pictish warrior illustrated appears to have long hair and no headgear.

Miss Smith was asked about the torches the figures she saw were carrying. She replied '. . . they were carrying very long torches in their left hands . . . [the torches were] *very* red . . . Afterwards,' she continued, 'I wondered what on earth they'd been made of – tar, I suppose. *Was* there tar in those days?' At the time of the interview McHarg assumed that Miss Smith meant that it had been the flames of the torches which had been unusually red, but she may equally well have meant that it had been their shafts. Enquiries revealed that torches in Scotland used to be made from the resinous roots of the Scots fir which, in their natural state, do indeed have a distinctive red colour which would perhaps be enhanced by torchlight. Such roots would have been available at Nechtanesmere, for Dunnichen Hill was crowned then, no doubt, as it is today, with the Scots fir of the old Caledonian Forest.

McHarg remarked that 'If all this is so, Miss Smith's surprise at the redness of the torches may be a point of significance because her supposition that they were made of tar clearly indicates that there had not been any preconceived idea, at the back of her own mind, that the torches would have been made of the roots of the Scots fir and, therefore, both "very long", and red in colour.'

He added that the activity of dealing with the dead after the battle, presumably by the Picts themselves, would no doubt have continued throughout the following night. Dr C. W. Fraser, of the Department of Astronomy at St Andrew's University, told him that on 20/21 May sunset would have been about 8.0 p.m. and that although after 10 May in that part of Scotland it is never completely dark at night it would become relatively dark (presumably requiring torches for any serious work) from about 9.15 p.m. until about 2.30 a.m. The time of the apparitional experience was shortly before 2.0 a.m. McHarg visited the site at 2.0 a.m. on the anniversary of the battle on 20/21 May 1976 in order to observe for himself the state of light at that time of the year.

Commenting on the case, McHarg wrote, 'I must emphasize that Miss Smith was in no sense a patient and that I did not, therefore, pursue those enquiries which would have been routine in a standard psychiatric assessment. At the same time, I must record that I detected nothing of a medical (i.e. neurological or psychiatric) nature to suggest temporal lobe epilepsy or any other relevant clinical condition which might have moved me to advise Miss Smith to seek formal medical advice.'

There seemed to be three basic possibilities, McHarg suggested. First, that there was no apparition at all, and that the whole thing had been a fraud or a hoax; second, that there was no apparitional experience, but that, without any question of a hoax, a false memory arose in Miss Smith's mind on the following morning, based upon mere musings she had had the previous night while passing the site of the ancient battle; and third, that she did have the series of visual experiences essentially as she had described it.

If the apparitional experience really did occur as described, it seemed probable to McHarg that Miss Smith had been in an 'altered state of consciousness' at the time, as suggested by the temporary suspension of her full reflective and critical faculties which made her, strangely, more concerned about waking the village than about the apparent fact that she was witnessing an event from so long ago. 'The cause of such an alteration in consciousness might have been related to exhaustion and cold and perhaps to the apprehension, at the start of the experience, which, she remembered, had prevented her from taking an otherwise tempting short-cut near the end of her long and tiring walk.'

Posing the question of how the 'elaborate content' of the

experience could be explained, McHarg asked if it could be based upon cryptomnesiac (hidden) knowledge acquired by a forgotten reading of Wainwright's paper, or by a forgotten hearing of discussion upon his findings or the survey work upon which they had been based. Miss Smith replied that she had previously heard about the battle of Nechtanesmere but had not known who were the contestants. She also said that she had heard of Wainwright, but had not met him before the experience, although she met him afterwards. Reminded by McHarg that Wainwright had published his paper just two years before her experience, and asked if she had any recollection of having seen, or heard of, the paper beforehand, Miss Smith answered, 'I had *not* seen it before I saw this. Someone gave it to me after, to read, but I merely told him I was one up on him!'

McHarg was impressed by the apparently correct locating by Miss Smith on the gently undulating landscape of the tip of the north-easterly finger of the mere – i.e. the point round which the moving figures, skirting the edge of the mere, seemed to move as they came towards 'the far corner of the field'. His opinion was that it would have required a practised map-reader, which Miss Smith certainly was not, to have transferred Wainwright's mapped information so precisely and so correctly on to the landscape as viewed from the part of the road where she was.

Some features of the apparitional experience appeared not to be related to explicit features of Wainwright's work and paper: 1. the extension so far east of the searching, presumably by the Picts, for their dead; 2. the details of clothing, and in particular, the curious detail of the headgear; and 3. the redness of the torches. 'Miss Smith did *not* report that she saw the "head-rings" being utilized for the transport of the bodies, by Picts working in pairs. It is surely possible, however, that the ancient Picts, like present-day Africans, were in the habit of carrying burdens on their heads and of wearing a hard ring on the head for this purpose. That corpses might have been carried in this way would seem to be the sort of detail which might conceivably receive future verification as a result of increased knowledge about Pictish practices.'

Having already considered the possibility that Miss Smith might have acquired, by telepathy, some knowledge from the work of Wainwright and his colleagues on the battle only three years earlier, McHarg considered that these additional features 'at least raised for consideration the possibility of a more general *psi*-hypothesis, in terms of retrocognition, and of some kind of collective knowledge and memory which, under certain circumstances, could be drawn upon.'

I asked him if he thought Miss Smith's attendance at a cocktail party the previous evening should be taken into consideration. He replied that he did not think this was relevant, as Miss Smith had stayed for dinner after the party and had left Brechin after midnight. She herself had said, laughingly, that her friends naturally told her she must have had too much to drink, but she had not. In any case, McHarg pointed out, an eight-mile walk would have sobered her up! 'But, more important, the idea that alcoholic *intoxication* [drunkenness] causes hallucinations is a fallacy – popular notion though it be. The notion is based, no doubt, on the visual hallucinations which do accompany alcoholic *delirium* [delirium tremens], which is a very different matter, and a disabling physical illness lasting for several days.'

Claims that someone has had a retrocognitive experience have always to be checked with great thoroughness. In the last enquiry into spontaneous cases, conducted by the SPR in 1959, Celia Green observed that the fifteen examples of ostensible retrocognition included 'a few extremely long-term perceptions which were not on the whole convincing, for in nearly every case they could be attributed to a scrap of information, perhaps picked up from a guidebook, which had been subconsciously retained' (27a p. 106). Miss Smith, it will be remembered, had heard about the battle of Nechtanesmere *before* she had her experience, but her description of it contained details that were most unlikely to have been in any account she had read. For instance, one item of information, the hard rolls stuck on the heads of the warriors, is presumably unknown to historians. Such rolls could blunt the impact of an axe or club.

The experience of Miss Smith is an excellent example of how, when hallucinating, a person may take the most extraordinary events for granted – although she did say to herself, when she first saw the torches in the distance, 'Well, that's an incredible thing.'

The differences between the two experiences recorded in this chapter will have been noted. The two ladies near Dieppe heard what they assumed were the sounds of battle but saw nothing; Miss Smith saw the figures of what, presumably, were Pictish warriors, but heard nothing, although the nearest figures were only fifty yards away.

The experience of the two ladies at Dieppe is much harder to assess than Miss Smith's. As Hastings rightly pointed out, the percipients were in a sufficiently normal state to be critical of their experience, which lasted about three hours. A possible explanation is that they were only partially hallucinated and were having the equivalent of what has been termed 'a lucid dream', during which the person concerned knows that he or she is dreaming. It should not be thought that the two ladies and the Eades family shared an experience, which they interpreted differently, on the same evening. The Eades family experience was towards the end of August, that of the two ladies early in the month. And Hastings's point that the two ladies, prior to their visit, were unacquainted with the normal sounds of the sea at Dieppe was incorrect; Mrs Norton had stayed there the previous Easter.

It may be argued that as the experience of the two ladies was at night most people would be asleep and could not be expected to share in it, but if we accept that the sounds heard by Mrs Norton and Miss Norton suggested those made by a raid on the coast, surely they should have been audible to others? The indications were that they were not. At least one other person in the house was awake at the time but she did not hear anything unusual, although the sounds were of 'amazing' loudness to the two listeners on the balcony. If the noises were 'real', in the popular sense of the word, other people in the house and the neighbourhood would also have heard them. When all the factors I have mentioned are taken into consideration, this remains a very puzzling case.

11 The Return of Grandfather Bull

If ever the Society for Psychical Research had the opportunity to investigate the persistent haunting of a family during the comparatively short period of two months it was in Ramsbury, Wiltshire, early in 1932. Eight months after Samuel Bull, a chimneysweep, had died of sooty cancer his apparition appeared to his widow and other members of his family, nine in all, dressed as he usually was in the evening after he had finished work. The apparition was seen at all hours of the day and at night by the light of candles. When asked about the duration of the appearances the dead man's daughter, Mrs Edwards, said that on one occasion the figure must have been visible for half an hour continuously. The local Vicar, the Rev. George H. Hackett, was told by the family, which lived in a 'dreadfully crowded and unhappy condition', that the figure appeared off and on during several hours. The hauntings stopped only five days before the arrival of two very experienced investigators, the second Earl of Balfour and Mr J. C. Piddington. Commenting on the case, which was published in the Society's Journal *for October 1932, the late Sir Ernest Bennett, M.P., a member of the Council, said in his* Apparitions and Haunted Houses *that the Society's slowness in starting the investigation after the haunting had been reported deprived it of the opportunity for obtaining evidence 'of quite exceptional value' (9 p. 73).*

On 21 June 1931 Samuel Bull, 'a man of very pleasant and high character', according to the Vicar, died of cancer, leaving in the house an aged widow and a grandson aged 21. In August Mrs Edwards, a daughter, came with her husband and five children to live with her mother and the grandson at the cottage in Oxford Street. Soon after, certain rooms of the cottage became unfit and unsafe for habitation, and as no alternative accommodation could be found, they had to live in squalor, a state of things which continued for several months, although continued efforts were made to find better housing. Added to this, the aged widow had become very ill and had been confined to her bed since very shortly after her husband's death.

Some time in February (1932) when some of the children had gone to bed, the mother (Mrs Edwards) was made anxious by their sleeplessness and restlessness. They complained that there was someone outside the door, and were very nervous. No one was there – that is, no visible presence – but the conditions continued, and a little later the dead man was seen to ascend the stairs and pass through a door, which was shut, into the room in which he had died, and in which Mrs Bull, the widow, had been lying for some time until it was condemned as unsafe, and which at the time of the apparition's first appearance was shut up and unused.

The first experience occurred after three of the children, who had previously been sleeping in the grandmother's bedroom, had been moved to a room downstairs because one, or perhaps two, of the children had got influenza. They had been downstairs at least a fortnight before they experienced anything unusual. It was when Mary, aged 13, was down with influenza (she was the last of the children to catch it) that the apparition was first seen by her and her mother. Shortly afterwards Mrs Edwards and the 21-year-old grandson, James Bull, saw the apparition together. Mrs Bull, when she heard that Mrs Edwards and Mary had seen the apparition, told her daughter that she had seen it before. At first everyone was terrified, and the children screamed. On subsequent occasions they were calmer, in a state of quiet awe.

When the apparition appeared all members of the family were able to see the figure equally well, including the smallest girl, about five years old, who recognized the apparition as 'Grandpa Bull'. The figure was seemingly solid, but the only person to have felt it was the dead man's widow. The apparition invariably went to a position by the bed and laid his hand upon her forehead. She said the hand was 'firm but cold'. The widow once heard the apparition say 'Jane', that being her name. Mrs Edwards told the Vicar that the thing which seemed to fascinate her most was the appearance of the apparition's 'poor hands' because the knuckles seemed to be protruding through the skin.

News of the haunting came to light on 3 April 1932 when the

Earl of Selborne was given a verbal account of it by Admiral Hyde Parker, who lived at Ramsbury. Lord Selborne then wrote to Lord Balfour, a vice-president of the SPR, to say that the Admiral would be willing to answer any communication from the Society. Lord Balfour sent a list of eight questions which were referred by the Admiral to the Vicar, who obtained the replies summarized above. In a letter dated 9 April, the Vicar remarked, 'There is some hope that the family might be moving into a council house in a few days' time, and in that case the apparition might cease to appear, especially as the owner intends to put the house into condition, which will involve very considerable disturbance of present conditions. So if the SPR propose to make any investigation there is no time to be lost.' As it turned out, the apparition was not seen after this date; but no one could have known this at the time.

On 14 April Lord Balfour and Mr Piddington went to Ramsbury and had a long interview at Admiral Hyde Parker's house with the Admiral and the Vicar, who said that Mrs Edwards had told him earlier that day that the appearances had taken a great deal out of the members of the family, and especially out of old Mrs Bull. She also told him spontaneously that Mrs Bull often saw the figure, and that the last appearance had been on 9 April. When asked whether any members of the family had been interested in spiritualism, the Vicar said 'no'; and he returned the same answer when asked whether any members of the family had previously had any experiences similar to the present one.

In reply to the suggestion that the whole story might have been concocted for the purpose of arousing sympathy with the family on account of the wretched conditions in which they were living, and so increase their chances of obtaining better accommodation, the Vicar said that he believed in the good faith of the witnesses, and that any such plot might well have had just the opposite result to that desired – though the family might, of course, have miscalculated the outcome of a manoeuvre of the kind. (The Vicar had said in his letter of 9 April that all the statements obtained at his interview bore testimony to the sadness of the apparition's appearance, which the family 'understood' to indicate that the deceased was grieved at their forlorn condition; but the fact that on his last two appearances he had changed considerably, and seemed 'much happier', was believed to be due to the possibility that the family might soon go into a council house, and so be in happier circumstances.)

The Vicar also noted that the family always knew the 'presence' was there for half an hour before anyone saw the apparition. They were conscious of a peculiar restlessness or stirring or expectancy. Mrs Edwards said, 'I feel as though I am expecting my brother from America, or something like that.' Samuel Bull had never said in life that he would try to reappear after death and the 'appearance' had come as a great shock to the family.

At 2.55 p.m. on 14 April Admiral Hyde Parker, Mr Hackett, Lord Balfour, and Mr Piddington called at the cottage, and had a minute or two's conversation with Mrs Edwards downstairs. Then they all went upstairs into a bedroom where Mrs Bull was lying in bed, and Mrs Edwards taking with her her youngest child, the only one of her children who was at home at the time. The investigators found the cottage completely dismantled, the only furniture left being the bed in which Mrs Bull was lying and a single chair; the family were actually engaged that day in moving into a council house.

The interview that took place in Mrs Bull's bedroom lasted about forty minutes. In the course of it a number of questions were put to Mrs Edwards, and answered by her, with Mrs Bull also answering one or two questions. The figure, Mrs Edwards said, appeared to be quite lifelike; it did not glide but walked, and seemed so solid; and when the appearances began, she was more frightened than the children. After describing the feeling of restlessness and expectancy that preceded her visions of the figure, she added that after the ghost had disappeared she felt more composed.

Mrs Bull said that she had twice felt the cold hand of the ghost on her brow, and once had heard the ghost call her 'Jane'.

When asked about the duration of the appearances, Mrs Edwards said that on one occasion the figure must have been visible for half an hour continuously. 'Mrs Edwards was a good witness,' the investigators agreed. 'She answered the questions put to her simply, naturally, readily, and briefly'; and in due course Mr and Mrs Edwards signed a statement prepared by Piddington.

Sir Ernest Bennett had some harsh things to say in his book about the Society's handling of the case:

Both the character and evidence of this bewildering case are quite unique. The figure which showed itself with such frequency seemed solid and lifelike, and I do not know of another narrative of this kind where the witnesses of a 'collective' apparition were so numerous — on some occasions no less than nine.

The unsatisfactory and extremely disappointing feature in this case is the inefficient and dilatory character of the investigation . . .

As it happened, this did not matter very much, as the haunting was already drawing to a close when it was notified to the Society, and nothing happened in the new house; so I doubt if the delay in the arrival of Lord Balfour and Piddington on the scene made much difference.

What is unusual about this haunting is the length and frequency of the appearances, and the fact that the apparition was visible to *all* members of the family. This suggests that the figure was of the kind Professor Price called 'a real object' (31b p. 238). An indication of the frequency of the apparition's appearances is contained in a letter in the archives from Lord Selborne who, describing the late Samuel Bull as 'a well-respected man but something of a character', said, 'According to the reports of every member of the family, the defunct sweep is quite constantly among them, moving all over the house and coming and going at all hours. They are not now in the least alarmed but were so when they first saw him but think him a bit of a bore. Apparently he never attempts to speak or appear to want any notice from anybody except his widow.' This is the first time I have ever heard a ghost being referred to as 'a bit of a bore.'

Readers will, of course, make up their own minds about this extraordinary case, but before they do so I suggest that they take into account the circumstances in which the haunting occurred.

Nine people were living in what the vicar described as 'a dreadfully crowded and unhappy condition' in a condemned cottage. Upstairs an old woman, worn out after nursing her husband for four years, was slowly dying. The time was February, when winter would be taking its toll. The children had influenza, and doubtless Mrs Edwards, as a good mother, was under strain as the result of having had to nurse them as well as Mrs Bull. The haunting started eight months *after* the chimney-sweep's death. Conditions, apparently, were not suitable for the appearances during the warm months of summer and the early autumn, but they could have been towards the end of winter when the vitality of the people in the cottage would be low as a result of living in such depressing and unsatisfactory surroundings. I have come across a few other cases in which people living in crowded conditions have experienced strange phenomena, although not as strange as those at Ramsbury. Such conditions favour, I believe, the spread of what may be described as 'psychic infection'. However, this is only a partial explanation of the extraordinary happenings that took place at Ramsbury. Thousands of families live in overcrowded and unsatisfactory conditions without experiencing hauntings by a deceased member of the family.

The Bulls' cottage, which stood at the junction of Oxford Street and Chapel Lane, was destroyed by fire during the last war, and a shop with a flat over it and an adjoining house stand on the site.

12 The Grey Lady of Cleve Court

The haunting of Cleve Court, near Minster, Kent, recorded here covers a period of sixty years and the evidence for this may, in my opinion, be considered good. An even longer tradition of haunting which goes back nearly two hundred years is attached to the house, but evidence for this is lacking. Information about the haunting of Cleve Court came to light when newspaper publicity was given to an experience by the owner of the house, Lady Carson, with the apparition of a woman in grey in 1949. Lady Carson was the widow of the famous Lord Carson, formerly Sir Edward Carson, a brilliant advocate and Parliamentarian, who became a champion of Ulster, where his name is still revered by the Protestant community. Lord Carson bought the house in 1920, a year before he was appointed a Lord of Appeal in Ordinary, and, when his period of office in that post ended in 1929, he enjoyed his retirement there, despite failing health, before his death in 1935 at the age of 81.

I published a paper on the haunting of Cleve Court in the SPR Journal (51e), based mainly on material supplied by Lady Carson in a long interview I had had with her three years earlier; but it also contained information supplied by her, and others, during the following three years. When I saw Lady Carson she thought that the phenomena had ceased, but it later transpired that the sound of footsteps for which no physical cause could be found still continued in another part of the house, and were even heard there after her death in August 1966. I have selected this case because it is modern, it allows discussion on how evidence given by children may be assessed, and because it contains a remarkable, and rare, example of retrocognition. This chapter contains considerably more information about Cleve Court, and some of the people who lived there, than was available when I wrote the account of the haunting for the Journal.

Cleve Court, a pleasant country house with ten bedrooms, was discovered by chance during one of Lord and Lady Carson's visits to Birchington, near the Kent coast. Lady Carson, who was sensitive to atmosphere, liked the house from the beginning: she refused to consider buying another house she and her husband had viewed because she thought the atmosphere there was sinister. They were not aware of any ghostly traditions in connection with the house, which is about 500 years old and was built in three different periods – there is a reference to the house in Henry VII's reign, then an Elizabethan section was added, and finally the 'new' part, which is early Georgian – but it was not long before the new owners were forced to consider the possible meaning of some strange happenings.

Lord and Lady Carson were both disturbed by the sound of footsteps, such as might have been made by a woman wearing high-heeled shoes, and taps on doors. Once, when they were in their bedroom, a tap sounded on the door and Lord Carson sang out 'Come in', but no one was there. Lord Carson believed that the noises were those made by an old house and refused to accept the theory of a haunting. Lady Carson, at that stage, was not so sure. She had discovered from a talk with a friend of the previous occupier, a woman, that strange things had happened in the house, but was never able to find out what they were because a planned meeting with this lady never took place.

A year after the Carsons bought Cleve Court a guest sleeping in the Elizabethan part had a restless night, being disturbed by sounds overhead of something being dragged and of drawers being opened and shut. In the morning she asked Lady Carson if the sounds were made by a footman packing before leaving. Lady Carson knew, however, that there was no bedroom above the guest room, that no servant was leaving, and that servants did not sleep in that part of the house.

When the Carsons bought Cleve Court their son, Edward, was not a year old. His bedroom was in the Elizabethan part of the house. When he was five or six years old he told his mother that he did not like the lady who walked in the passage from which his room opened. Lady Carson asked, 'What is she like, Ned?' The boy replied, 'I don't know. She only walks away.' The light was always left on for him in the passage after that. Lady Carson added that the sound of footsteps had frequently been heard in this passage from the Georgian part of the house, where she and her husband had their bedroom.

Patricia Miller, a great-niece of Lord Carson, was four when she stayed at Cleve Court. Her bedroom was in the Elizabethan section at the end of the passage. Lady Carson was with Patricia when she started to talk about the 'lady' who was there. In reply to the question 'What lady?' by Lady Carson the child answered, 'The lady who stands by my bed. There she is.' The child pointed to a corner of the room but no one was there. The child persisted in her view that the 'lady' was present and became cross because Lady Carson could not see her. This room became known to the family as the 'ghost room'. According to Lady Carson, dogs would not enter it at that time, and she was once amused by finding a servant going to the room at night to carry out some duty there escorted by another with a broom. On my visit Lady Carson's two spaniels who went with us through the house entered the room without hesitation.

Another child who stayed at Cleve Court and had an experience with the apparition was Diana Colvin. When, aged five, she was invited back in 1945 she asked if the 'poor lady' would be there. Asked 'What poor lady?', she replied, 'The poor lady who walks in and out. No one speaks to her and no one tells me who she is.' This 'poor lady' was, apparently, invisible to others. Further questioning revealed that she was referring to the 'poor lady's' movements in the drawing-room in the Georgian part of the house. (In my first report of this case in *The Unexplained* (51a), and in the *Journal*, I gave the name of the child concerned as Joanna Wilson. This information was supplied by Lady Carson but Mrs Heather Carson, Lady Carson's daughter-in-law, has told me that Diana Colvin, Joanna's cousin, was the one who spoke about the 'poor lady'.)

Mrs Carson, who married the Hon. Edward Carson in 1943, had an alarming experience at Cleve Court in 1949. One evening, when the household was asleep, she was coming out of a bathroom when she heard footsteps coming towards her down the passage, although no one was visible. She went quickly to her bedroom, slamming the door after her.

Although Patricia Miller had tried to point out the apparition to Lady Carson, she had been unable to see the figure until she had her own visual experience one December morning in 1949. At 1.30 a.m. she was awakened by her spaniel, Susan, who obviously wanted to be let out of the house. She put on her dressing gown and, leaving one light burning on the landing by the bedroom, went down the stairs accompanied by the dog, in the process of which she accidentally turned off the light as she brushed past a switch. When she was at the foot of the stairs the dog did not go to the door but ran whimpering back up the stairs. Lady Carson switched on all the lights and saw, to her astonishment, a woman coming down the stairs from the direction of her room. She was wearing a very full grey skirt which covered her feet, she had a piece of white lace on her head, and seemed to have a fichu of very pale grey matching the rest of her dress. Her face was averted but she appeared to be young. Lady Carson's first reaction was that she was seeing an intruder. She told me that she was about to shout 'What are you doing here?' when she realized that the woman was moving noiselessly, walking, not floating, and that she was seeing an apparition. In her own words, 'I was terrified; I went cold. I thought that ghosts were transparent but this one looked quite material in every way.' While Lady Carson stood at the foot of the stairs the figure turned at the landing above and walked through the open door to the Elizabethan part of the house.

After an account of Lady Carson's experience appeared in the press a representative of a society in London rang Lady Carson and offered to send three people to the house to carry out a ceremony of exorcism. She refused, telling her caller that she rather liked the ghost. But, most interesting of all responses to the publication of the account was a letter from a woman, 'E.C.', with an address in West Hampstead, London, dated 1 January 1950 (the SPR has the name and address).

My Lady,
The article in the newspaper last week concerning the ghost at Cleve Court greatly interested me, and I thought that perhaps the following might be of a little interest to you.

Many years ago, forty-five to be exact, I was fifteen years of age, and had decided to go into domestic service, and my first job was as an under-maid at Cleve Court. A Mrs Garrard and a companion lived there with about five maids and a butler. Guests were expected and I was given a room to prepare as a day nursery.

It was in the old part of the house, at the end of a passage. I was very busy about 7 o'clock one morning when I heard footsteps coming along the passage. I looked up expecting to see one of the maids, but to my surprise it was a lady in an old-fashioned dress. As I got up to leave the room she just waved one hand and went away. When the maid came to inspect my work and I told her of the lady she was most indignant.

It was neither of the two old ladies who lived there, and as there were no other guests at the time, as she pointed out to me, I must be telling an untruth. However, I still stuck to my story, and I am wondering now if it was the Gay [*sic*] Lady I saw. I have often wondered who she really was, and never for one moment did this solution come to me.

I trust you will not consider it a liberty, but it was such a very uncommon experience I felt I had to write to you. I would like to know that the other maid may have read it, although I am afraid she would now be too old.

Yours very respectfully,
E.C.

Lady Carson sent this letter to an official of the Society who had been in touch with her, and it was copied for the records before being returned. An experienced member of the Society interviewed E.C. but she could not add any further details. I called at the house in West Hampstead in the autumn of 1965, hoping to get some details of the 'old-fashioned dress', but the occupants there knew nothing about E.C., who had left at some earlier date.

The Carson family physician, Dr E. G. Moon, who practised from Broadstairs, knew about the legend attached to the property because he once asked Lady Carson if she 'minded' the ghost. She replied that she did not, and remarked, 'She must be a very nice one because the atmosphere here is so pleasant.'

Dr Moon told Lady Carson of a strange experience of his own at Cleve Court. He had been asked to call on Lord Carson one day in 1930, and, after attending him, paused at the front door, looking down, while he considered whether he should have prescribed a stronger tonic. When he looked up a totally different scene from what had been there when he arrived was before his eyes. His car, which had been standing in the small drive before the house, had vanished, as had the thick hedge which is between the two sets of gateposts. Instead of the lane which he had driven down that day there was a muddy cart track. Coming towards him was a man who was wearing a coat with many capes, a short top hat, and gaiters at which he flicked noiselessly with a hunting crop.

The man stared at Dr Moon who, not believing the evidence of his eyes, decided to go back into the house. There he decided to have another look from the doorway. When he did so the car was where he had left it, the scenery of the present day was restored, and there was no sign of the man who had stared so intently at him. Dr Moon made Lady Carson promise not to relate this experience of his until his retirement or death, and she kept this promise. He died in 1937.

Before I called on Lady Carson in 1963 she wrote, 'I think our ghost has gone away because I haven't heard or seen her since December 1949.' She repeated that statement during the long interview I had with her; but the haunting was not yet over, as Lady Carson was to realize. In the autumn of 1965 her grandson, Rory Carson, then aged 15, was in a bedroom in the oldest part of the house with a big dog, half-Labrador and half-Alsatian, when he was disturbed by the sound of footsteps and movement overhead, where there was only an empty attic. He was then given a bedroom in another part of the house. It transpired in correspondence, too, that servants who lived in the oldest part of the house had often heard the sound of footsteps, 'but there were so many of them they didn't mind.'

Lady Carson added a postscript to a questionnaire to say that 'an ex-hospital sister came to stay here when she hadn't been well and she asked my housekeeper one day if my gardener had gone by her room very late at night and she, fearing to frighten her, said he had gone to shut a window beyond thinking it might have been left open.' This was my last communication from Lady Carson. She died on 7 August 1966, aged 85.

Additional evidence came from Mr and Mrs Rigden, who had been on Lady Carson's staff for twenty-eight years at the time of her death: Mrs Rigden as personal maid and Mr Rigden as gardener. They did not sleep in the very old part of the house but had both heard footsteps there, from 1940 onwards, 'most times after midnight and at times very plain.' They confirmed Lady Carson's account of the experience of the ex-hospital sister, gave her name, and said the footsteps were heard about midnight. 'She asked me if I came through the house late at night because she had heard footsteps and I said to her that I did come through because I had forgotten to shut a window.'

Footsteps continued to be heard at Cleve Court after Lady Carson's death. In a letter to me dated 18 December 1966 Mr and Mrs Rigden wrote, 'About the footsteps at Cleve Court, yes, they are still heard, and very plain at times. You hear them come to the bedroom doors in the old part of the house, mostly after midnight . . . These footsteps were heard last week by a woman now living in the old part and she told us both that she had heard footsteps.' I wrote to this woman, who was, apparently, a new member of the staff, seeking her own account, but unfortunately did not receive a reply; and Mr and Mrs Rigden left Cleve Court early in 1967.

The identity of the apparition is not known, but according to local legend the figure is that of an heiress who was unhappily married. The story was told to Lady Carson in 1922 by a man in his eighties from the neighbouring village of Monkton. He said he had been told the story by his father, who had heard it from *his* father. If this were so, the legend had been circulating in the neighbourhood for nearly 200 years. The heiress, it was said, had lived at Cleve Court and the property had become her husband's on their marriage. He had built an extension onto the Elizabethan part of the house against her wishes. According to the legend, the husband used to lock up his wife while he caroused with drinking companions and women. The wife was also unhappy because she had wanted children and her husband had not. After her death she haunted the house and children saw her. Lady Carson pointed out to me a strange, old-fashioned bolt *outside* a room in the new part of the house.

Some information about Cleve Court is given in Edward Hasted's *History of Kent* and Samuel Bagshaw's *History, Gazetteer, and Directory of the County of Kent*. Hasted attributes the building of the 'present seat' to James Ruck, a London banker, who died on 15 January 1739. In 1758 Ruck's youngest son, George Ruck, sold the house to Josias Farrer, of Doctors Common, London, for £5,800. Farrer died in 1762, aged 53, leaving 'very considerable property in estates and money' to his only son, Josias Fuller Farrer, then a minor.

A highly-coloured account in the *Thanet Magazine* for August 1817 tells how young Josias Fuller Farrer managed to dispose of his fortune by converting Cleve Court 'into a scene of riot and extravagance almost incredible'. He kept a kind of open house, where all visitors who could amuse or be amused were welcome.

He also kept hounds and hunters 'and even a seraglio of women for the accommodation of his visitors'. When his cellars overflowed with wine, butts were deposited to ripen in the out-offices, and when required for use were too frequently found emptied 'by the train of rascal attendants'. A brewer's dray regularly conveyed three butts of ale to his vaults in a fortnight, and the consumption occasionally exceeded even that amount. Brewers' bills amounted to £400 or £500, and other tradesmen's in proportion. In this 'riotous waste' a fortune of more than £100,000 was dispersed in a very few years and the thoughtless proprietor was reduced to comparative want. He afterwards retired to France, and, it was said, occupied a post in the establishment of the famous Duke of Orleans. Later he returned to England and died at Douglas, in the Isle of Man, about 1804. At his death the remains of his ample property passed to his son of the same name who disposed of the whole in 1807 to a Mr Pett Hannam of Northburn Court, for £15,000.

The origin of the legend attaching to Cleve Court may without much doubt be traced to that young profligate, Josias Fuller Farrer; but there are some contradictions. His wife was not childless, and the extension to the house was built by a previous owner, but it is quite possible that she was locked in her room during the 'orgies'. It is thus possible that the apparition is that of the wife of Josias Fuller Farrer, who must have suffered much in the house.

The dress worn by figures reportedly seen at a haunted site may help to date the period concerned. According to a specialist in costume at the Victoria and Albert Museum, London, the dress of the woman described by Lady Carson – a full skirt and white cap – could have been worn over a very long period; and, if the woman was elderly and partial to old-fashioned dress, the span could be extended even further. Nevertheless, in general terms, such dress was commonest between 1660 and 1790, and between 1840 and 1875 (Josias Farrer lived at Cleve Court in the 1760s). The costume of the man described by Dr Moon to Lady Carson seems to belong to a slightly later period. As early as the first quarter of the nineteenth century cloaks with multiple capes were very fashionable, and gaiters and top hats were also worn. However, I was told at the Museum, it must be borne in mind that caped coats, top hats and gaiters continued to be worn throughout most of the nineteenth century, and coachmen's overcoats, from the mid-nineteenth century, particularly, were often caped.

The figure seen by Dr Moon suggests that of a country landowner, or farmer, rather than a young rake such as Josias Fuller Farrer was.

Cleve Court has had many owners, some of whom occupied it for only a few years. It is, I think, significant that Cleve Court changed hands five times in the seventy-five years before Lord Carson bought the house. When a house is haunted most people prefer to keep the fact to themselves so as not to discourage a possible purchaser and quietly move out. However, rumours about a property being haunted cannot always be contained. Lady Carson was amused, she told me, in the early years of their occupancy when she heard two women outside the walls of the ground discussing how she 'dared' to live there.

In H. Montgomery Hyde's book *Carson* (35) it is stated that Lord Carson was 'delighted' with the purchase of Cleve Court, 'which included twenty acres of land and only cost him altogether £2,500.' This price, which was confirmed by Mrs Carson, was indeed extremely low for such a fine property when it is considered that it was sold to Hannam for £15,000 in 1807, when the pound was worth much more than it was in the 1930s. The low price may have been due to the house having a tradition of being haunted and therefore difficult to sell.

When we look back on this case it will be seen that the haunting followed a typical pattern: footsteps for which no physical explanation could be found (there is no underground water), dragging sounds overhead, knocks on doors when no one was there (a comparison may be made with a similar phenomenon in the account of the haunted vicarage in Chapter 5), and the appearance of apparitions. The haunting was also typically aimless. One of the noteworthy features of this case is that most of the appearances of the 'lady' were to children. Many people will want to ascribe this to imagination, but this view may not be correct in the majority of cases described here. That very experienced investigator, W. H. Salter, has said (76a p. 42) that 'young children's experiences are particularly valuable, as they are too unsophisticated to have any bias for or against what adults may classify as "supernatural"'. Lambert, an equally experienced investigator, pointed out in his foreword to my book *Apparitions and Ghosts* that when a child not known to be dreamy or fanciful says that it has just seen 'so-and-so' in the garden, and that person is miles away, the statement should be noted and not brushed aside as mere nonsense. 'Children know a limited number of persons by sight and so not often make mistakes in identifying persons they know well' (51c p. 11). The children at Cleve Court did not know the 'lady', in the usual sense of the word, but nevertheless she was real to them.

The account of Dr Moon's experience by Lady Carson is, of course, secondhand; but his reluctance to make it known during his lifetime is understandable. Any doctor would go to great lengths to avoid a reputation for 'seeing things'. It is very rare, in modern times, to receive details of an experience in which the present-day landscape and objects in it, such as a car, are obliterated, and the landscape of a former age substituted, with the addition of a figure in the clothes of that period.

The letter from the former maid, E.C., to Lady Carson is most valuable from an evidential viewpoint. The room she was given to prepare as a day nursery was 'in the old part of the house, at the end of a passage'. The room where Patricia Miller tried to point out the 'lady' to Lady Carson was in the old part of the house at the end of a passage – i.e. the same room. Could E.C. have come across a reference to this room in a local or national paper? I made most careful enquiries, but could not find any such reference. The maid's experience is also significant in that she thought the figure was that of a living person. When Lady Carson saw the figure she thought that the 'woman' was an intruder. So much for the common belief that apparitions are wispy or transparent.

Confirmation of some of the events described here is contained in a letter from Mrs Carson in July 1980. She said that her son, Rory Carson, who had just visited her, 'well remembers the night he and his dog (Bobby) flatly refused to stay in the room in the old part any longer.' The Hon. Edward Carson added a note. 'You are quite correct in saying that in after years my mother told me that I had always told her that a lady stood by my cot in the room in question and no one who came in ever spoke to her.'

Mrs Carson said that after Lady Carson's death in 1966 the house was divided. She and her husband lived in the Georgian part of the house, her parents in the Elizabethan section; and there were separate owners of the old cottage and the stable block. In 1975 Mr and Mrs Carson moved to Sevenoaks. Mrs Carson said that 'The odd thing was that after the division I don't think we ever heard or felt anything. Certainly I loved the house and garden very much . . . whatever or whoever it was was quite harmless and benevolent and I never felt any fear even when I was alone at night.'

I have made enquiries by telephone and none of the present occupants of Cleve Court has been disturbed by phenomena of the type reported by members of the Carson family and their household; something that can be expected when a house has been divided.

13 A Night Visitor in Cambridge

For some forty years Professor F. J. M. Stratton of Gonville and Caius College, Cambridge, President of the SPR from 1953 to 1955 and a noted astronomer, was keenly interested in stories of alleged happenings at Abbey House, Abbey Road, Cambridge. After Professor Stratton's death in 1961, his file on Abbey House was passed to the Society, with a few small additions, by Professor C. D. Broad. Abbey House stands close to the site of the former Barnwell Priory, a twelfth-century Augustinian foundation. In the main it is the work of three periods: the late sixteenth, the late seventeenth and the early eighteenth centuries. Stratton believed that publication of the stories about Abbey House might contaminate the testimony of possible future witnesses and although he talked about the alleged haunting at various private gatherings, he only once referred to Abbey House in print and then not by name. However, the stories about Abbey House have figured several times in the press, and are so well-known in Cambridge, that Dr Alan Gauld, of Nottingham University, a member of the Society's Council, considered that there seemed little point in withholding the original accounts, and published a paper under the title of 'The Haunting of Abbey House, Cambridge' in the Society's Journal *(23b). The narrative that follows is based on Gauld's account, but I have been able to add to it some most interesting information given to me by Professor Peter Danckwerts, F.R.S., who, with Mrs Danckwerts, now lives in the house. Professor Danckwerts, who was Shell Professor of Chemical Engineering at Cambridge University from 1957 to 1977 and is now Emeritus Professor, tells me that Abbey House was given to the Cambridge Folk Museum by Lord Fairhaven in 1945, and the freehold was subsequently given by the museum to the City Council in 1973. However, the museum has in fact never occupied any part of the house, which formed three dwellings until 1964, when Professor Danckwerts and his wife took a long lease on Nos 1 and 2 Abbey House and threw them into one. In 1977 they took a long lease on the whole house, although No. 3 remains a separate dwelling. The house has been used as a dwelling by owners or tenants uninterruptedly since it was built (c. 1580?) and extended (1678). Gauld's report suggested to me that the haunting of the house was not as pronounced as it had been in the past, and might possibly have stopped, but the experience of an elderly lady in the house as recently as June 1980, an account of which was sent to me by Professor Danckwerts, is an indication that the haunting is not yet over.*

The earliest rumours in connection with Abbey House to be mentioned in the file date from the 1860s, but the earliest first-hand testimony comes from the beginning of this century, when the house was occupied by J. C. Lawson (1874–1935) of Pembroke College, Cambridge, and his wife and family. Lawson was a distinguished classical scholar, a fellow of Pembroke College from 1899 until his death, and a College and University lecturer in classics. He was Junior Proctor in 1909 and Senior Proctor in 1912. His *Modern Greek Folklore and Ancient Greek Religion* remains a classic in its field. The knowledge of modern Greek which he acquired while collecting materials for this book enabled him to carry out valuable work for Naval Intelligence in the Aegean during World War I. The Lawsons occupied what are now Nos. 1 and 2 Abbey House (see plan below). No. 3 was

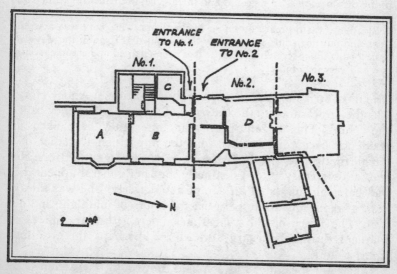

Ground floor plan of Abbey House, Cambridge

then known as Abbey Cottage and was occupied by a Mr and Mrs Kingsnorth.

The Lawsons moved into Abbey House (then known as 'The Old Abbey') in October 1903. They had two children, John (*b.* June 1901) and Mary (*b.* October 1902). During their tenancy, which lasted until 1911, two further children were born, Jane (*b.* January 1904) and Arnold (*b.* July 1906). Their arrival was marked by an alarming incident, which Mrs Lawson described as follows:

The very first night we spent in the house the maids were disturbed about midnight by a tremendous bang at their doors, the noise seeming to start high up on the door and continue downwards. Two maids were sleeping in one room and opposite them the nurse and two children slept. The noise was first on the nurse's door and then repeated on the other. They were all terrified at first, but the cook suddenly thought the nurse perhaps needed something and had banged for them and so together they went across to her room to find her quaking in bed and far too terrified to try and console the two children, waked and howling disconsolately. They all three spent the night in terror in her room, and next morning all decided they could not possibly sleep another night in the house, until I was able to persuade them that it was our great dog [a Newfoundland] anxious about the children and trying the doors to see if he could find them. They were finally satisfied and we have heard no more from any servants sleeping in those rooms.

But there was no mark on either of the doors. The paint was new and thick and our dog could not possibly have banged at them in the way they described without scratching it as he had been chained up for some months and had very long nails.

The most striking phenomenon in the haunting of Abbey House was the appearance to the Lawsons of a figure which they called the 'Nun'. This began three years after they had taken up residence. According to Lawson, the apparition was that of a female figure clad in a darkish robe, rather like a nun's dress. Her features were never seen distinctly, but her general appearance and carriage suggested an age of about thirty. She was always seen at night, generally between the hours of midnight and 4.0 a.m. The times of her appearances were irregular, but more frequent during February and March, perhaps three or four times a month.

Generally speaking, Lawson said, he would be awakened by the sound of heavy footsteps which resembled those of a policeman and would see and hear the figure walking across the room from the door to the foot of the bed, where it would remain for half a minute, apparently staring at the occupants. Then it would turn and go to the window and disappear in the curtains there. In almost all instances the figure could be distinguished plainly in the usual night illuminations. More than once Lawson saw the silhouette against the night sky. It was occasionally seen by moonlight. There was no illumination emanating from the figure, which presented the appearance of an ordinary person.

Twice the figure was questioned but without any response. In the Lent term in 1906 a third sense was concerned in the hallucination. The figure, when standing at the foot of the bed, apparently bent forward and Lawson distinctly felt a pressure on his foot. This was the only time he felt any sense of alarm. After the touch Lawson saw and heard the 'nun' walk as usual to the window curtain and vanish.

Lawson saw the figure more than a dozen times, he estimated. It was seen more frequently during the earlier part of the tenancy, possibly because with custom the noise of the footsteps ceased to arouse him.

Although Lawson never saw the door open when the figure appeared, Mrs Lawson saw it both open and close; and she never heard the loud footsteps which her husband described. (The Lawsons occupied a large bedroom immediately above room A on the plan, which was their drawing-room.) For some time Mrs Lawson merely felt the presence but later began to see a distinct dark form. Lying awake, she would see the door open a little and the figure come through and the door close (the door, she said, made a loud crack when really opened, but there was no sound these times). The figure stood for different lengths of time at the bottom of the bed, but always, it seemed to her, until it had attracted definite attention; then it would move slowly across to the curtains by the window opposite the door and not come out again.

'I never felt the least afraid or troubled by it,' Mrs Lawson said. 'Sometimes I would wake, and feel it staring and say to myself "You can just go on staring. I'm bothered if I'll look up," but I always did in the end and then it moved on. As the nights grew lighter I thought it was distinctly a woman's form and from the bulky look might have been a nun, though the white part of the headdress did not show.'

When Mrs Lawson was ill for many weeks she found the 'night visitor' very tiresome.

... seeming to grudge me any comfortable long sleep and standing for so long at the foot of my bed and latterly sighing – the only sound I heard from it. And at last one night I said quite slowly and distinctly, 'In the name of the Holy Trinity, poor soul, rest in peace.' It went away to the curtain and I have never seen or heard it since. That same night it appeared to my husband who was sleeping in the bedroom upstairs, where the steps are heard – stared at him and disappeared. He has not seen it since. The nurse, who was looking after me and then sleeping in the room opposite with both our doors open, came across to me for a few minutes after I spoke to it. She said, 'Oh, I had to come in, to make sure you were all right – I woke in such a fright thinking I felt you standing by my bed.' She had not heard me speak, so it must have gone to her after that although it disappeared into an outside wall at the opposite end of the room.

There were indications that two of the children were troubled by the apparition. The youngest girl, Jane, who slept in her mother's room for a time, told her one morning that something came and stared at her; she was sure it was a big bear. The child was moved at once to another room. That same night Mrs Lawson heard her complaining about her experience to her brother John, who replied, 'You're a great goose to be frightened at that. I *used* to be afraid of it when I was little, but I'm not now, because I know it's just God walking about and looking after us and He sometimes forgets to be quiet, when He thinks we're all asleep.'

Nothing was known by the Lawsons about the apparition before they took the house, but after they had both seen the 'Nun', and christened her as such, they heard that the house was popularly supposed in the neighbourhood to be haunted by a nun. Local legend connects the phantom nun of Abbey House with a bricked-up opening still to be seen in the cellars. This was supposed to mark the end of a tunnel which allegedly ran from Barnwell Priory to the nunnery which occupied the site of Jesus College prior to 1496. If, which may be doubted, there is such a tunnel, it certainly did not run in the direction of Jesus College.

In addition to the 'Nun', the haunting of Abbey House

included appearances of a phantom animal, described by Lawson as resembling a large-sized hare, with close-cropped ears, and named 'Wolfie' by the children. It was always seen and heard running about on its hind legs, the patter of its footsteps being very distinct and characteristic. It was never seen standing still or moving slowly. Its haunts were the downstairs rooms – drawing-room (A) and dining-room (B) – the stairs, the up-stairs passage, and the central parts of the house, parts which the 'Nun' never seemed to visit. It was generally seen in twilight but it was also seen quite clearly by artificial light in the drawing-room.

Once Lawson heard the animal coming along the passage and, turning after it had passed, saw it between himself and the light at the end of the passage. He convinced himself of its hairy outline and of its apparent solidity. The animal was once seen by one child when a second and elder child saw nothing. He estimated that it was seen about as often as the 'Nun' – about thirty times – but never by two people at the same time.

According to Mrs Lawson, the first appearance of the animal was to her son John in the spring or summer of 1904, when he was nearly three. She went to fetch him out of the nursery (D on plan) and he ran in front of her into the drawing-room (A), where he stood looking round with a puzzled expression and said at once, 'Where's it gone, Mummy?' Questioned, he described seeing a 'little brown thing' which ran to the curtain and disappeared. Mrs Lawson, thinking that her son must have seen a strange cat or dog, searched for an animal without success. She later saw the 'animal', which was a brown, furry thing about two feet high, moving quickly. Once, when she opened the door at the bottom of the steps to go up, it seemed to come rushing down the stairs and went clean through her.

Mrs Lawson's notes were written in the spring of 1908, and the animal was seen a number of times after that date, for in June 1913, she appended the remark: 'I may add that after this was written I often saw the Brown Thing about the house.'

It has several times been asserted in the press that 'Wolfie' was the ghost of a pet dog owned by a certain Squire Butler, an eighteenth-century owner of Abbey House. Butler, who was a man of huge proportions and great eccentricity, allegedly taught his dog to walk on its hind legs. Many of the stories about Squire Butler seem to originate from an anonymous Cambridge pamphlet of 1806, *The History of Barnwell Abbey near Cambridge with the Origin of Sturbridge Fair*. The account mentions Butler's favourite dog, but says nothing about his having trained it to walk on its hind legs. These stories were drawn up by A. B. Gray in his *Cambridge Revisited* (26), and it appears to have been Gray who first linked Butler's dog with the animal ghost. The suggestion that Butler had trained his dog to walk on its hind legs seems to be a journalistic superaddition to Gray's story.

Footsteps were heard by the Lawsons and others. Lawson said that heavy footsteps were frequently heard in the next bedroom (over the dining-room [B]), apparently from the floor of the room above. They seemed unduly loud for a carpeted floor and were not, so far as was known, heard by the servant sleeping in the room above. Several times, when sitting up late downstairs after his wife had retired, Lawson would hear footsteps apparently descending the stairs and the rustle of a dress. Though he sometimes went to the door he never managed to see anyone. The Newfoundland dog occasionally seemed to share the experience, going out apparently to look for someone and coming back disappointed.

Early in their tenancy Mrs Lawson was always awakened at night by the sound of someone walking up or down stairs, and although she invariably went out to look at once, never saw anything. In the drawing-room (A) she often had the feeling of there being someone else sitting there as well as herself. When her brother slept in a room at the top of the house he was disturbed by what he assumed was the ghost walking around the room all night, 'and when I was surprised at anything short of an earthquake being able to wake him – he vowed it started off by falling over his boots and making a "most unholy" noise, though it avoided them throughout the rest of "its" perambulations. The next night he heard nothing.'

Mrs Lawson added:

Most people using the room below, our spare-room, have heard the footsteps above, and have had to be persuaded it was a cook with toothache, or told the truth, according to their temperaments. At one time my husband being very ill and laid up in the spare-room, his night-nurse came across to me in the night to ask if she could go up and see what was the matter, as the tramping up and down was so pathetic. She also heard a clanking of chains, voices and many other creepy sounds during her night-watches and was altogether very miserable and nervous, though we assured her nothing was ever felt or seen in the spare-room itself.

The Abbey House file contains reports of a great many different phenomena alleged to have occurred there between 1911 and 1916. The phenomena concerned include apparitions, poltergeist effects, mysterious lights, smells of burning, footsteps, sounds of musical instruments, the stopping of a clock, and disappearance and reappearance of objects. Gauld said, 'Many of the reports are secondhand, and in most cases the incidents concerned would probably have been forgotten had the house not already gained the reputation of being haunted.'

Others shared the apparent experience of the Lawson family of an 'animal'. For instance, a young returned officer, G. Granville Sharp, moved with his wife and little daughter, Charmian, into the south end of Abbey House in August 1920. He was at that time President of the Union and was reading for the Bar, at which he later had a distinguished career. He reported that he had been in the house only a week when he found Charmian in the doorway of the dining-room (room A on plan, the Lawsons' drawing-room) crying hard, with tears rolling down her cheeks, having been frightened by an 'animal'. She was then under three years old and had never been told about the ghostly 'animal'. Later that year Charmian started talking about 'mummies' (her name for any lady was a 'mummy') who came and leant over her cot and looked at her after her mother had gone downstairs. Her cot was in the room where Mr and Mrs Lawson had seen the 'nun'.

In 1947 a small boy aged two ran into the kitchen in Abbey House (C) and called out, 'Oh look! tiny doggie,' but no animal was there.

Miss L. Chimney (pseudonym), a health visitor who lived at No. 1 Abbey House from 1952 to 1955, had an alarming experience there. When she arrived at the house to take up residence in December 1952, she was told about the queer happenings that had taken place, but took very little notice as she was tired, and retired to bed (in room A). Having gone to bed and fallen asleep, she was suddenly awakened by a metal object being forced down on her face and thought at the time it might have been a metalwork tray. She came to this conclusion as she had to place her hands underneath the rim of the tray to push it away from her face. Having pushed away the tray, Miss Chimney had the impression that it had been held down by a human figure (sex unrecognizable), which appeared unable to obtain sufficient leverage to exert the full pressure downwards. It was as if the figure were standing on a higher level than the present floor and as a result seemed to have to lean down, extending its arms forward to exert pressure. The figure and tray just disappeared, and upon switching on the light Miss Chimney saw nothing in her room, the door being shut. The next morning she related this affair to the other occupants of the house and recognized the metal tray concerned; it was in another room.

Another health visitor who shared No. 1 Abbey House with Miss Chimney was Miss Roberts (pseudonym). Miss Chimney used room A as a bed-sitting room, and Miss Roberts apparently slept in the Lawsons' former bedroom, which had been sub-divided. Miss Roberts was awakened one night in 1952 by the bedclothes flapping at the end of the bed. She sat up and whilst in this position the eiderdown was pulled over her head. She pushed it back but it came up again. This happened several times. She distinctly remembered having made the bed in hospital fashion before retiring and was at a loss to understand how the bedclothes could have been so disturbed. She described the flapping of the clothes as being similar to somebody standing at the end of the bed, holding the clothes at the end, and shaking them about. No figure, however, was seen on this occasion.

In 1959 the teenage daughter of the then occupants of No. 1 described how, when she was climbing the second flight of stairs to her bedroom in the attic, she saw reflected in the mirror of a wardrobe which stood at the top of the second flight the figure of a nun. The experience so upset her that she returned downstairs, told her mother, and would not return until accompanied by a friend.

The latest report on Abbey House comes from the present occupants, Professor and Mrs Danckwerts. In February 1975, Professor Danckwerts wrote to the Librarian of the SPR, Mr N. Clark-Lowes, 'My wife and I have lived here (in the same parts of the house as the Lawsons) since 1965, and there have been numerous children, adults and animals staying here. Apart from some dubious bumps and "atmosphere" experienced by suggestible people, there have been no phenomena to report. No. 3 Abbey House to some extent overlaps No. 2, which may account for unexplained footsteps.' However, when I got in touch with Professor Danckwerts in the summer of 1980, there was something to report. In reply to a letter of enquiry from me he wrote on 11 July that 'By a strange coincidence the first significant "phenomenon" since Gauld wrote occurred two weeks ago. An elderly lady now uses as a bed-sitting room what was the Lawsons' bedroom, haunted by the "nun" until informally exorcized by Mrs Lawson. I enclose her account. She is not "spooky" and has never previously seen an apparition. She was not upset by the episode. She says the door was "open", but it was closed before and after the episode. The "brilliant white light" cannot be accounted for by the lighting arrangements in the neighbourhood and the principal individual seen was extraneous to the household. The episode might be worth a note in the *Journal*.'

The elderly lady's account is in her own handwriting:

At approximately 3.30 a.m. on 26 June 1980 I was in bed but awake when suddenly the figure of a man appeared in the doorway. The door was open and the figure was framed in brilliant white light. A piece of furniture across the room obscures from the bed the lower part of the body from just above the waist and it was so in this case. The man was conventionally dressed in light grey jacket, light coloured shirt and dark tie. The complexion was ruddy, rather mottled, and the eyes were dark. The hair was grey and wavy. Every detail was quite distinct. He did not move but looked straight at me. I suppose it was a matter of seconds until the figure and light vanished. Immediately afterwards a 'procession' of whitish nun-like figures passed quickly across the room in front of the door in an arc formation as if climbing up a step or two and down the other side. About 5 or 6 passed in this way and then all was normal.

It is clear from this lady's account that the 'man' was a contemporary figure. The experience was committed to writing soon after the event.

The Abbey House case provides an excellent example of poltergeist-type phenomena, such as the movement of the bedclothes, being combined with the more usual haunted house-type phenomena. It should be noted how many of the phenomena occurred in what was the Lawsons' bedroom. From time to time cases are reported in which phenomena of a certain type are restricted to one part of a house. The 'nun' appeared to be almost a substantial figure, with a tread like a policeman's, and, like the phantom at Cheltenham, seemed to come within the category of what H. H. Price called a 'real object', although obviously not a physical one. The apparent movement of the door, reported by Mrs Lawson, was almost certainly hallucinated.

An amusing aspect of this case, and one I had not come across before, was the belief of Mrs Lawson's brother that the ghost had fallen over his boots! This, I feel, was his interpretation of a loud noise heard in his room, which, he believed, could have been caused by someone, or something, falling over his boots in the darkness. It showed considerable fortitude on his part to remain in the room after that.

The quickness of the movements of the little brown 'animal' will have been noted. The clairvoyante, 'Jane', remarked on the quick movements of a phantom animal in the haunted Mill House at Willington. It is possible that observations such as this will one day throw more light on the phenomena we have been studying.

What I find particularly convincing about this case is the evidence of the Lawsons. Describing them, John Lawson, their son, said in a letter to Gauld that they were staid Edwardians with a staid Victorian upbringing. 'I feel quite sure that neither was over-imaginative or predisposed towards belief in the supernatural. I am sure that prior to their own experiences they would have considered such events to have no place outside fiction or folklore. My father had considerable critical ability and would not have accepted his own experiences and recorded them without having carefully tested and cross-examined himself. My mother was a religious woman who would have been naturally unwilling to accept such events and would not have accepted them without considerable self-examination.'

Gauld talked to a number of persons who knew Lawson and none regarded him as credulous or fanciful, though Dr E. J. Dingwall, whose tutor Lawson was, felt that Lawson let slip an 'unequalled opportunity' to arrange a scientific investigation of the phenomena.

It is possible that we have not yet heard the end of the haunting of Abbey House.

14 Two Modern Hauntings

The two cases in this chapter concern families living in very different circumstances — one in a prosperous suburb in outer London and the other in a house in a mining village in South Yorkshire. The London case came to light quite by chance. The veteran Dutch parapsychologist George Zorab, when in England, met some members of the Graham family which had recently left a house which they had occupied for thirty years and which they had reason to believe was haunted. While still in residence Mrs Graham, who lived there with her husband and three daughters, had compiled an account of the hauntings to which she added notes from time to time as incidents occurred. This was signed by all members of the family except one daughter, who was away at the time, and by the home help, Mrs Turner (pseudonyms have been provided for all the people concerned), but publication was not intended.

Realizing the significance of the account, however, Zorab sent it with Mrs Graham's permission to the editor of the SPR Journal for publication, adding that he found Mr and Mrs Graham 'absolutely ignorant in the matter of psi and haunting but intelligent and completely trustworthy.' Zorab had mentioned the case to me at a conference, I made further enquiries, and as a result a report of the case, with discussion on various aspects of it, appeared under both of our names in the Journal (51h). I had two interviews in depth with the youngest of the three Graham daughters, Thelma, and these suggested to me psychological factors which should, in my opinion, be taken into account in assessing such cases.

The Yorkshire case involved a short haunting which affected two families who lived in a house owned by the National Coal Board. It is not dramatic, but it is of particular interest as the account, by K. H. Turner, of 'A South Yorkshire Haunt' in the SPR Journal (90), contains details of instruments used by the investigating group. This study will be of value to researchers and those who rightly believe that the testimony of people involved in a haunting should, wherever possible, be supported by scientific evidence.

* * *

The house in the London haunting was built around 1871 and was formed from what were originally two cottages. It is a substantial detached building, standing on high ground facing a park, and the exterior does not contain any cracks such as would occur had the house been affected by subsidence or 'settling' of the foundations. It is believed that before the cottages were converted into one dwelling they were occupied by employees of a large estate. During World War II the building was used for commercial purposes. Mr and Mrs Graham took up occupation in 1946. Their eldest daughter was born in May 1947 and the second in May 1950. Neither of these daughters noticed to any extent the phenomena experienced by the youngest daughter Thelma, who was born on 24 July 1955, and by others in the household.

'Countless times', Mr and Mrs Graham, sitting in the lounge downstairs, heard the sound of footsteps going upstairs and noises in the five upstairs bedrooms just as if someone was walking around up there. On these occasions Mr Graham went immediately to investigate, going into every room to check that a burglar had not entered the house, but there was never any trace of an intruder. Mrs Graham had always insisted that the back door to the garden should be kept locked in the evening, and when these noises were heard she checked that the door was indeed locked.

The eldest daughter Helen married George Wells (pseudonym) and they came to the house on 8 December 1973 to spend some months while the house they had bought was undergoing alterations. Shortly after this Wells, who was occupying with his wife a bedroom into which a street light allowed a certain amount of illumination, woke between 3.0 and 4.0 a.m. to see the seemingly solid figure of a young woman reaching upwards towards the wardrobe as though she were dusting. She was wearing a long, faded, washed-out-looking rust-coloured dress and a long white apron. Her sleeves were rolled up and her hair was dressed in an upswept fashion. The dress suggested that of a domestic of the last century.

Wells had a sideways view of the figure, which showed no awareness of him, for three or four minutes before it faded away. He did not wake his wife. He had not seen an apparition before and until then had been, in his own words, 'always very

ceptical' of such experiences. He related what had happened the
next day, and according to Mrs Graham, 'It was only then that
we began to put two and two together and realized that what we
had been hearing all these years could in fact be a ghost. She does
not worry us at all as she is not a nasty character, nor does she do
malicious things, but just makes her presence felt.' (This was
written early in 1975.)

Mrs Turner, who worked for Mrs Graham as a home help for
ten years, beginning in 1965, also had strange experiences. She
came two or three mornings a week, and from the beginning had
felt there was a presence in the house, often having the sensation
that someone wanted to pass her on the stairs. She had once felt
something 'flit' from the bedroom at the end of the corridor
occupied by the second daughter, Clarice, to the bathroom at a
time when she had a friend staying with her; she thought that
this was Clarice, who had slept rather late that day; but it was
neither Clarice nor the friend.

Mrs Turner had never mentioned these impressions to Mrs
Graham until quite by chance on one occasion, when both heard
a noise, Mrs Graham said jokingly, 'Perhaps it's our ghost', and
Mrs Turner looked at her without surprise and said, 'Oh, so you
do know.' Matters came to a head later in 1975 when Mrs
Turner experienced what she described as a 'physical push'
when she was walking along the upstairs landing. 'It was quite a
nasty experience,' she said later. Mrs Graham said in her
narrative that when she entered the house she found Mrs Turner
in 'an extremely shocked state.'

Thelma Graham's first visual experience was probably in
1973 – she did not make a note of the happening. She was sitting
downstairs when she had the impression of a woman gliding
silently up the stairs. She knew the figure was that of a woman
because of the clothes. Later in the same year she had gone to her
mother's bedroom upstairs to telephone and, on emerging into
the corridor, she saw the bottom part of a bright-coloured skirt
disappearing round the corner into her own sitting-room (her
bedroom adjoined). She was 'quite dumb-founded'. She did not
follow the figure but went downstairs to tell her parents what had
happened. She felt she could not go into her room.

In 1972 Thelma was alone one evening in the house; this did

not worry her. She usually went to bed between 12.30 a.m. and
1.0 a.m. and had been in bed 'quite a time' when she became
aware of noises downstairs. Her bedroom was directly above the
kitchen and it seemed to her that at least three people were
chattering there, the conversation being accompanied by bangs
and crashes as if saucepans were being replaced on the metal
shelves of the dresser. She was 'really frightened', she told me,
when she heard heavy footsteps, such as those made by a man,
coming up the creaking stairs; and was 'absolutely petrified'
when the footsteps stopped outside her door, where there was a
creaky floorboard. She went under the blankets. She could not
remember if she heard the footsteps retreating. Eventually she
went to sleep. She was convinced at the time that burglars were
in the house. When she went downstairs in the morning she
expected to find 'total destruction' because of the loud noises she
had heard, 'but everything was absolutely normal. Nothing had
been moved. I could not believe it.'

Another strange incident happened when she was in her
sitting-room making a necklace from small beads in a box which
was on the sewing machine. She left the room and when she came
back the box was gone. She went downstairs to tell her parents,
but when she returned five minutes later the box was back in its
former position. She was asked if it were possible that the box
had been there all the time. Her answer was that this was
something she could not have mistaken.

Thelma heard footsteps many times. One weekend when she
had a friend staying with her, occupying a separate room, both
heard footsteps in the corridor in the night but did not investigate.

The opening and closing of doors without apparent psychical
agency was a puzzling phenomenon in this case. Early in 1975
Mr Graham was in the bedroom one Friday evening when he
heard a door bang and assumed it was Thelma back from her
class, but on investigating found that all the doors of the rooms
were open, and that his daughter had not come in. Another
door-banging occurred on 14 January 1975. It was not the
draught, said Mrs Graham, as all the windows were closed and
no one had come into the house. Another Friday evening when
Mr Graham returned home, the house was empty, and the street
door and all the windows were closed. As he stood on the landing

at the top of the stairs, the five open bedroom doors banged shut one after another.

In September 1976, Mrs Graham had what she described as 'the strangest and most frightening experience of all.' While she was speaking to a friend on the telephone upstairs the bedroom door opened about a foot, closed again, then opened: this went on four or five times. Mrs Graham was 'petrified', stopped the conversation abruptly, and went to investigate the windows for draughts, but they were all firmly closed. She went downstairs to tell her husband what had happened. He was watching TV, the two cats were peacefully curled up in the hall, and no one was upstairs. 'The door of the bedroom I was making the telephone call in was ajar when it swung open and closed,' Mrs Graham added. 'No windows were open so there was no draught. I know this for an absolute fact, as the whole experience is extremely vivid in my mind and was the only one that really frightened me.'

As I was unable to examine the doors personally I addressed a number of questions to Mrs Graham, asking in particular if the door catches had weak springs and if the build-up of air pressure could have resulted in a sequence of door openings. Mrs Graham replied that the living room door had rising butts. All the other doors, including the bedroom doors, had orthodox hinges. The springs were not weak. The house was so solidly built that it was virtually impossible to drive a nail into the wall. The doors were heavy and solidly panelled appropriate to the age of the house.

Mrs Graham's last experience was just before the family moved in April 1977. She thought her husband had entered the living room, and heard the sound of a book or some other article of that weight being placed on the small round coffee table. She was aware of a form in a black cloak, and turned round, but there was nobody in the room and nothing on the table.

I will consider some of the implications of this case at the end of the chapter.

The next report of an investigation, by the now defunct Doncaster Group for Psychical Study, will be reassuring to readers who think that too many of the Society's investigations are conducted in large detached houses where the occupants live in comfortable circumstances, often with servants. Askern is a large mining village on the A19 road about seven miles north of Doncaster and occupies the site of a once fashionable spa. With the development of the South Yorkshire coalfield in the early years of the present century, the spa and its mineral springs were allowed to fall into disuse. Rich farmland and private estates were acquired by the newly formed colliery companies who needed all available ground to house miners and their families. In the first two to three decades of the present century some 300–400 houses were built at Askern, one of which, No. 11 West Grove, was the subject of the Group's enquiry. West Grove is one of several intersecting streets or red-brick houses situated on high ground one-third of a mile to the south-west of Askern Colliery. The colliery and its adjacent coke-oven plant are not directly visible from the house (No. 11), but occasionally mechanical sounds from the plant carry as far as the Grove, depending on wind direction. The author of the paper describing the investigation, Kenneth H. Turner, is a corporate member of the Royal Society of Chemistry (LRSC), and for the past thirty years has been employed as a chemist, mainly in the glass and steel industries.

Records of occupation at No. 11 West Grove, which was built between 1925 and 1928, are unfortunately incomplete. Nothing is known of the earliest occupants or their period of occupation. During the war years the house became empty and was used for billeting soldiers. Between 1956 and 1962 it was occupied by Mr and Mrs Holt and their three children. On moving into No. 11 Mrs Holt was ill for several months and felt unhappy in the house. Awakening suddenly one night she was startled to see a figure bending over the child's cot. When she aroused her husband, the figure disappeared into the fireplace. Holt regarded the figure as a figment of his wife's imagination and the incident was soon forgotten. No further visitation occurred and although the bedroom always felt cold, the atmosphere improved so that Mrs Holt was quite content to live there for a further five years.

Mr and Mrs Brown, a young couple in their early twenties then living at Hill Drive, Askern, exchanged houses with the occupants of No. 11 (Mr and Mrs Jarvis) in 1963. For five years the Browns, who had two children, lived quite happily at No. 11 until in the spring of 1968 a series of inexplicable events disturbed the domestic equilibrium.

Ornaments were displaced in the living-room china cabinet; a crucifix and chain draped itself over a photograph on the sideboard. In the front bedroom a pair of basket chairs turned to face each other, while visitors to the house commented on the cool breezes circulating in the living room, although a good fire was burning at the time. Metallic clicks, tappings and scraping sounds were heard about the house: several times a double click resembling an electric light switch being turned on and off was heard from the direction of the landing although no one was upstairs at the time.

One evening shortly after the family had gone to bed, Brown, who was still awake, became aware of a figure crossing by the bed. The figure paused by the dressing table as if looking for something; then, turning to its right, moved towards the curtained alcove in the bedroom, at which point it vanished. In the feeble light from a street lamp outside the figure resembled that of a youngish man with prominent chin and fair hair. The style of dress was contemporary, i.e. short coat and narrow trousers.

Convinced that this was a real intruder, Brown was quickly out of bed, switched on the lights and searched the alcove, bedroom, and the rest of the house without success. Following this incident Mrs Brown was reluctant to sleep in the house, so for the next few weeks the family spent their nights with relatives, although continuing to use the house during the day.

Mr Holmes, an uncle of Brown, remained sceptical of the whole affair and to reassure his nephew offered to sleep in the house himself. A miner in his mid-fifties, Holmes had spent his working life at Askern Colliery and knew the village well. He was unaware of any previous disturbances in West Grove and did not believe in ghosts or other paranormal phenomena.

Fully dressed and smoking a cigarette at the time, Holmes rested on the Browns' bed one evening while Brown and his wife sat in the living-room below. Suddenly he felt a cold sensation and almost immediately the side of the bed away from the door was pressed down as though someone or something had sat on it. For a moment Holmes was petrified, then jumping up he switched on the light and searched the bedroom. After satisfying himself that no one else was present, he descended to the living-room. When he entered the room Mr and Mrs Brown remarked that he looked 'as white as a sheet' and jokingly asked whether he had seen a ghost. He recounted what had happened, and the Browns confirmed that no one had entered the house or had been upstairs at the time.

From then onwards the house was not occupied at night. The local police were informed and they agreed to keep an eye on the premises in order to discourage intruders.

Evidence was given to the investigating group by two neigh-bouring families. Mr and Mrs Ford had occupied the adjoining house (No. 9) for more than twenty years. They had not heard of any unusual incidents at No. 11 until 1 April 1968 when the above disturbances began. Ford stated that they had heard clicking noises at night but attributed this to an electrical junction box fixed to the outer wall just below the eaves of the house. They appeared to be friendly towards the Browns and sympathetic regarding their problem.

Mr and Mrs Carlin had lived at No. 13 West Grove for about twenty years. They confirmed the previous testimony regarding absence of disturbances during this time, adding that they had not heard any clicks or other metallic noises. Carlin visited No. 11 during the first two weeks of April 1968, and felt a definite cold sensation in the living-room, although a good coal fire was burning in the grate at the time.

Mrs Carlin and her niece were called into No. 11 one day by Mrs Brown, who asserted that the basket chairs in the bedroom had moved. Mrs Carlin placed a piece of card under the foot of one of the basket chairs and encircled the foot. The three ladies then went into the children's bedroom; after a few minutes Mrs Carlin returned to the front bedroom and found that the foot of the chair was not coincident with the circle but was slightly displaced to one side. Carlin pointed out that the floorboards in the bedroom run from left to right across the room so that it would be difficult to tread down a board which could later click back into place on walking into the room from the door.

Following reports of these disturbances, the owners of the property, the National Coal Board, examined the house for structural defects, faulty wiring, loose boards, etc. Nothing was found to account for the phenomena and it was concluded that everything was in order. No further investigation seems to have taken place until 11 May 1968 when members of the Doncaster Group visited the house with Mr Brown.

The purpose of the investigation was twofold: first, to record any physical changes such as temperature, noise, vibration, etc.; second, to seek possible natural causes whether peculiar to the house itself or of geographical origin.

The investigators were in the house for only seven nights, during a comparatively short period – from 11 May to 8 June 1968 – and the family was not in residence at night. After that the investigation had to be abandoned.

Tests on the electric light switches in the bedrooms and on the landing and staircases showed that firm pressure would be needed to operate each one, but their action was barely audible to anyone standing more than a few feet away. Two tape recorders were used, one to pick up any sounds in the front bedroom–landing area, the second to pick up any noise within the children's bedroom, which was sealed during the period of observation. Temperature measurements were made with six thermometers, three in the bedroom, two in the living-room and one fixed outside the living-room window in such a position that it could be read from within the room by means of a torch. A check on the external temperature was thus provided, although in the event the variations from this source were less than expected.

Additional equipment used as and when required included two microphones with extension cables and amplifiers linked to meters and headphones at the central panel, vibration and sound-level meters, cameras with normal and infra-red film, a thermograph, mercury dishes, levelling devices, measuring tape, etc. Iron powder was sprinkled around a number of marked objects as an indicator of lateral displacement.

From the results of the investigation two types of phenomena predominated – thermal and acoustic. The thermal phenomena consisted of cold sensations and cool breezes, sometimes but not always coincident with sudden falls of temperature. The acoustic phenomena took the form of sporadic clicks of measurable intensity, and extraneous sounds of natural origin.

Some, at least, of the cold sensations, particularly those in which changes of temperature took place, may have been due to changes in temperature and/or humidity of the circulating atmosphere. When no change of temperature occurred, the cause, if natural, remained obscure unless of psychological origin, Turner considered. No satisfactory explanation of the double clicks was found.

When we look back on the case concerning the Graham family we realize that it started with the unexplained sound of footsteps which the parents did not associate with the haunting; but, as the children grew up, there was the introduction of other phenomena experienced by other members of the household but not by the two elder daughters. That there are such exceptions is not unusual. The American parapsychologist, W. G. Roll, commented in his book *The Poltergeist* (74), 'It is characteristic of haunting cases that only one or a few people experience the ghost, footsteps, and so on, and this may suggest a genuine case rather than one produced by trickery.' We must, of course, consider whether there could have been a physical explanation for the footsteps heard by different members of the household. When you live in a block of flats, or in adjoining premises, it is easy to make a mistake about where a sound is coming from; but the Grahams lived in a detached house, with a park facing them and quite a large back garden, so it is difficult to assume a physical cause for the footsteps that were heard so often.

There are parallels to Thelma Graham's frightening experience of hearing what seemed to be the clatter made by people at night in the kitchen below her bedroom. I showed her an account in A. A. MacGregor's *Ghost Book* of an experience by Lady Leslie, wife of Sir Shane Leslie, of Billingham Manor, Isle of Wight, during six weeks' tenancy in 1929. In the early hours there came from an adjoining room 'the most terrific commotion.' It sounded as though bodies were being hurled about, there were loud thumpings on the wall and on the door leading to the hall, where most of the phenomena sounded as if they were taking place, a metallic sound such as might have been made by a sword being withdrawn from, or being returned to, its scabbard, and the noise of furniture being moved. Lady Leslie said, 'Ghosts never entered my head, but that some evil marauder had broken into the house I was certain. So I sat shivering until dawn, then went downstairs to explore. To my amazement, nothing was touched, no chairs or tables were overturned, the silver remained in the dining-room, the doors and windows were all locked. I went outside and examined the flowerbeds under the windows, and found no footprints, so I was more puzzled than ever' (49). Miss Graham commented on the similarity of Lady Leslie's experience to her own. She thought that burglars were in the house, and that in the morning she would find 'total destruction', but nothing had been moved. The chapter on the haunting of Beavor Lodge in this book gives an example of the sounds of 'roystering' being heard downstairs by an occupant of the house but, in fact, no physical acts that could account for the sounds had taken place.

I discussed with Thelma Graham a phrase from Roll's book – 'The red thread running through most of the cases I have investigated, or am familiar with, is tension in family situations', and this evoked an immediate response. She said that when she was between 13 and 17 (1968 to 1972), and to a lesser extent in 1973, she was very disturbed and caused her family much anxiety. She went out too often, did not eat enough because she thought she was overweight (she dropped over 20 pounds in weight), and had emotional problems. Her parents wondered what she was doing and would ask her sister Clarice if she could throw any light on what was going on. Clarice, however, was having her own problems. She had married in 1972 but her marriage broke up three years later. She came home at weekends during this period. Mrs Graham confirmed that Thelma had had 'a very difficult adolescence'. It is obvious to me that there was considerable tension in the household from 1968 onwards.

In his contribution to the discussion of this case in the *Journal* Zorab said:

In the course of the last two decades I have become more and more convinced that in haunting cases as well as in poltergeist cases there was a certain living person who should be regarded as the 'energy centre' producing the phenomena observed and that the same paranormal faculties are involved in both types of spontaneous case. Haunting and poltergeist phenomena are brought about by potential 'mediums', 'psychics', etc., living in or frequenting certain premises or localities. If Mr Roll writes that the thread running through most of the cases was 'tension in family situations', I can agree with him to a certain degree. I think, however, that he misses the most important point by not remarking that one or more members of the family must have been paranormally gifted.

That such poltergeist and haunting phenomena were produced by paranormal means, Zorab felt, implied that the phenomena in hauntings, such as the hearing of footsteps, all kinds of noises, opening and shutting of doors, and even apparitions, need not be of a purely subjective, hallucinatory nature. All the phenomena listed were paralleled by phenomena reported to have been experienced in the séance room during sittings with such powerful mediums as D. D. Home, Eusapia Palladino, and a few others.

In Zorab's opinion, apparitions, though they may vanish through thick walls and walk through thin black threads stretched across a staircase without displacing any of them (56 p. 321), need not be considered figments of the imagination or subjective hallucinations. Such apparitions may possess mass and objectivity. At many Home séances, for instance, 'spirit hands and arms' often appeared out of the void and would disappear in the same manner after being felt, shaken hands with, and transporting objects. It is necessary to add, however, that one very seldom receives reports of 'spirit hands and arms' from reliable sources today.

It may be possible, at some time in the future, to make discreet enquiries on whether the phenomena experienced by the Graham family have been experienced by the new occupants, who have children. I have withheld the address in order that privacy may be preserved.

In both cases in this chapter there were physical phenomena – the opening and shutting of doors in the Grahams' home and the displacement of objects in the house at Askern. What I found particularly interesting in the latter case were the reports of cold breezes and sensations of cold. Cold breezes are often reported at séances or on occasions when a medium, or potential medium, is present. When the amateur medium 'Mrs Willett' (Mrs Coombe Tennant) was visiting Fishers Hill, Surrey, the residence of the Earl of Balfour, during his last illness and was in the sickroom, she complained to his brother, Gerald Balfour, of feeling cold, and declared there was 'an icy wind' blowing between them, although he felt nothing (4).

15 A Field for Research

In the preceding chapters dealing with hauntings we have been presented with evidence – and I do not think this is too strong a word – of some extremely strange phenomena. Apparitions, we have discovered, need not necessarily be the figures of the known dead; for instance, the little boy in the haunted mill house at Willington [Chapter 4] saw the figure of a boy who resembled him, and other haunting apparitions have a certain 'family resemblance' in that they are in the form of women with part of the face concealed and given to the habit of staring. Haunting figures of men are much less common. These figures are not confined to physical space or time; indeed, it is far from certain that some were ever 'in the flesh'. As our minds are attuned to a certain manner of thought which, we like to think, conforms to the reality of the nature of the physical world, we tend to recoil from accounts of experiences which suggest that the world is really much more complex than we had imagined, or could imagine.

The realization of this is, naturally, most disturbing. Many people – perhaps the majority – will tend to reject the evidence for haunting collected by the Society for Psychical Research, since it was founded a century ago, on the grounds that 'it can't be true' or 'there must be a natural explanation for these happenings the Society has investigated', but the indications are that the experiences took place as described, and if there is an explanation for the sounds of footsteps, knocks on doors, dragging sounds as if furniture was being moved, and the appearance of apparitions, it has so far eluded us, even when every allowance has been made for a natural cause and human weaknesses in observation and memory of events. Indeed, it is the persistence of the pattern in hauntings that leads us to believe in the reality of the phenomena described by those who have experienced it.

On the last page of her long study of Phantasms of the Dead (81a p. 150), Mrs Sidgwick said:

There are numerous cases of seemingly similar apparitions seen in particular houses, without apparently any possibility of the similarity being the result of suggestion or expectation; but the evidence connecting such haunting with any definite dead person is, on the whole, very small; and the evidence for the operation of any intelligent agency in the haunting, at present absolutely nil; and until we can discover more about the laws that seem to govern such haunting, we are hardly justified in forming any theory as to the cause, except as a provisional hypothesis.

We are still ignorant of the laws which govern hauntings, if indeed there are such laws. Nearly a hundred years after Mrs Sidgwick wrote those words, we know very little about hauntings themselves, principally because the subject has been neglected by serious researchers. I find myself in agreement with Mrs Sidgwick's conclusions. There does not seem to be evidence for the operation of any intelligent agency in most hauntings, though in the occasional case in which there is a response to questions or taunts in the form of raps (Chapter 5) there are indications that a rudimentary form of intelligence may be operating. That experienced investigator W. H. Salter has pointed out in *Zoar* that in certain forms of automatism (table-tilting and planchette, for example) 'an *ad hoc* intelligence emerges which is not the intelligence of any single member of the group', but he stressed that what emerged was too rudimentary and transient to be called a personality (76b p. 216).

It seems to me, after studying a great many cases of haunting, that what is in operation is a subtle interaction between a person, or family, and a house or area. Some places are imbued with feeling or atmosphere – call it what you will – which may be experienced by a sensitive person, although not by others, and this interaction of person and place can result in hallucinations in which apparitions are seen or footsteps or strange sounds heard. Such apparitions may not be those of persons who ever lived in the house, or frequented a certain spot; but when descriptions of the figure seen are in general agreement, as in the Cheltenham case, it is possible that the apparition is that of a former resident. But what is one to make of dragging sounds, or noises which suggest the movement of objects, so often heard in a haunting? Is the haunting figure trying to draw attention to itself, or is some sort of disturbance set up in the mind of the listener? I cannot even venture an answer.

I am attracted by Professor Price's concept of telepathically charged images being significant factors in some hauntings, so that when a sensitive person enters a house or place scenes of the past, or events, are animated again. Some families, obviously, do not have this power of animating a place. For instance, the Unthank family lived in the mill house at Willington for twenty-five years without any untoward happening; but when the Proctors moved in, the series of disturbances set in motion made life intolerable, so that eventually they had to leave. The Richmond family, too, were almost driven from Beavor Lodge by the disturbances that took place there.

The accounts of apparitions and hauntings published by the SPR during the past century have been, in the main, plain, unadorned narratives with emphasis on evidential aspects of the case. In this, I feel, the various editors of the *Journal* and *Proceedings* have been wise; what has been needed has been evidence, rather than theory, if a sceptical world was to be convinced of the reality of such happenings. But now, surely, the time has come for more emphasis to be placed on theoretical aspects of this branch of psychical research and on the psychological background of certain cases in which the influence of stress will obviously have to be taken into account. The Bull Case (Chapter 11) is an example. Here we had a large family living in a condemned cottage in winter. Conditions were propitious for the appearance of the apparition of a dead father and grandfather who, it was believed, had the welfare of his family at heart, even after death. On the other hand, the Cheltenham case suggests the wanderings of the apparition of an unhappy woman who was rejected by the children of her husband's first, happy, marriage. Other examples could be given.

But close scrutiny of a particular case can be time-consuming, and in a field in which there are, as yet, too few researchers it is understandable that some cases have not had the necessary amount of attention they deserve devoted to them. 'The long and complicated task of mathematical assessment' of cases in the

1959 report of enquiry into spontaneous cases carried out by the late Sir George Joy, then Honorary Secretary of the SPR, and Celia Green worked out very roughly as seventy man-hours per case (82d p. 96), and Rosalind Heywood has related that Edward Osborn told her that his investigation of The Woman in Brown, which he ultimately traced to psychological causes only, took him about 200 hours (82d p. 95).

Dr D. J. West, who is a psychiatrist, has pointed out in his *Psychical Research Today* (93b p. 34) that 'It would be a help if investigators always had a sound practical knowledge of psychology, so as to recognize when an explanation in terms of abnormal mental processes will cover some seemingly mysterious experience.' This, he said, was well brought out in the case of 'The Woman in Brown' (62), which might easily have been put down as a psychic experience had it not come into the hands of an investigator who carried out, with psychiatric consultation, a painstaking psychological enquiry.

The Woman in Brown was an apparition seen thirteen times between November 1948 and May 1949 by someone who in the report is called Miss Benson. She worked in a London office, and it was always there that she saw the figure. The office building, badly damaged by a flying bomb in 1944, was practically rebuilt in 1948. One of the office workers, Mrs Johnson, was 'very psychic' and had seen many spirit faces and heard many footfalls. On her first visit to the office the thought came to her that someone may have died in the blitz. Her imagination was fed still more by a workman's dramatic story of the casualties and devastation caused by the flying bomb in 1944. Very soon Mrs Johnson was saying she had seen in the basement a man in a boiler suit who was 'not of this earth'.

Miss Benson said she had not heard Mrs Johnson's story when first she saw the woman in brown, but when she was told about it she was inclined to accept the suggestion that both apparitions were ghosts of war victims. Mrs Johnson, having heard of the woman in brown, then saw a man in brown in the cloakroom, but not everyone took this seriously, as Mrs Johnson was so well known for her tall stories.

After Miss Benson had seen her apparition four times, another office worker, Miss Dixon, became nervous of being on the top floor alone. One evening she felt she had 'walked into someone' who looked like a tall woman in brown. Edward Osborn, the SPR investigator, stood at the same spot and saw a shadow cast by the street lamp on a cupboard. It grew darker as it was approached and could easily have given the impression Miss Dixon described.

Osborn thought that an explanation of the genesis of Miss Benson's hallucinations might lie in what she was thinking about just before she saw the figure. He found that Miss Benson was suggestible and could easily be hypnotized. He made use of this to put her in a state of mind in which she could tell him things which ordinarily she would say she could not remember. Osborn discovered that her hallucination was each time preceded by some thought connected with an emotional complex from which she was suffering.

Miss Benson's complex was one in which ideas of guilt and death were intermingled. She told her superior, Miss Watson, and later repeated in greater detail to Osborn, a story about a bombing incident during which she had been on duty at a Report Centre at Southwood and had cycled to a post which had been hit and where a woman named as Miss Thorpe was lying in a pool of blood. Not knowing what to do, Miss Benson gave prior attention to a man whose arms were badly cut. Ever after she felt guilty, thinking that she had not done what she should to save Miss Thorpe's life.

Investigation revealed that Miss Benson's story was a fantasy. The bombing incident had taken place, although not quite as she had described it, but she had never been there herself and had only heard about it. Her fantasy must have been what psychologists call a 'screen memory', that is, a false picture unconsciously fabricated in order to blot out a more guilt-ridden memory. The guilt feeling becomes more bearable when attached to the screen memory instead of to its true object. Possibly the memory that her fantasy was trying to conceal was that of her mother's death. Miss Benson was seventeen at the time and passionately attached to her mother. She was brought home to find her mother's body lying on the floor covered over with a dark rug. Miss Benson was so affected that she could not at first accept that her mother was dead, and since then she had never been able to speak about it.

Osborn made Miss Benson recall, under hypnosis, the circumstances in which she saw the apparition, and the thoughts she had

had in mind at the time. On several occasions she saw the apparition just after the telephone rang. Telephone ringing was for her associated with the succession of telephone calls when she was waiting at the Report Centre. It was also a telephone call that had summoned her home to find her mother dead. West said:

It was clear that the 'apparition' was only one of a number of signs of mental conflict and understandable, not in terms of ESP or ghosts, but in terms of Miss Benson's own anxieties. Working in bomb-damaged premises no doubt stimulated her guilt fantasies, while her ghost-seeing colleagues provided the background for the onset of the hallucinations. But for the investigation under hypnosis, this interpretation would not have been at all obvious. This case brings home the need for a psychological approach, which should be applied to all spontaneous cases irrespective of ESP content. Such cases as that of Lt. McConnel [Chapter 2] would be far more interesting if the percipient's mental state at the time of seeing the apparition could have been explored (93b pp. 36–7).

I agree with West on the need for a psychological approach to all spontaneous cases, and that is why I have given the case of The Woman in Brown at some length, but surely the cases of Miss Benson and Lieut. Larkin, who saw the apparition of McConnel, are quite different. There was never, so far as we know, a Woman in Brown; but, unknown to Larkin, his room-mate McConnel was dying, or had just died, when his apparition was seen. Miss Benson was burdened with a load of guilt; Larkin was a young flyer, physically fit, and probably as extrovert as most young airmen are. This is not to say that he did not have anxieties or suffer from stress, but this is common to the human race. The 'apparition' Miss Benson saw was a fantasy, but all reports of apparitions cannot be dismissed as fantasies. Some convey information which is afterwards found to be correct.

The idea that 'ghosts' are the spirits of the dead is so widespread, and so deeply implanted in what may be termed the collective unconscious, that it has been rejected by many, in a secular age, as being unworthy of discussion on the grounds that it was all very well for primitive people to hold such a belief but science has cleared away 'all such nonsense'. However, once we put aside the conception of apparitions, and hauntings, as *invariably* being manifestations of activity by the dead, and accept that it is capable of different interpretations, we see the subject from a different angle. Most apparitional experiences, I suggest, should be regarded as dreams when awake, but with the important difference that when we see an apparition we usually do so as an observer, and are not part of the apparitional scene, whereas in dreams we are active participants in the drama being played out in our sleep. However, certain cases suggest that when people are awake, but in an altered state of consciousness, they can become participants in an apparitional drama. An example is provided by the Versailles Case in which Miss Moberly and Miss Jourdain, during their walk through the park of the Petit Trianon, conversed with figures seen there.

The significance of dreams as hallucinations has been realized from the earliest days by the SPR but differences in classification have developed. In her introduction to her long paper on *Phantasms of the Living* (81f pp. 27–8) Mrs Sidgwick said that Edmund Gurney had treated separately dreams, 'borderland' cases (that is, experiences occurring when the percipient was in bed but believed himself to be awake), and hallucinations when the percipient was up and about, while she treated these three classes together. For the sake of argument at least, she said, we could assume that Gurney's book had accomplished its object and that telepathy was proved, adding, 'In speaking of telepathy as proved, I do not of course mean that it is yet accepted by the scientific world. Much more accumulation of well-evidenced instances will be required before this can be claimed. But we want more than the mere piling up of facts. Our facts will be the more readily accepted, the more we can compare them, and, provisionally assuming telepathy, show when and how it occurs.'

During the past century views on how telepathy operates have changed. In her presidential address for 1980, Dr Louisa E. Rhine, who has collected thousands of spontaneous cases, said that when she examined all the cases she had classified as telepathic, because the unexpressed thought of one person had been received by another, she found three different situations. In one an agent had 'sent' his thought; in a second, he had not consciously done so but had been thinking of the percipient; in the third, he had not even thought of the percipient, and in some cases he did not even know him. 'The percipient received the thought, thus making the "sending" irrelevant. The conclusion had to be that the telepathic process was not necessarily different from that in clairvoyance and precognition.'

Dr Rhine's conclusion from this was that 'the assumption that the idea originated with the agent was unnecessary. The percipient, not the agent, could be the author of the entire phenomena. By ESP he could secure unconsciously the pertinent information without an agent, just as in the other two types [clairvoyance and precognition].'

Dr Rhine argued that this change in the concept of the telepathic process, of course, affected the interpretation of the line of evidence that had earlier been taken as a possible sign of survival, that of apparitions; and while it was still true that influence from the discarnate could have a part in structuring the hallucinatory effect, the assumption that it necessarily did so was no longer necessary, 'for the combination of ESP and the percipient's ability to hallucinate could produce the effect. The suggested evidence of survival in apparitions was thereby deflated . . .'

In his summing up of the McConnel case to which I have already referred, West asked, 'What was the connection, if any, between McConnel's death and Larkin's experience? The theory favoured by most investigators is that Larkin became aware, subconsciously, and by means of ESP, that McConnel had been killed, and that this subconscious knowledge, striving to gain expression, gave rise to the hallucination' (93b p. 28).

Dr Rhine and Dr West are substantially in agreement on this, but I have reservations because both are assuming considerable powers of extrasensory perception among ordinary people, which are seldom apparent in other situations. Indeed, West points out, 'Larkin stated that the experience *was* for him quite exceptional. There is no doubt that had he been questioned on the point he would have vigorously denied that he was subject to hallucinations, expectant or otherwise.'

I feel that we must leave the question of agency in apparitional experience open, bearing in mind Dr Rhine's statement in her address that 'as yet, however, no method has been found to trace the source of *psi*.'

In some respects the pattern of apparitional cases, but not of hauntings, has changed in the past century. Experimental cases are now few and far between, and crisis cases do not comprise as high a proportion of all cases as they did, although they are regularly reported. Examples of apparitions of the living are still reported in considerable numbers, and I am surprised that the significance of this has not received more attention because, if we are to accept the reports of such cases, they may indicate that man has an etheric body. It will be remembered that the scholars who contributed to the debate on various theories to account for apparitions ended up with what they termed 'a revised "etheric-object" hypothesis' and, on the evidence for apparitions of the living, I find myself in agreement with their conclusion (31b pp. 228–31). It seems to me that in many respects there is a 'family likeness' between apparitions of the living and out-of-the-body experiences, to which Celia Green has already drawn attention (27b); but I will not dwell on this, as Dr Susan Blackmore is contributing a book on out-of-the-body experiences to this series.

When I first studied apparitions, I thought the evidence pointed to their being, in the main, subjective experiences, but gradually my view has changed until I now accept that some apparitions might be what Professor Price calls 'real objects . . . neither mental nor physical, but betwixt and between' (31b p. 238). It is difficult to accept as purely hallucinatory the figure of the tall woman in black seen so often at Cheltenham, once for half an hour. The solicitor, George Gooding, accepted as quite natural the figure he saw as a child at the house *before* the Despard family took up residence. On one occasion, probably after the Despards had arrived, a ring was made round the figure 'from which she appeared merely to walk out between two people and then disappeared', according to Gooding. I have quoted the secondhand report in *Light* of how it used to be 'quite a common experience' for boys in Cheltenham to go and see the ghost dancing across the lawn. As I have been able to interview three reliable people about a figure resembling the tall woman in black being seen at night at two different houses in Cheltenham, it does seem that there is some evidence for this haunting being continued in the Pittville neighbourhood, and the persistence of the figure suggests that it might be akin to a 'real object'.

If some apparitions are 'real objects' might it not be possible to detect their presence with instruments? This is the hope of Dr Karlis Osis, Chester F. Carlson Research Fellow at the American Society for Psychical Research (ASPR), who has recently issued a call for cases of apparitions, asking for help in what he termed 'breathtaking research possibilities' (63). Osis, with whom I discussed apparitions at some length during two of his visits to London, has appealed for cases where there is more than one person, or pet, present. He has developed a research model which elucidates four basic kinds of apparitions and enables us to search for the roots of these phenomena. 'Since the turn of the century, investigators have realized that apparitional phenomena may hold the key to fuller understanding of human personality, but methods were lacking for solving the mystery. We now have methods and equipment, developed in out-of-the-body and near-death research at the ASPR and elsewhere, for finding out the meaning and value of these varieties of apparitional experiences. We hope to gain essential insights into that part of our being which seems to be relatively independent of the body and which may even continue after corporeal death.'

I asked Osis for details of his project which, he replied, was still at the planning stage. The four groups of apparitions were those collectively perceived, with a here-and-now orientation; singly received, with a here-and-now orientation; collectively perceived, orientated to the past; and singly perceived, orientated to the past. He predicted that collective cases, in which two or more persons observed an apparition which reacted to the present environment, might be registrable by instruments, similar to those developed by the ASPR's out-of-the-body research project. High sensitivity (.05 foot-candle) video recording had been explored, but experience showed that a lower light was needed, possibly .001 f.c.

The ASPR expects two parallel approaches: a large-scale survey when the project is funded, and an intensive study of apparitional cases now in progress. The latter, it is believed, will have considerable emphasis on the search for new hypotheses.

In his letter to me Osis commented, 'We hope to find more clarity and consistency when viewing different kinds of separate groups of apparitions rather than the whole bag. I do believe that striving for a unified view of all apparitions has been a handicap even for so brilliant a mind as Tyrrell's. It could be that Myers and Gurney are both right – but concerning apparitions of different origins. I am personally most interested in Myers's type – intruding in the external space of the observer – rather than the telepathy or retrocognition types.'

The Gurney hypothesis interpreted apparitions as mental hallucinations, created by individual percipients in response to telepathic impulses directly or indirectly received from the appearer; the Myers-Price theory, which has been further developed by Raynor C. Johnson, suggested that apparitions are etheric images, created currently, or in the past, by some mental act. I agree with Osis when he says that 'striving for a unified theory of apparitions has been a handicap' because apparitions vary so widely. For every one which suggests a 'real object' of a very strange type there were scores which suggest nothing more than a psychic husk, wandering aimlessly at a certain spot.

In his Myers Memorial Lecture in 1952, of which an extract is quoted in Chapter 3, Thouless suggested that in order to have a really illuminating investigation of a good haunting a prolonged occupation of the house by a team of research workers with full equipment of recording devices would be necessary. The Society, however, has never been in a financial position to buy haunted houses, and the ASPR is planning to carry out its investigations in a laboratory, although recording equipment could be installed in a haunted house if necessary. This American initiative in research is to be welcomed, and if eventually it shows results the SPR in London, and research institutes on the Continent, could join in.

Before the American project for the investigation of apparitional experiences gets under way, however, some thought needs to be given to problems associated with haunted houses or areas. It has been shown time and again that when people sit up waiting for a ghost to appear nothing happens. The reason, obviously, is that alertness is a deterrent. In the last chapter I outlined steps taken by a research group in South Yorkshire to investigate phenomena in a miner's house with the aid of instruments *but without the presence of the usual occupants of the house at night.*

In my opinion, a haunting is the result of a family's interaction with a house and, if the family is removed, although only temporarily, little can be expected. Whatever it is in a house that gives rise to the phenomena, it can hardly be expected to react automatically to the efforts of a group of alert technicians, even if led by an experienced and sympathetic investigator.

Is there an answer to this problem? I suggest that when a haunted house is investigated the necessary equipment should be installed without undue fuss and with the least possible noise and that the family should remain in residence. Very often the presence of one particular person is necessary before phenomena occur, whether it be table-turning, the operation of a ouija board, a successful séance, the hearing of the sound of footsteps without apparent physical cause, or the appearance of an apparition to different people. Sometimes the presence of a particular individual inhibits the production of phenomena. I can envisage a situation in which an aggressive and unsympathetic investigator at the head of a group of technicians could so create a feeling of hostility in a house by his desire to demonstrate that *he* was the one to make an experimental breakthrough in this highly controversial field, that nothing whatever could happen.

What is needed in the investigation of a haunted house is close co-operation between the family in residence and the experimenters, with possible changes in the investigating team when no results are being achieved. If nothing happens the experiments should not be blamed; in all hauntings the phenomena are intermittent. By sheer good luck the investigators with their recording instruments could be present when phenomena were occurring. The subjective or objective nature of what was taking place could then, provisionally, be established. For instance, an investigator, and members of the household, might hear footsteps which were not recorded; but this would not necessarily mean that the experience was purely subjective – it might prove possible to record the sounds on a more sophisticated instrument.

The possibility of achieving a breakthrough in some fields of psychical research by the use of instruments should not be underestimated. An example of this is provided by Dr Morton Schatzman, M.D., an American psychiatrist working as a psychotherapist in London, in his book *The Story of Ruth*, a summary of which he has provided in an article in *The New Scientist* (77c). Schatzman says by way of introduction that in childhood his playmates and he occasionally asked each other, 'Do you believe in ghosts?' He supposed that the question referred to a belief that 'ghosts' were entities which actually existed outside the minds of those who experienced them. He did not believe in 'ghosts' in that sense then, and he did not think he did now, but added, 'If I were asked now, "Do you believe that people experience apparitions?" my answer would be, "Yes. People sometimes see, hear, smell, or feel the presence of someone who is not really there."'

Schatzman described how a young American woman, whom he called Ruth, who was not insane or suffering from an organic disorder, told him that she often perceived figures of people who were not really there. These figures looked as real to her, Ruth told him, as live persons. She could perceive them voluntarily and to some extent could direct their behaviour; they talked just like live persons; the sound of their voices hindered her perception of actual sounds; they cast shadows; and they blocked from her view objects and walls behind them.

Was she telling the truth? To answer this question Dr Peter Fenwick, a neurophysiologist and psychiatrist at the Institute of Psychiatry and at St Thomas's Hospital, London, used a method based upon visual-evoked and auditory-evoked responses. If a normal person looks at a television screen displaying a chequerboard pattern in which the white squares repetitively change to black ones and the black ones to white ones at a rate of about one a second, or looks at a flashing stroboscopic light, electrical reponses to the stimuli are evoked in the occipital cortex, the part of the brain concerned with receiving visual information. These responses, when recorded on an electroencephalogram (EEG), are called visual-evoked responses. Clicks delivered through headphones to the ears of a normal person elicit responses in the cerebral cortex which, when recorded on an electroencephalogram, are called auditory-evoked responses. Fenwick and Schatzman asked Ruth to produce an apparition between her eyes and the reversing chequerboard pattern on the television screen. She had alleged that apparitions blocked objects behind them; this indicated that an apparition might interfere with her experiencing the stimulation of the chequerboard pattern. What would her visual-evoked response show? Would the apparition inhibit it, in the same way as a real person or object; or would her brain continue to respond to the stimulus?

When Ruth looked at the reversing chequerboard pattern on the television screen and did not hallucinate, she showed a normal visual-evoked response with an amplitude of 18 microvolts. When she hallucinated the figure of her eight-year-old daughter sitting on her lap, so that the head of the figure blocked Ruth's perception of the screen, her visual-evoked response was absent. When on a further trial she reported that the head of her daughter did not fully cover the screen, the amplitude of the evoked response was reduced to only 8 microvolts. According to Schatzman, 'Ruth's reports of how completely the screen in front of her was obstructed consistently corresponded to how much the visual-evoked response displayed on the oscilloscope behind her was inhibited.'

The two doctors did control experiments to determine whether pupillary convergence, or not paying attention to the stimulus, each of which reduces the visual-evoked response, could have been responsible for her absent visual-evoked response, and they found that they were not. Other tests revealed that the blocking of Ruth's visual-evoked response had occurred by pathways to the brain other than those controlling the adaptation of the pupils to darkness and light.

In Fenwick's laboratory, Ruth sat with headphones listening to clicks being delivered at a rate of about two a second. Her auditory-evoked response was normal. Fenwick suggested to Ruth that she have the apparition of her daughter turn down the volume control on the machine producing the clicks to the point where Ruth could not hear them, and he showed Ruth the control knob. When Ruth tried this, her auditory-evoked response was completely absent. In blocking her responses, Schatzman commented,

. . . she had produced electrical events that were measurable objectively and corresponded with hallucinatory experience. How had she managed to do it? Probably she had an unusually good capacity to focus her attention where she wanted and to exclude thereby things around her. Whether other hallucinators can inhibit their evoked responses may depend on whether they can control their hallucinations to the degree that she can.

Could the entities Ruth allegedly saw and heard, Schatzman wondered, be in some sense real? 'I did not see how that was possible – folklore notwithstanding – but nothing would be lost by performing a few tests. I tried to record with a Polaroid camera and a video camera the visual image of an apparition she saw, but when I did, neither she nor anyone else saw the apparition on the photographs or the videoscreen. I also tried to tape-record the sounds of an apparition she heard talking, but when I played the tape back neither she nor anyone else heard anything.'

Reports of experiences with apparitions since the earliest days of the SPR have included details of how the seemingly solid figure obscured objects behind it; but this is the first time, so far as I know, that experimental proof in support of this claim has been obtained. Schatzman thought that Ruth probably 'had an unusually good capacity to focus her attention where she wanted and to exclude thereby things around her.' I agree, but even more remarkable is her ability to hallucinate at will. In the early SPR publications stress is often placed, in reports of crisis cases, on the fact that this was the only hallucinatory experience the percipient had ever had. I have had many letters from people who claim to have had several experiences with apparitions but never one from a person who said that he or she could produce an apparition at will. The lesson to be drawn from this is that progress in parapsychology will, to some extent, depend on the availability of exceptional experimental subjects such as Ruth.

It is significant that Schatzman was unable to photograph a figure which, Ruth claimed, was in a certain spot. Could the figure have been photographed with more sophisticated equipment than that used by Dr Schatzman? We do not know, but Ruth would obviously be a very good subject for Karlis Osis's forthcoming series of tests. Although photographs of white, misty figures in a building are produced from time to time as proof that 'ghosts' can be photographed I am very doubtful about such claims. It has still to be proved, to my satisfaction and that of many other open-minded students of this subject, that apparitions can be photographed; but they are none the less real for that. The heading placed on Schatzman's article in the *New Scientist* was 'Evocations of Unreality', which, to say the least, is strange, considering the experimental findings by Schatzman, Fenwick, and others named in the article.

Scientific investigations of spots said to be haunted can be carried out without the use of instruments. An account of one such study has been published by the psychologist Dr Gertrude R. Schmeidler, a well-known figure in parapsychology in the United States (78). Three members of a family of four reported that certain places in their home were haunted, and that they agreed in their accounts of the ghost's age, sex, and personality. They marked on a floor plan of the house the places occasionally haunted and frequently haunted; and they scored a personality check list for traits characteristic of the ghost and opposite to the ghost. Nine sensitives toured the house, marked copies of the floor plans for locations they considered haunted, and scored the check list. Two of the sensitives' locations were similar to the family's and to each other's – a sensitive was defined as someone who thought himself (or herself) capable of sensing a ghost – and four other sensitives' personality descriptions were similar to the family's. The remaining five sensitives described two different types of ghost personality. [Eleven sensitives agreed to take part, but two did not return usable reports.] Dr Schmeidler's conclusion was that 'A family's reports of the location of hauntings and of the personal characteristics of a ghost were confirmed by sensitives at a high rate of statistical significance. The question of what the family and the sensitives were responding to is still open.' (One of those who visited the house, but did not take part in the experiment, was a distinguished sensitive, Eileen Garrett; she reported that there was no ghost in the house.)

An attempt was made to identify some dead person with the ghost's characteristics who was associated with the family, the house or the site, or who was likely to try to deliver some message through these appearances. 'Casual enquiries along these lines came to a dead end. There was no hint of a message; no such person (a man who was forty-five or older, meek, gentle and anxious) was associated with the family; and so far as the inhabitants of the house knew, no such person was earlier associated with the house or the site.'

In her interpretation of the data, Dr Schmeidler considered that an autonomous or semi-autonomous 'presence' may have been created by the strong needs of a living person; and it may have been this presence to which some of the family and some of the sensitives were responding, but she considered this suggestion 'highly speculative'.

Pointing out that the question 'Whose ghost was there?' could be restated in the more general form 'Who created the ghostly impression?', Dr Schmeidler considered that in this form it was clearly parallel to questions often raised about poltergeist phenomena. There was perhaps a tenuous clue or two to connect the phenomena with the friend who had reported the case to her.

It was she who first felt the haunting and who later felt such strong anxiety about it that she ran from the house; it was she who, as it were, socialized the ghost by telling about it and offering it up to research; and after she had done this it was she who rid herself and her children of it by ordering it to leave her. She seems to have initiated, directed, and terminated the events. She also seems to have considerable psychic ability, evidenced by a number of vivid and detailed experiences that may well be telepathic. All these comments are consonant with the conclusion reached by Mrs Garrett when she toured the house: that the lady of the house was 'eminently psychic . . . she might be producing the shadows'.

These odd bits and pieces may lead us to wonder whether a ghostly presence could be created unconsciously by a person with strong psychic abilities, and whether this presence could be perceived by others. The line of speculation suggests that, if poltergeist phenomena may be created by a living person's repressed hostility, apparitions may be created by other repressed needs of a living individual.

It is interesting that Mrs Garrett should have used the word 'shadows'. In the account of the haunted mill house at Willington in Chapter 4, the clairvoyante 'Jane', asked to describe the apparition, said 'she is just like a shadow', suggesting a figure without even a vestige of personality. However, as other figures do suggest something more 'real', an umbrella term cannot be used to cover all types of apparitions. Some apparitions may be created unconsciously by a person with strong psychic abilities, as Schmeidler has suggested; certainly this suggests a line for future research.

Unless they have had personal experiences of the hauntings described in this book, many readers will consider them to conflict with the generally accepted view of the nature of reality. But scientific opinion in this field is changing. As the physiologist

Dr Kit Pedler has pointed out in the *Guardian* of 18 June 1980, discoveries in modern physics could provide an intellectual framework in which such things as ghosts and poltergeists can be explained.

The real trouble is that people won't believe anything they can't explain. The old rules of physics – where God winds up the system to let it run like clockwork – may produce new technical advances. But they just can't contain the new discoveries. Ghosts, for instance, may be like a footprint which some event has left imprinted in time. I don't know. But refusing to believe can be just as dogmatic as faith.

Pedler's conception of ghosts as being like footprints which some event has left imprinted in time is not unlike Price's, except that the latter has preferred to think in terms of images. It has often seemed to me that some apparitions may be thought of as memory traces which can be animated under certain circumstances.

In his booklet *Psychology and Psychical Research*, Professor Sir Cyril Burt pointed out that the most outspoken critics of parapsychology, such as Professor C. E. M. Hansel, took their stand on the old materialistic assumptions which formed the basis of 'classical' physics. The universe was regarded as essentially a purely physical world, and by this they meant a completely mechanical world (14a p. 61). As it is obviously important for us to try to fit phenomena of the type described in this book into a framework for which some scientific support can be claimed, let us go into this matter in some detail. I take as my guide Professor Paul Davies, who holds the chair of theoretical physics at Newcastle University. He is not, so far as I know, involved in parapsychology, but what he has to say in his recent book *Other Worlds* does have a bearing on the matters we have been discussing.

Professor Davies claimed that the greatest scientific revolution of all time, which took place between 1900 and 1930, had gone largely unnoticed by the general public, not because its implications were uninteresting, 'but because they are so shattering as to be almost beyond belief – even to the scientific revolutionaries themselves.' The revolution was the development of what is known broadly as the quantum theory, which began with an attempt to explain certain technical aspects of subatomic physics by postulating the existence of other worlds parallel to ours. Science, it had been believed, helped to build a picture of objective reality – the world 'out there'. 'With the advent of the quantum theory,' Davies pointed out, 'this very reality appears to have crumbled, to be replaced by something so revolutionary and bizarre that its consequences have not yet been properly faced . . . one can either accept the multiple reality of the parallel worlds, or deny that a real world exists at all, independently of our perception of it' (18 pp. 11–15). These studies showed that reality, inasmuch as it had any meaning at all, was not a property of the external world on its own but was intimately bound up with our perception of the world – our presence as conscious observers. Quantum theory reinstated the observer at the centre of the stage. Indeed, some prominent scientists had even gone so far as to claim that quantum theory had solved the riddle of the mind and its relation to the external world, asserting that the entry of information into the consciousness of the observer was the fundamental step in the establishment of reality. 'Taken to its extreme, this idea implies that the universe only achieves a concrete existence as a result of this perception – it is created by its own inhabitants!'

Maintaining that the inherent uncertainty of nature was not confined to matter, but even controlled the structure of space and time, Davies argued:

Space and time can change their shape and extension – crudely speaking they move about – and like sub-atomic matter their motion is somewhat random and uncontrolled . . . Our experiences of time lie closest to our perception of reality, and any attempt to build a 'real world' must come to grips with the paradoxes of time. The most profound puzzle of all is the fact, that, whatever we may experience mentally, time does not pass, nor does there exist a past, present and future. These statements are so stunning that most scientists lead a sort of dual life, accepting them in the laboratory, but rejecting them without thought in daily life. Yet the notion of a moving time makes no sense at all in daily affairs, in spite of the fact that it dominates our language, thoughts and actions. It is here, perhaps, that new developments lie, in unravelling the linkage between time, mind and matter.

The weird world revealed by the investigations of those engaged in psychical research has been matched by the equally weird, or even weirder, world of the physicist. Such discoveries as those related here will be met not so much by scorn, as in the past, but by incomprehension, so limited is our grasp of the conceptions involved.

It has been argued, Davies admits, that the other universes are not real, but only contenders for reality – failed alternative worlds: but they cannot be ignored, 'for it is central to the quantum theory, and can be checked experimentally, that the alternative worlds are not always completely disconnected from our own: they overlap our perceived universe and jostle its atoms.'

Some cases of haunting, such as that at Versailles, where figures in the costume of a bygone age are seen from time to time, suggest the possibility of fragments of life from an overlapping world. We have noted that apparitions are not in physical space and time: certain experiences involving retrocognition certainly suggest adjustments to time. I do not think it is an exaggeration to say that in the light of quantum mechanics, parapsychology makes much more sense than before.

In his *Wholeness and the Implicate Order*, David Bohm, Professor of Theoretical Physics at Birkbeck College, London, has described his work on non-locality (or 'action at a distance'); and his wedding of physics and consciousness have caused some parapsychologists to look to his theory for an explanation of such phenomena as telepathy, precognition and psychokinesis. According to Danah Zohar, commenting on the idea, Bohm does not repudiate this interpretation, but maintains neutrality: 'Unlike classical physics, the Implicate Order doesn't make the existence of these phenomena conceptually impossible,' he told her; 'but neither does it make any explicit statement about them.' The Implicate Order (from the Latin 'to be enfolded') is a level of reality beyond our normal everyday thoughts and perceptions, as well as beyond any picture of reality offered by a given scientific theory (11).

Before the discovery and development of quantum theory the pioneers of psychical research sought, with only partial success, to form a theory to account for the phenomena reported to the Society. This search is still proceeding; and as new discoveries, such as those outlined here, are made, the quest for an adequate theory becomes even more difficult because of the increasing complexity of the data. But what is important is that the search for a theory began when the Society for Psychical Research was formed in 1882. The hypotheses discussed in the thick pages of *Proceedings* before the end of the century, and the rather thinner pages since, have been of the greatest value to modern theoreticians and experimenters, as talks with Karlis Osis and others have confirmed for me. Now the field to be explored, first outlined by pioneers such as Myers, Gurney, Podmore, and the Sidgwicks, has been widened by the researches of physicists, as well as those of psychologists, physiologists and biologists. There is great scope for research in parapsychology by scientists of different disciplines in the Society's second century.

When I first started writing about apparitions I made the mistake of studying them in isolation, rather than as part of the structure of psychical research as a whole. Through reading the works of G. N. M. Tyrrell, and talking over the subject with Rosalind Heywood, particularly during the last year of her life, my outlook gradually changed. I eventually realized that instead of asking, 'What is an apparition?' I should be asking, 'What is man?' It was as if we were discussing the nature of shadows instead of the nature of who or what casts the shadows. When I put this conclusion to Mrs Heywood her reply was 'But of course' (51i).

In the book from which I have quoted, Davies said, 'The grey area between mind and matter, philosophy and physics, psychology and the objective world is only on the threshold of exploration, yet any ultimate picture of reality cannot omit it' (18 p. 199). The Society for Psychical Research provides a meeting place for those who are prepared to take part in the exploration.

This is the end of my quest for the present. I hope to publish other studies in due course. As explained earlier, the Society does not hold or express corporate views and those given here are my own responsibility. More case material is always welcome. I shall be grateful to readers with experience of hauntings and apparitions if accounts of such experiences are sent to me at The Society for Psychical Research. 1 Adam and Eve Mews, London W8 6UG. Accounts of experiences at Versailles or Cheltenham will be particularly welcome. Dr Karlis Osis requests American readers to send accounts of their experiences to him at The American Society for Psychical Research, Inc., 5 West 73rd Street, New York, N.Y. 10023.

Acknowledgements

I wish to thank the Council of the Society for Psychical Research for permission to quote from the *Journal* and *Proceedings* of the Society and from material in the archives: the Secretary, Miss Eleanor O'Keeffe, for her invariable helpfulness; and in particular the Librarian, Mr Nicholas Clark-Lowes, for the many hours he has spent in helping me to trace material in the archives. I am most grateful to Mr G. W. Lambert who, over the past twenty years, has given far more help than I could reasonably have expected in the interpretation of some of my own cases and those in the Society's collection. In the Cheltenham case I have been greatly helped by the late Dr Rosina Despard's niece, Mrs Joyce Rynd; by Henry Swinhoe's granddaughter, Mrs Violet Rhodes James; by a local investigator, Mr W. P. Bond; and by Dr Michael Martyn and his associates at Weston House. Mrs Nancy B. Pringle, local history librarian at the Cheltenham Library, provided some most useful information about former residents of Pittville Circus Road and the neighbourhood.

In the Willington case (Chapter 4) I am most grateful for the help given by Mr Eric Hollerton, local studies librarian at the North Tyneside Metropolitan Borough Council's central library at North Shields, and by Miss E. Mallabar, area librarian at Wallsend; in the Beavor Lodge Case (Chapter 6) for the help given by Mr T. J. Rix, librarian of the London Borough of Hammersmith and Fulham and by the local history assistant, Miss Bull; in the Snettisham Case (Chapter 7) for the help given by Mr D. G. Bell, of the County Library, Wesgate, Hunstanton, Norfolk; in the Versailles Case (Chapter 9) for the help given by Mr Lambert, M. François Chapon, Conservator of the Bibliothèque Littéraire Jacques Doucet, Paris, and by the staff of the library of the Institut Français du Royaume-Uni in London; in the Cleve Court Case (Chapter 12) for the help given by Mrs Heather Carson, formerly of Cleve Court and now of Sevenoaks, Kent, by Mr J. P. M. Richards, local history librarian of the Kent County Library, Springfield, Maidstone, and by Miss G. M. Wyatt, divisional reference librarian, Thanet, Kent; in the Abbey House, Cambridge, Case (Chapter 13) for the help given by Dr Alan Gauld, Mr A. D. Cornell, and Professor P. V. Danckwerts, F.R.S.; and in the closing chapter for the help given by Dr Karlis Osis, Chester F. Carlson Research Fellow of the American Society for Psychical Research. Dr James McHarg, of Dundee, is thanked for his advice on medical aspects of some of the cases.

I wish also to thank J. M. Dent and Sons for permission to quote from Professor Paul Davies's book *Other Worlds*; Messrs Duckworth for permission to quote from Dr D. J. West's *Psychical Research Today* and from Dr Morton Schatzman's *The Story of Ruth*; also *New Scientist* for permission to quote from Dr Schatzman's article based on his book; Messrs Robert Hale for permission to quote from Mrs A. M. W. Stirling's *Ghosts Vivisected*, and Messrs Sidgwick and Jackson for permission to quote from W. H. Salter's *Ghosts and Apparitions*. The Editor of *Encounter* is thanked for permission to quote from Dame Joan Evans's article 'An End to An Adventure'.

Selective Bibliography

For those who wish to undertake a reading course may I suggest that it should include Dr Gauld's book *The Founders of Psychical Research* for a description of the early days of the Society; *Phantasms of the Living* because of the pattern of the early cases submitted to the Society (an abridged edition was published by Mrs Sidgwick in 1918, but this does not include the paper by Myers 'On a Suggested Mode of Psychical Interaction' which was in the original edition in two volumes); *Human Personality and its Survival of Bodily Death* by Myers for its background of the first twenty years of the Society's existence, its case material, and for the discussion of the important issues involved in psychical research; Sir Ernest Bennett's *Apparitions and Haunted Houses* (1939) for his survey, with informed comment, of more than one hundred cases; Tyrrell's *Apparitions* for his discussion on theoretical aspects of apparitional experiences, but it should be read in conjunction with the paper on 'Six Theories About Apparitions' in *Proceedings*, Volume 50, for his theory to be compared with others; my books *The Unexplained* and *Apparitions and Ghosts* for discussion of evidential material; and Celia Green's and Charles McCreery's *Apparitions* for classification of types of apparitional experience. Bennett received nearly 1,300 letters as the result of a BBC radio broadcast on 'Apparitions and Haunted Houses' in 1934 and included some fifty narratives 'of adequate merit as regards the evidence' in his book, the rest being taken from the publications of the SPR. Most of his cases are concerned with the evidence for, and explanations of, apparitions of the dead. Important issues of *Proceedings* are Volumes 3 and 33 for Mrs Sidgwick's papers on phantasms, Volume 6 for the debate between Myers and Podmore on phantasms, Volume 10 for the results of the great Census of Hallucinations, Volume 45 for Professor Price's discussion on hauntings, and, in particular, Volume 50 for the views of some distinguished scholars in 'Six Theories about Apparitions'.

Informed comment on cases in the Society's collection is contained in D. J. West's *Psychical Research Today* and in W. H. Salter's *Zoar*. Salter's *Ghosts and Apparitions* is also to be highly recommended. Tyrrell's *The Personality of Man*, C. D. Broad's *Lectures on Psychical Research*, and Sir Cyril Burt's *Psychology and Psychical Research* throw light on the complexities of psychical research.

In the list that follows I have included issues of *Proceedings* for readers interested in the wider aspects of psychical research.

* * *

1. Amadou, R., Moberly, C. A. E., and Jourdain, E. F. *Les Fantômes de Trianon* (Paris: Editions du Rocher, 1978).
2. Ashby, R. H. *The Guidebook for the Study of Psychical Research* (London: Rider, 1972).
3. Balfour, Earl of, and Piddington, J. W. 'Case of Haunting at Ramsbury, Wilts', *Journal SPR*, 1932, vol. 27, pp. 297–304.
4. Balfour, Jean (The Countess of Balfour). 'The Palm Sunday Case: New Light on an Old Love Story', *Proc. SPR*, 1960, vol. 52.
5. Barlow, F., and Rampling-Rose, W. 'Report on an Investigation into Spirit Photography', *Proc. SPR*, 1932–3, vol. 41, pp. 121–38.
6. Barrett, Sir William. a) 'Poltergeists Old and New', *Proc. SPR*, 1911, vol. 25, pp. 377–412.
   –. b) 'Investigation of a Haunted house in Worcestershire', *Journal SPR*, 1915–16, vol. 17, pp. 34–42.
7. Barton, N. *The Lost Rivers of London* (London: Phoenix House. Leicester: University Press, 1962).
8. Beloff, J. a) ed. *New Directions in Parapsychology* (London; Elek Science, 1974).
   –. b) 'On Trying to make Sense of the Paranormal', *Proc. SPR*, 1976, vol. 56, pp. 173–95.
   –. c) 'Could There be a Physical Explanation for Psi?' *Journal SPR*, 1980, vol. 50, pp. 263–72.
9. Bennett, Sir Ernest. *Apparitions and Haunted Houses* (London: Faber, 1939).
10. Besterman, T. a) *Crystal Gazing* (London: Rider, 1924. New York: University Books, 1965).
    –. b) 'The Psychology of Testimony in Relation to Paraphysical Phenomena', *Proc. SPR*, 1931–2, vol. 40, pp. 363–87.
11. Bohm, D. *Wholeness and the Implicate Order* (London: Routledge and Kegan Paul, 1980). Reviewed by Danah Zohar in the *Sunday Times* of 27 July 1980.
12. Bozzano, E. *Les Phénomènes de Hantise* (Paris: Alcan, 1929).
13. Broad, C. D. a) 'Phantasms of the Living and of the Dead,' *Proc. SPR*, 1953–6, vol. 50, pp. 51–66.
    –. b) 'Dreaming and Some of its Implications', *Proc. SPR*, 1959, vol. 52, pp. 53–78.
    –. c) *Lectures on Psychical Research* (London: Routledge and Kegan Paul, 1962).
14. Burt, Sir Cyril. a) *Psychology and Psychical Research* (London: The SPR, 1968).
    –. b) *ESP and Psychology*, edited by Anita Gregory (London: Weidenfeld and Nicolson, 1975).
15. Carington, W. *Matter Mind and Meaning* (London: Methuen, 1949).
16. Collins, B. Abdy *The Cheltenham Ghost* (London: Psychic Press, 1948).
17. Crowe, Catherine M. *The Night Side of Nature* (London: Newby, 1848), two vols.
18. Davies, P. *Other Worlds* (London: Dent, 1980).

19. Davies, W. 'Notes on Reports of The Society for Psychical Research', *Journal SPR*, 1884–5, vol. 1, pp. 400–7. This is a critical review to which Myers replies (pp. 407–16). Many reports of cases received by the Literary Committee are given here.

20. Dingwall, E. J., Goldney, K. M., Hall, T. H. a) 'The haunting of Borley Rectory. A Critical Survey of the Evidence', *Proc. SPR*, 1956, vol. 51, pp. 1–181. Also published by Duckworth, London, 1956.
– and Hall, T. H. b) *Four Modern Ghosts* (London: Duckworth, 1958). The introduction contains a chapter on possible physical factors in a haunting.

21. Evans, J. a) Preface to fifth edition of *An Adventure* (London: Faber, 1955).
–. b) 'An End to An Adventure', *Encounter*, October, 1976.

22. Flammarion, C. a) *The Unknown* (London and New York: Harper Brothers, 1900).
–. b) *Haunted Houses* (London: T. Fisher Unwin, 1924. New York: D. Appleton and Co., 1924).

23. Gauld, A. a) *The Founders of Psychical Research* (London; Routledge and Kegan Paul, 1968. New York: Schocken Books).
–. b) 'The Haunting of Abbey House, Cambridge', *Journal SPR*, 1972, vol. 46, pp. 109–23.
– and Cornell, A. D. c) *Poltergeists* (London: Routledge and Kegan Paul, 1979). Two chapters concern hauntings.

24. Gibbons, O. A. and M. E. *The Trianon Adventure, A Symposium* (London: Museum Press, 1958).

25. Grasset, J. 'The History of a Haunted House', *Proc. SPR*, 1903–4, vol. 18, pp. 464–80.

26. Gray, A. B. *Cambridge Revisited* (Cambridge: Heffer, 1921).

27. Green, C. a) 'Report (1959) on Enquiry into Spontaneous Cases', *Proc. SPR*, 1960, vol. 53.
–. b) *Out-of-the-Body Experiences* (Oxford: Institute of Psychophysical Research, 1968).
– and McCreery, C. c) *Apparitions* (London: Hamish Hamilton, 1975).

28. Gurney, E., Myers, F. W. H., Podmore, F. *Phantasms of the Living* (London: The SPR and Trubner and Co., 1886), two vols. Abridged edition by Mrs Sidgwick (London: Kegan Paul and Trubner and Co. New York: E. P. Dutton, 1918).

29. Hall, Radclyffe. 'A Veridical Apparition', *Journal SPR*, 1921, vol. 20, pp. 78–88.

30. Hardy, Sir A. *The Spiritual Nature of Man* (Oxford: Clarendon Press, 1979).

31. Hart H., and Ella B. a) 'Visions and Apparitions Collectively and Reciprocally Perceived', *Proc. SPR*, 1932–3. vol. 41, pp. 205–49.
– and associates. b) 'Six Theories About Apparitions,' *Proc. SPR*, 1953–6, vol. 50, pp. 153–239.

32. Hastings, R. J. a) 'An Examination of the Borley Report', *Proc. SPR*, 1969, vol. 55, pp. 66–175.

–. b) 'An Examination of the Dieppe Raid Case', *Journal SPR*, 1969, vol. 45, pp. 55–66.

33. Haynes, R. a) *The Hidden Springs* (London: Hollis and Carter, 1961. New York: The Devin-Adair Co., 1961).
  –. b) *The Seeing Eye The Seeing I* (London: Hutchinson, 1976).

34. Huby, P. M. 'New Evidence about Rose Morton,' *Journal SPR*, 1970, vol. 45, pp. 391–2.

35. Hyde, H. M. *The Life of Sir Edward Carson* (London: Heinemann, 1953).

36. Heywood, R. a) *The Sixth Sense* (London: Chatto and Windus, 1959. New York: E. P. Dutton, 1961, retitled *Beyond the Reach of Sense*).
  –. b) *The Infinitive Hive* (London: Chatto and Windus, 1964. New York: E. P. Dutton, 1964, retitled *ESP: a Personal Memoir*).

37. Inglis, B. *Natural and Supernatural* (London: Hodder and Stoughton, 1977).

38. Iremonger, L. *The Ghosts of Versailles, A Critical Study* (London: Faber, 1957).

39. Jaffé, A. *Apparitions and Precognition. A Study from the Point of View of C. G. Jung's Analytical Psychology* (New York: University Books, 1963).

40. James, W. a) *The Principles of Psychology* (London: Macmillan, 1890. New York: Henry Holt and Co., 1890), two vols.
–. b) *William James on Psychical Research*, editors Gardner Murphy and R. O. Ballou (New York: Viking Press, 1960. London: Chatto and Windus, 1961).

41. Johnson, R. C. *The Imprisoned Splendour* (London: Hodder and Stoughton, 1953. New York: Harper and Row, 1953).

42. Jullian, P. *Un Prince 1900 – Robert de Montesquiou* (Paris: Librairie Academique Perrin, 1965. London: Secker and Warburg, 1967, under title of *Robert de Montesquiou, a Fin-de-Siècle Prince*).

43. Jung, C. G. a) 'The Psychological Foundation for Belief in Spirits', *Proc. SPR*, 1921, vol. 31, pp. 75–93.
  –. b) *Memories, Dreams, Reflections* (London: Collins and Routledge and Kegan Paul, 1953. New York: Pantheon, 1963).
  –. c) *Synchronicity* (London: Routledge and Kegan Paul, 1972).

44. Lambert G. W. a) 'The Use of Evidence in Psychical Research', *Proc. SPR*, 1956, vol. 50, pp. 275–93.
  –. b) 'Antoine Richard's Garden: a Postscript to "An Adventure"', *Journal SPR*, 1953, vol. 37, pp. 117–54.
  –. c) 'Antoine Richard's Garden: a Postscript to "An Adventure"' (continued) *Journal SPR*, 1954, vol. 37, pp. 266–79.
  –. d) 'Antoine Richard's Garden. A Supplementary Note', *Journal SPR*, 1955, vol. 38, pp. 12–18.
  –. e) 'Richard's Garden Revisited', *Journal SPR*, 1962, vol. 41, pp. 279–92.
  –. f) 'Phantom Scenery', *Journal SPR*, 1963, vol. 42, pp. 5–6.
  –. g) 'The Cheltenham Ghost. A Reinterpretation of the Evidence', *Journal SPR*, 1958, vol. 39, pp. 267–77.
  –. h) 'Beavor Lodge: an old ghost story retold', *Journal SPR*, 1964, vol. 42, pp. 273–82.
  –. i) 'An Apparition of a Child: the case of Johnnie M.', *Journal SPR*, 1966,

vol. 43, pp. 428–31. Also, MacKenzie, A., *Frontiers of the Unknown* (London, 1968), pp. 148–57.

–. j) 'The Dieppe Raid Case. A collective auditory hallucination', *Journal SPR*, 1952, vol. 36. With Hon. Mrs Kathleen Gay.

45. Landau, L. 'An Unusual Out-of-the-body Experience', *Journal SPR*, 1963, vol. 42, pp. 126–8.

46. Lang, A. a) *Cock Lane and Common-Sense* (London: Longmans, 1894. New York: AMS Press, 1970.)

–. b) *The Book of Dreams and Ghosts* (London: Longmans, 1897. New York: AMS Press, 1970).

47. LeShan, L. *The Medium the Mystic and the Physicist* (New York: Viking Press, 1974. London: Turnstone Press, 1974).

48. McCreery, C. *Science, Philosophy and ESP* (London: Faber, 1967).

49. MacGregor, A. A. *The Ghost Book* (London: Hale, 1955). He quotes from Chapter Six of Mrs Shane Leslie's *Girlhood in the Pacific* (London: Macdonald, 1943).

50. McHarg, J. 'A Vision of the Aftermath of the Battle of Nechtanesmere, AD 685', *Journal SPR*, 1978, vol. 49, pp. 938–48.

51. MacKenzie, A. a) *The Unexplained* (London: Arthur Barker, 1966. New York: Abelard-Schuman, 1970).

–. b) *Frontiers of the Unknown* (London: Arthur Barker, 1968. New York: Popular Library).

–. c) *Apparitions and Ghosts* (London: Arthur Barker, 1971. New York: Popular Library).

–. d) *A Gallery of Ghosts* (London: Arthur Barker, 1973. New York: Taplinger, 1973).

–. e) 'A Case of Haunting in Kent', *Journal SPR*, 1967, vol. 44, pp. 131–49.

–. f) Review of Peter Underwood's *Hauntings* (London: Dent, 1977), in *Journal SPR*, 1978, vol. 49, pp. 837–41.

–. g) Review of Amadou's *Les Fantômes de Trianon* in *Journal SPR*, 1979, vol. 50, pp. 187–9.

–. h) 'A Modern Haunting' (with Zorab, G.), *Journal SPR*, 1980, vol. 50, pp. 284–93.

–. i) 'Talks with Rosalind Heywood', *Journal SPR*, 1980, vol. 50, pp. 523–6.

52. Maitland, R. W. *The Snettisham Ghost* (London: Psychic Press, undated, but probably 1956).

53. Marillier, L. 'Apparitions of the Virgin in the Dordogne', *Proc. SPR*, 1891–2, vol. 7, pp. 100–10. A valuable paper because of what the author calls the 'contagious character' of the appearances.

54. Matthews, W. R. 'Psychical Research and Theology', *Proc. SPR*, 1940–1, vol. 46. He refers to Price's views on haunting on pp. 13–15.

55. Moberly, C. A. E., and Jourdain, E. F. *An Adventure* (London: Macmillan, 1911. Fifth edition, Faber, 1955).

56. 'Morton', R. C. 'Record of a Haunted House', *Proc. SPR*, 1892, vol. 8, pp. 311–32.

57. Moss, T. *The Probability of the Impossible* (Los Angeles: J. P. Tarcher, 1974. London: Routledge and Kegan Paul, 1975).

58. Mundle, C. W. K. 'Strange Facts in Search of a Theory', *Proc. SPR*, 1973, vol. 56.

59. Murphy, G. *Challenge of Psychical Research* (New York: Harper and Row, 1961).

60. Myers, F. W. H. a) *Human Personality and its Survival of Bodily Death* (London: Longmans, 1903. New York: Longmans, 1954, with intro. by Gardner Murphy). Abridged editions in one volume have been published.
–. b) 'On Apparitions Occurring Soon After Death', by Gurney, completed by Myers, *Proc. SPR*, 1888–9, vol. 5, pp. 404–85.
–. c) 'On Recognized Apparitions Occurring more than a Year after Death', *Proc. SPR*, 1889–90, vol. 6, pp. 13–65, and 'A Defence of Phantasms of the Dead', pp. 314–57.
–. d) 'On Indications of Continued Terrene Knowledge on the part of Phantasms of the Dead', *Proc. SPR*, 1892, vol. 8, pp. 170–252.
–. e) 'The Subliminal Self. The relation of supernormal phenomena to time', *Proc. SPR*, 1895, vol. 11. This is a most important paper dealing with Retrocognition and Precognition.

61. Nicol, J. F. 'The Founders of the SPR', *Proc. SPR*, 1972, vol. 55.

62. Osborn, E. 'The Woman in Brown', *Journal SPR*, 1949, vol. 35, pp. 123–53.

63. Osis, K. 'Call for Cases of Apparitions', American SPR Newsletter, July 1980, vol. 6, no. 3.

64. Owen, A. R. G. *Can We Explain the Poltergeist?* (New York: Garrett Publications, 1964).

65. Parker A. *States of Mind: ESP and Altered States of Consciousness* (London: Malaby Press, 1975).

66. Podmore, F. a) *Telepathic Hallucinations. The New View of Ghosts* (Halifax: Milner and Company, undated).
–. b) *Apparitions and Thought-Transference* (London: Walter Scott Ltd, 1894. New York: Charles Scribner & Sons).
–. c) *Studies in Psychical Research* (London: Kegan Paul, Trench, Trubner and Co., Ltd, 1897).
–. d) 'Phantasms of the Dead from Another Point of View', *Proc. SPR*, 1889–90, vol. 6, pp. 229–313.
–. e) 'Poltergeists', *Proc. SPR*, 1896–7, vol. 12, pp. 45–58.

67. Price, H. H. a) *Perception* (London: Methuen, 1932).
–. b) 'Haunting and the "Psychic Ether" Hypothesis', *Proc. SPR*, 1938–9, vol. 45, pp. 307–41.

68. Procter, E. 'The Haunted House at Willington', *Journal SPR*, 1892, vol. 5, pp. 331–52.

69. Rey, L. *Le Petit Trianon et le Hameau de Marie-Antoinette* (Paris: Archiviste Paléographe, Pierre Worms, ed., 1936).

70. Rhine, Louisa B. a) *ESP in Life and Lab* (New York: Macmillan, 1967).
–. b) *Psi* (New York: Harper and Row, 1975).
–. c) 'Letters and Comments', *Journal of Parapsychology*, June 1970, pp. 143–63. A most interesting exchange of views on the significance of spontaneous cases between Dr Rhine and Professor Ian Stevenson.

71. Richardson, M. A. *A Local Historian's Table Book* (London: 1843, Legendary Division, vol. 1).

72. Richmond, Sir A. *Twenty-six Years, 1879–1905* (London: Geoffrey Bles, 1961).

73. Rogo, D. S. *Phantoms* (New York, Taplinger, 1974. Newton Abbot: David and Charles, 1976).

74. Roll, W. G. *The Poltergeist* (New York: New American Library, Signet Books, 1974. London: Wyndham Publications, a Star Book, 1976). There is a useful appendix 'On meeting ghosts and poltergeists'.

75. Sabine, W. H. W. 'Is there a Case for Retrocognition?', *Journal* American SPR, April, 1950, vol. 44, pp. 43–64.

76. Salter, W. H. a) *Ghosts and Apparitions* (London: Bell, 1938.)
–. b) *Zoar* (London: Sidgwick and Jackson, 1961).
–. c) ' "An Adventure": a note on the evidence', *Journal SPR*, 1950, vol. 35.

77. Schatzman, M. *The Story of Ruth* (London: Duckworth, 1980). The book is summarized in the *New Scientist* of 25 September 1980, pp. 935–7, and reviewed in the April 1981 *Journal* of the American SPR by T. C. Goodsort, and in the June 1981 *Journal* of the SPR by A. Gauld.

78. Schmeidler, G. R. 'Quantitative Investigation of a "Haunted House"', *Journal* American SPR, 1966, vol. 60, pp. 138–49.

79. Schouten, Sybo A. 'Analysis of spontaneous cases as reported in *Phantasms of the Living*', *European Journal of Parapsychology*, May 1979, pp. 408–55.

80. Sidgwick, H. a) Second Presidential Address, *Proc. SPR*, 1882–3, vol. 1.
–. b) 'The Canons of Evidence in Psychical Research, *Proc. SPR*, 1889–90, vol. 6, pp. 1–6.
– (and committee), c) 'Report on the Census of Hallucinations', *Proc. SPR*, 1894, vol. 10, pp. 25–422. Appendix G is a paper by Myers on 'A proposed scheme of apparitions'.

81. Sidgwick, Mrs H. a) 'Notes on the Evidence, Collected by the Society, for Phantasms of the Dead', *Proc. SPR*, 1885, vol. 3, pp. 69–150.
–. b) 'On Spirit Photographs', *Proc. SPR*, 1891–2, vol. 7, pp. 268–89. There is correspondence on this paper in the *Journal*, vol. 5, for November 1891, to which Mrs Sidgwick replies (pp. 153–60).
–. c) 'On the Evidence for Clairvoyance', *Proc. SPR*, 1891–2, vol. 7.
–. d) Presidential Address, *Proc. SPR*, 1908, vol. 22, pp. 1–18.
–. e) Review of *An Adventure*, *Proc. SPR*, 1911, vol. 25, pp. 353–60.
–. f) 'Phantasms of the Living', *Proc. SPR*, 1923, vol. 33, pp. 23–429.

82. Society for Psychical Research. a) Report of the Literary Committee, *Proc. SPR*, 1882–3, vol. 1.
–. b) Report of Council for Year 1915, *Journal SPR*, 1915–16, vol. 17.
–. c) 'A Case of Apparent Retrocognition', *Journal SPR*, 1947–8, vol. 34, pp. 74–80.
–. d) 'Report (1959) on Enquiry into Spontaneous Cases', *Proc. SPR*, 1960, vol. 53.
–. e) 'Experiments in Thought Transference', *Journal SPR*. 1893–4, vol. 6.
–. f) 'Experiments in Thought Transference at a Distance', *Journal SPR*, 1895–6, vol. 7, pp. 234–8.

–. g) 'Second Report of the Committee on Haunted Houses', *Proc. SPR*, 1884, vol. 2.

–. h) 'Cases. Collective Apparition from Miss M. W. Scott', *Journal SPR*, 1893–4, vol. 6.

–. i) *Journal SPR*, 1899–1900, vol. 9.

–. j) *Journal SPR*, 1968, vol. 44.

–. k) *Notes for Investigators of Spontaneous Cases* (1968).

83. Smith, W. Whately. 'The Reality of Psychic Phenomena', *Proc. SPR*, 1920, vol. 30, pp. 306–33.

84. Smythies, J. R. ed. *Science and ESP* (London: Routledge and Kegan Paul, 1967).

85. Stevenson, I. a) 'Letters and Comments', *Journal of Parapsychology*, June 1970.

–. b) 'The Blue Orchid of Table Mountain', *Journal SPR*, 1964, vol. 42, pp. 401–9.

86. Stirling, A. M. W. a) ed. *The Richmond Papers* (London: Heinemann, 1926).

–. b) *Ghosts Vivisected* (London: Robert Hale, 1957).

87. Tart, C. T. 'Application of Instrumentation in the Investigation of Haunting and Poltergeist Cases', *Journal* American SPR, 1965, vol. 59, pp. 190–201.

88. Thouless, R. H. a) *Psychical Research Past and Present* (London: SPR booklet, 1952).

–. b) *From Anecdote to Experiment in Psychical Research* (London: Routledge and Kegan Paul, 1972).

89. Thurston, H. *Ghosts and Poltergeists* (London: Burns, Oates, 1953. Chicago: Regnery, 1954).

90. Turner, K. H. 'A South Yorkshire Haunt', *Journal SPR*, 1970, vol. 45, pp. 325–53.

91. Tyrrell, G. N. M. a) *Grades of Significance* (London: Rider, 1930).

–. b) *Science and Psychical Research* (London: Methuen, 1938. New York: University Books, 1961).

–. c) *The Personality of Man* (London: Allen and Unwin, 1946. Baltimore: Penguin, 1960).

–. d) *Apparitions* (London: Duckworth, 1953. New York, University Books, 1961.) There is an excellent Preface by Professor Price.

92. Wainwright, F. T. 'Nechtanesmere', *Antiquity*, 1948, vol. 22. pp. 82–97.

93. West. D. J. a) 'The Investigation of Spontaneous Cases', *Proc. SPR*, 1946–9, vol. 48, pp. 264–300. Salter's comments on this paper are on pp. 301–5.

–. b) *Psychical Research Today* (London: Duckworth, 1954).

94. Whiting, J. Sturge. *The Mystery of Versailles* (London: Occult Book Society, 1937).

95. Zorab, G. 'A Modern Haunting' (with MacKenzie), *Journal SPR*, 1980, vol. 50, pp. 284–93.

Index